Lecture Notes of the Institute for Computer Sciences, Social Informatics and Telecommunications Engineering 464

The LNICST series publishes ICST's conferences, symposia and workshops. It reports state-of-the-art results in areas related to the scope of the Institute.

LNICST reports state-of-the-art results in areas related to the scope of the Institute. The type of material published includes

- Proceedings (published in time for the respective event)
- Other edited monographs (such as project reports or invited volumes)

LNICST topics span the following areas:

- General Computer Science
- E-Economy
- E-Medicine
- Knowledge Management
- Multimedia
- Operations, Management and Policy
- Social Informatics
- Systems

Zygmunt J. Haas · Ravi Prakash ·
Habib Ammari · Weili Wu
Editors

Wireless Internet

15th EAI International Conference, WiCON 2022
Virtual Event, November 2022
Proceedings

 Springer

Editors
Zygmunt J. Haas ⓘ
The University of Texas at Dallas
Richardson, TX, USA

Ravi Prakash
The University of Texas at Dallas
Richardson, TX, USA

Habib Ammari ⓘ
Texas A&M University-Kingsville
Kingsville, TX, USA

Weili Wu ⓘ
The University of Texas at Dallas
Richardson, TX, USA

ISSN 1867-8211   ISSN 1867-822X (electronic)
Lecture Notes of the Institute for Computer Sciences, Social Informatics
and Telecommunications Engineering
ISBN 978-3-031-27040-6   ISBN 978-3-031-27041-3 (eBook)
https://doi.org/10.1007/978-3-031-27041-3

This Springer imprint is published by the registered company Springer Nature Switzerland AG
The registered company address is: Gewerbestrasse 11, 6330 Cham, Switzerland

Preface

Welcome to the 15th edition of the 2022 European Alliance for Innovation (EAI) International Conference on Wireless Internet Conference (EAI WiCON), which was held virtually on November 17, 2022, in Dallas, Texas, USA.

We are delighted to introduce the proceedings of EAI WiCON, which focuses on various aspects of wireless technology. EAI WiCON 2022 aimed to tackle the challenges of wireless Internet communications, covering topics ranging from technology issues to new applications, especially focusing on current, novel, and future next-generation wireless Internet technologies, 5G, 6G, IoT, Industrial IoT, Healthcare IoT, and related topics. This conference has brought researchers, developers and practitioners around the world to share their experiences and research findings on all aspects of Wireless Internet Communications. Furthermore, EAI WiCON 2022 offers a leading interdisciplinary forum for academics, educators, and practitioners to present and discuss the latest technologies, developments, practical challenges, and approaches to Wireless Internet.

The technical program of EAI WiCON 2022 consisted of 16 full research papers on the above research issues, which form 4 oral presentation sessions, each of which includes 4 papers. The conference sessions were: Technical Session 1 - Security and Privacy; Technical Session 2 - Blockchain and Wireless Networks; Technical Session 3 - Resource Management, Routing; and Technical Session 4 - Social Networks and Learning. The research papers collected in this international conference were rigorously reviewed by the scientific program committee members. Aside from the high-quality technical paper presentations, the technical program also featured one keynote speech, titled "Connected World: Past, Present, and Future". This keynote was delivered by Dr. Samee Khan who is the James W. Bagley Chair Professor and Department Head of Electrical & Computer Engineering at the Mississippi State University. Dr. Khan was Cluster Lead (2016–2020) for Computer Systems Research at the US National Science Foundation (NSF).

Many people have kindly helped us prepare and organize the EAI WiCON 2022 Conference. First of all, the coordination with the general chairs, Dr. Zygmunt Haas and Dr. Ravi Prakash was essential for the success of the conference. We sincerely appreciate their constant support and guidance. It was also a great pleasure to work with such an excellent organizing committee team for their hard work in organizing and supporting the conference. In particular, we are grateful to the EAI Conference Manager, Ms. Veronika Kissova, for her constant support and efforts. In addition, we would like to thank all contributing authors for producing high-quality papers to be presented at EAI WiCON 2022, and all the TPC members for their timely reviews and constructive feedback in the peer-review process of technical papers, which helped make a high-quality technical program.

We strongly believe that EAI WiCON 2022 conference provided a good forum for all researchers, developers, and practitioners to discuss all science and technology aspects that are relevant to Wireless Internet Communications. Furthermore, we expect that future EAI WiCON conferences will be as successful and stimulating, as indicated by the contributions presented in this volume.

November 2022

Zygmunt Haas
Ravi Prakash
Habib M. Ammari
Weili Wu

Organization

Conference Organization

Steering Committee

Imrich Chlamtac	University of Trento, Italy
Der-Jiunn Deng	National Changhua University of Education, Taiwan

Organizing Committee

General Chairs

Ravi Prakash	University of Texas at Dallas, USA
Zygmunt Haas	University of Texas at Dallas, USA

TPC Chairs and Co-chairs

Habib M. Ammari	Texas A&M University-Kingsville, USA
Weili Wu	University of Texas at Dallas, USA

Publicity and Social Media Chair

Eirini Eleni Tsiropoulou	University of New Mexico Albuquerque, USA

Publications Chairs

Xiao Li	University of Texas at Dallas, USA
Weili Wu	University of Texas at Dallas, USA

Web Chair

Michelle Posamentier	University of Texas at Dallas, USA

Technical Program Committee

Chris Poellabauer	Florida International University, USA
Hirozumi Yamaguchi	Osaka University, Japan
Jianping Wang	City University of Hong Kong, China
Jianxiong Guo	Beijing Normal University at Zhuhai, China
Jun Luo	Nanyang Technological University, Singapore
Liqiang Zhang	Indiana University South Bend, USA
Malek Khan	Texas A&M University-Kingsville, USA
Michele Polese	Northeastern University, USA
Nan Cen	Missouri University of Science and Technology, USA
Pengjun Wan	Illinois Institute of Technology, USA
Qiang Ye	Dalhousie University, Canada
Qianping Gu	Simon Fraser University, Canada
Qilian Liang	University of Texas at Arlington, USA
Rong Jin	California State University, Fullerton, USA
Smita Ghosh	Santa Clara University, USA
Stefano Basagni	Northeastern University, USA
Tariqul Islam	Syracuse University, USA
Wiem Abderrahim	KAUST, Saudi Arabia
Xiang Li	Santa Clara University, USA
Xiaohua Jia	City University of Hong Kong, China
Xiuzhen Cheng	Shandong University, China
Yi Li	University of Texas at Tyler, USA
Yuqing Zhu	California State University, Los Angeles, USA
Zakirul Alam Bhuiyan	Fordham University, USA
Zhangyu Guan	University at Buffalo, The State University of New York, USA
Zhipeng Cai	Georgia State University, USA

Contents

Social Networks and Learning

Security and Privacy

Preventing Adversarial Attacks on Autonomous Driving Models

Junaid Sajid[1], Bareera Anam[1], Hasan Ali Khattak[1(✉)], Asad Waqar Malik[1], Assad Abbas[2], and Samee U. Khan[3]

[1] National University of Sciences and Technology (NUST), Islamabad, Pakistan
{jsajid.msit20seecs,banam.msit20seecs,hasan.alikhattak}@seecs.edu.pk
[2] Department of Computer Science, COMSATS University Islamabad, Islamabad, Pakistan
assadabbas@comsats.edu.pk
[3] Electrical and Computer Engineering, Mississippi State University, Starkville, USA
skhan@ece.msstate.edu

Abstract. Autonomous driving systems are among the exceptional technological developments of recent times. Such systems gather live information about the vehicle and respond with skilled human drivers' skills. The pervasiveness of computing technologies has also resulted in serious threats to the security and safety of autonomous driving systems. Adversarial attacks are among one the most serious threats to autonomous driving models (ADMs). The purpose of the paper is to determine the behavior of the driving models when confronted with a physical adversarial attack against end-to-end ADMs. We analyze some adversarial attacks and their defense mechanisms for certain autonomous driving models. Five adversarial attacks were applied to three ADMs, and subsequently analyzed the functionality and the effects of these attacks on those ADMs. Afterward, we propose four defense strategies against five adversarial attacks and identify the most resilient defense mechanism against all types of attacks. Support Vector Machine and neural regression were the two machine learning models that were utilized to categorize the challenges for the model's training. The results show that we have achieved 95% accuracy.

Keywords: Autonomous driving models · Autonomous driving system · Adversarial attacks · Support vector machine

1 Introduction

Applications of artificial intelligence (AI) and deep neural networks (DNN) are growing in the field of autonomous driving systems (ADS) as they provide intelligent transportation systems. The field of pervasive computing is developing quickly, especially with ADS. Various prediction and categorization issues are used in several ubiquitous computing applications of deep learning. CNN-based

© ICST Institute for Computer Sciences, Social Informatics and Telecommunications Engineering 2023
Published by Springer Nature Switzerland AG 2023. All Rights Reserved
Z. J. Haas et al. (Eds.): WiCON 2022, LNICST 464, pp. 3–13, 2023.
https://doi.org/10.1007/978-3-031-27041-3_1

regression models can be used to forecast when the car will collide and prevent it from being involved in accidents [1]. Response time and throughput are the main parameters that must be considered in the design of ADMs. The globe presently has a large number of autonomous vehicles. By placing sensors such as camera and LiDAR, autonomous vehicles may gather data that is then fed into systems to execute judgments [2].

Autonomous automobiles also help to enhance the driving skills of a driver [3]. However, they must be tested several times to ensure safety. It even now requires a few critical actions to increase their precision and drive to avoid dangerous collisions. Most of the world is yet to work to install autonomous driving systems on autonomous unmanned aerial vehicles to enable them to take off unassisted by pilots as generic model of autonomous vehicle is shown in Fig. 1. However, to prevent any threat, humans should make sure it is fully established [4]. Deep neural networks have become well-known for their use in autonomous driving functions in intelligent transportation systems. However, safety regulations, as well as comfort and functionality, are essential [5]. Despite their significant contribution to autonomous vehicle visual perception, DNNs are easily fooled by adversarial attacks [6]. These attacks can alter the prediction of autonomous cars by bringing minor changes in the pixels of the images. In this way, neural networks fail by making incorrect predictions [7].

Many adversarial attacks have been studied, and their defense methods to improve adversarial robustness [8]. Some adversarial strategies have already been put forth and shown to be successful against image classifications [9,10] and several mechanisms to strengthen neural networks have already been suggested to protect against adversarial threats [11]. But prior studies have mostly concentrated on image classifications. The effectiveness of such adversarial attacks and responses against regression models is unknown, such as ADMs. These ambiguities highlight possible privacy threats and expand the field of study. Intruders may potentially trigger road collisions and endanger human protection if adversarial assaults on ADS are effective. It is essential to propose a defensive technique appropriate for ADMs if present defensive strategies cannot be modified to protect against attacks on regression models.

In this paper, some adversarial attacks are analyzed given in Sect. 3 in this investigation. Those adversarial attacks were defended using four strategies. These tests employ Nvidia DAVE-2, Epoch, and VGG16 as the ADMs. The Nvidia DAVE-2 ADMs for autonomous cars are well-known in the community, Additionally, in the Udacity dataset, Epoch is seen to behave effectively, and VGG16 employs the extremely reliable framework of neural networks that are widely utilized in transfer learning for image categorization. Neither of the four defense strategies can successfully stop all five types of attacks. According to adversarial training and defensive distillation, only the IT-FGSM and an optimization-based strategy are capable of lowering the effectiveness of the attacks. Those two attacks, as well as AdvGan, can be successfully detected using a mechanism that recognizes unusual device status. Considering appropriate conditions, feature squeezing can identify all five attacks with significantly higher than 78% accuracy, although it has a significant false positive rate. This suggests that to develop a strong defensive mechanism against different threats, a system or middleware must employ many security techniques simultaneously.

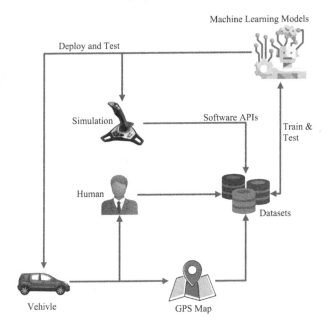

Fig. 1. Generic autonomous driving model based on machine learning

Structure of the Paper: The introduction of this paper is presented in Sect. 1. The rest of the paper is organized as follows: Literature Review is covered in Sect. 2. The methodology is represented in Sect. 3. The Sect. 4 provides the results, and the paper is concluded in Sect. 5.

2 Literature Review

2.1 Autonomous Driving Systems

Autonomous vehicles, which are developed on various ADMs, represent one of the finest competent and fascinating examples of innovation that has been rapidly evolving around the globe. The very first autonomous driving competition was organized in 2005, which goes by the name of DARPA [12] While following, the topic has experienced tremendous expansion, and several ADS proposals have been made. One of the essential elements that support this reason is DNN-based LiDAR-based item identification [13,14]. Additionally, TESLA uses a variety of deep neural networks and learning models for its AutoPilot capabilities. It goes without saying that every technique that incorporates a learning model is going to provide various flaws and be vulnerable to adversarial assaults [11]. This typically happens whenever the initial forecast differs from reality and the actual prediction that exceeds the adversarial threshold.

2.2   Adversarial Attacks on ADS

In [15], an examination of common autonomous vehicle weaknesses is provided. The study in [16] states that adversarial attacks might potentially be successful against every legitimate input or successful against a certain parameter alone. To execute these assaults, there are primarily two types of approaches: those depending upon optimizing methods and those dependent upon the fast gradient step method. Both types of attacks discussed above may be conducted using optimization-based techniques. L-BFGS, which was suggested by the authors of [17], is one illustration. The Fast gradient step method and its expansions, such as iterative-based-FGSM, and momentum-based iterative-FGSM, are those techniques [18].

The patch attack only impacts a limited percentage of image dots. The variations in image pixels are considerably bigger than those caused by the perturbations assault, which often impacts most of the pixels inside of the source picture. These assaults examined some operational components required for vision-based ADMs. For instance, the patched attack has been investigated concerning lane changing in [19], and 2D item identification in [20]. The other attacks were studied, considering symbol categorization in [21] and 2D item identification in [22]. Neither of the aforementioned research specifically examines how the assaults affect ADS safety and driving patterns.

2.3   Adversarial Defences

In general, preemptive defense and responsive defense are two categories of the various strategies that have been put forth to counter adversarial assaults. The goal of preemptive defenses is to increase the neural network's durability versus adversarial examples. The typical approach is to add batch normalization elements into the baseline models [23] or train the system employing datasets containing adversarial cases [11]. Defensive distillation was also presented by the authors in [24]. This hardens a neural network by increasing the size of signals to the soft max by altering a factor termed temperature. Conversely, responsive approaches look for adversarial cases. By examining the characteristics of the incoming pictures [25] and monitoring the state of the soft max [26], DNN might be utilized to ascertain if the network is being attacked. In this paper, the goal is to analyze some possible adversarial attacks versus some different CNN-based ADMs, present four countermeasures to counteract such attacks, and then present the best countermeasure versus these five attacks.

3   Proposed Methodology

3.1   Adversarial Attack

In image classification models, adversarial assaults are extremely effective. While this differs beyond the underlying model's forecast, perhaps we may conclude that adversarial attacks are effective and productive in undermining the models. There are three different forms of adversarial attacks that are based on the perturbation generation approach. The Fast Gradient Sign-Based technique (FGSM) executes assaults by applying the signature of the loss gradient to every pixel inside this baseline picture. Confrontational instances are produced using an optimization-based strategy. Using compositional models' capabilities, generative model-based methodology creates adversarial instances. There are some distinct adversarial attacks known as universal attacks. This produces a solitary adversarial case to screw up the whole database or every sample of the data.

ITFGSM. IT-FGSM [27] is an adversarial attack, and a special kind of FGSM. In this type of attack, every pixel of the source picture may have an additional signature added to it to create adversarial attacks, and as the term implies, the adversarial attack is strengthened by applying the targeted fast gradient sign method more than once.

Opt. This type of attack [28] is yet an additional technique for producing adversarial assaults. By using the equation underneath to solve the optimization issue, it determines the adversarial perturbation ϵ.

$$argmin_\epsilon ||\epsilon||_2 \ s.t. \ f(x + \epsilon) = b \ , x + \epsilon \, \epsilon[0, 1]^m \tag{1}$$

In this analysis of, we modify the b to $f(x) + \delta$ and both the aforementioned equation and the following equation.

$$argmin_\epsilon ||\epsilon||_2 \ + Z_\theta \left(Clips(x + \epsilon), f(x) + \delta\right) \tag{2}$$

AdvGAN. AdvGAN [9] provides the adversarial instances by implementing other objective $J_y = Z_\theta \left(G(x), f(x) + \delta\right)$ through initial picture into the objective function $J_{AdvGAN} = J_y + \alpha J_{GAN}$, where α is the thing which determines how important each target seems to be. Once learning is finished, the produced G can provide new adversarial attack examples that resemble our initial picture however can also update the forecast or produce forecasting which deviates by *delta* from $f(x)$.

Opt-uni. An Opt-uni [29] attack is a type of optimization-based approach.For that kind of attack, we disrupt a picture initially, then each picture in the database individually at a time. By converting v to $v + \delta v$, we determine that the least difference is δv. The general disturbance was obtained by repeatedly performing this assault across the entire data set.

AdvGAN-uni. This is the variant of the Advance GAN method [9]. Rather than creating the distinct perturbations $G(x)$ per each picture within the data as is the case in that sort of attack, we suggested utilizing GAN to produce the general perturbations. An overall disturbance is produced by the generators.

Table 1. Methodology and their capabilities

Method	Comments
Regression model	This model is weak to adversarial attacks
Classification model	This model is highly successful against adversarial attacks
Adversarial training	In contrast to other sorts of attacks, adversarial training is particularly successful against ITFGSM and opt
Defensive distillation	This defensive technique works well versus ITFGSM and certain similar types of attacks, although not versus others
Feature squeezing	This method is effective in detecting an adversarial attack. However, it is not well enough in defense
Anomaly detection	Although this defensive technique can identify adversarial attacks, and also it has several drawbacks by itself

3.2 Adversarial Defenses

As we know, each model has a defense strategy for all kinds of attacks. To defend against adversarial attacks on ADMs, we incorporated four defenses in this investigation as given in Table 1. All four techniques are given below:

Adversarial Training. In order to defend against this, we first create adversarial instances and attempt to relearn the existing system using hostile instances. By using this strategy, the models would understand the characteristics of adversarial cases, resulting in resilient and universally applicable models.

Defensive Distillation. The defensive distillation [24] type of approach uses the original model's prediction of class probabilities to train a new model.

Anomaly Detection. Continually checking the conditions of the automobile and ADMs is a live supervision mechanism found in autonomous driving systems. In order to identify possible additional deaths brought on by adversarial attacks, we initially evaluate the model's forecasting after they are applied. We next utilize NvidiaSMI to analyze the processor and memory usage. This anomaly detection method analyzes GPU utilization and forecasting times for each picture, either using adversarial instances or without them.

Feature Squeezing. This methods have two types of techniques [30] in order to facilitate defense versus adversarial attacks. A picture's native 24 bit color is reduced in the first technique to 1 bit or 8 bit color. While the bit quality declines, one could more easily foresee an adversarial attack. By our next technique, median temporal flattening, we move the strainer to change the main pixel number to the average of the pixel number. Thus, one may state that there is a chance of an adversarial attack if there is a gap between the forecast of the source picture and the estimation of the compressed picture that surpasses the cutoff value.

3.3   Neural Regression

The Keras library supports a neural network regression model to provide the solution to the regression problems. We needed to determine or forecast the accuracy of the trained models using a few dependent variables.

3.4   SVM Classification

A support vector machine classification is just the model's discrete observations coordinated together. It belongs to the class of supervised machine learning, which is utilized for issues involving the categorization of distinct categories. It has been employed in this study since we needed to ensure whether the methodology backed training models.

4   Results

A thorough examination of adversarial attacks and countermeasures against ADMs To achieve this, we applied four defensive techniques and five adversarial attacks to three convolutional neural network-based driving models. According to the study's findings, all three driving models aside from IT-FGSM are not resistant to these adversarial attacks, whereas neither of four defensive strategies can counteract all five of them. Following a thorough analyzation of every attack, we discovered that CNN based training is particularly susceptible towards the attack we mentioned in the article because they have a strong achievement percentage when used against regressors. As a result, they are not appropriate for use when training against such attacks.

	precision	recall	f1-score	support
0	0.97	0.93	0.95	1074
1	0.82	0.93	0.87	354
accuracy			0.93	1428
macro avg	0.90	0.93	0.91	1428
weighted avg	0.94	0.93	0.93	1428

Fig. 2. Accuracy of the trained model

Models for classifying attacks defend well against adversarial attacks. The outcomes also demonstrate that defensive distillation and adversarial training are only somewhat successful against IT-FGSM and opt attacks, however, hardly versus alternative forms of attacks. Feature squeezing and defensive distillation, additional major defense strategies, are also capable of spotting certain attacks, although each has its particular drawbacks and restrictions.

4.1 Accuracy and Prediction Error

In the Fig. 3, two images have been shown. On the left image the results of the training model are shown when the models are being trained. It is observed that at start the error rate was very high, as the model continue training, the error rate are reduced down linearly. In the right image, the total performance of the 1428 samples have been discussed. It is observed that, more that 95% samples did not deviates from the attacks when defensive techniques are being used as shown in the Fig. 3.

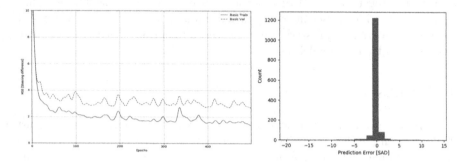

Fig. 3. The results of the simulation with 1428 samples

4.2 SVM Classification

The results of the SVM classification on the testing samples are given in Fig. 2. There are two classifications in this diagram; '0' and '1'. The normal behavior of the ADMs is categorized as '0', and the other behaviors are categorized as '1' where the infraction of the vehicles is greater than 0. Precision, recall, f1-score, and support are used as measurement metrics. The support for 0 is 1074 and the support for 1 is 354. This means that we have 75% support for autonomous models. The precision score was 0.97, the recall of our model was 0.93, and the f1-score was 0.95. That means that, collectively, the performance of the classification model was 95.7%.

4.3 Perturbations and Decision Boundary

In Fig. 4 two results have been shown: steering angle difference and infraction of the vehicle. We used two types of graphs to find the difference and infraction in the form of decision boundary and perturbation. Color is given on the Y-axis, width is given on the X-axis, steering angle difference, and infraction is on the Z-axis in the three-dimensional graph. On the other side of the image, few color combinations show different types of results. The dark color shows that there is no attack on the surface, and the lighter color shows the region where adversarial attacks happen. The color that is in the middle acts as the decision boundary between the two regions where adversarial attacks happen and the safe region.

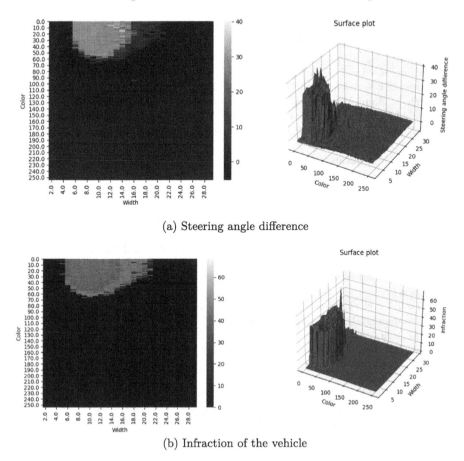

(a) Steering angle difference

(b) Infraction of the vehicle

Fig. 4. Difference of Steering Angle and Infraction of the Vehicle

5   Conclusion

In this research, we examine several of the adversarial attacks against ADMs as well as defense methods to identify and thwart these assaults. We employed neural regression and support vector machines as our two models for training samples. As we can observe, classifiers are far better adapted to adversarial assaults than regressors. Neither of the four defense strategies can successfully stop all five types of attacks. According to the adversarial training and defensive distillation, only IT-FGSM and optimization-based strategy are capable of lowering the effectiveness of the attacks. Those two attacks, as well as AdvGan, can be successfully detected using a mechanism that recognizes unusual device status. This suggests that in order to develop a defensive mechanism that is strong against different threats, a system or middleware must employ many security techniques simultaneously. The findings reveal that, out of 1428 testing examples, 95.7% of the specimens in SVM demonstrate that there is no divergence beyond +0.5 and −0.5.

References

1. Mozaffari, S., Al-Jarrah, O.Y., Dianati, M., Jennings, P., Mouzakitis, A.: Deep learning-based vehicle behavior prediction for autonomous driving applications: a review. IEEE Trans. Intell. Transp. Syst. **23**(1), 33–47 (2020)

2. Singh, S., Saini, B.S.: Autonomous cars: recent developments, challenges, and possible solutions. In: IOP Conference Series: Materials Science and Engineering, vol. 1022, no. 1, p. 012028. IOP Publishing (2021)

3. Raja, F.Z., Khattak, H.A., Aloqaily, M., Hussain, R.: Carpooling in connected and autonomous vehicles: current solutions and future directions. ACM Comput. Surv. **1**(1), 1–35 (2021)

4. Ni, R., Leung, J.: Safety and liability of autonomous vehicle technologies. Massachusetts Institute (2014)

5. Yuan, T., da Neto, W.R., Rothenberg, C.E., Obraczka, K., Barakat, C., Turletti, T.: Machine learning for next-generation intelligent transportation systems: a survey. Trans. Emerg. Telecommun. Technol. **33**(4), e4427 (2022)

6. Malik, S., Khattak, H.A., Ameer, Z., Shoaib, U., Rauf, H.T., Song, H.: Proactive scheduling and resource management for connected autonomous vehicles: a data science perspective. IEEE Sens. J. **21**(22), 25151–25160 (2021)

7. Kyrkou, C., et al.: Towards artificial-intelligence-based cybersecurity for robustifying automated driving systems against camera sensor attacks. In: 2020 IEEE Computer Society Annual Symposium on VLSI (ISVLSI), pp. 476–481. IEEE (2020)

8. Deng, Y., Zheng, X., Zhang, T., Chen, C., Lou, G., Kim, M.: An analysis of adversarial attacks and defenses on autonomous driving models. In: 2020 IEEE International Conference on Pervasive Computing and Communications (PerCom), pp. 1–10. IEEE (2020)

9. Poursaeed, O., Katsman, I., Gao, B., Belongie, S.: Generative adversarial perturbations. In: Proceedings of the IEEE Conference on Computer Vision and Pattern Recognition, pp. 4422–4431 (2018)

10. Xiao, C., Li, B., Zhu, J.-Y., He, W., Liu, M., Song, D.: Generating adversarial examples with adversarial networks. arXiv preprint arXiv:1801.02610 (2018)

11. Goodfellow, I.J., Shlens, J., Szegedy, C.: Explaining and harnessing adversarial examples. arXiv preprint arXiv:1412.6572 (2014)

12. Buehler, M., Iagnemma, K., Singh, S.: The 2005 DARPA Grand Challenge: The Great Robot Race, vol. 36. Springer, Cham (2007)

13. Cao, Y., et al.: Adversarial objects against lidar-based autonomous driving systems. arXiv preprint arXiv:1907.05418 (2019)

14. Arnold, E., Al-Jarrah, O.Y., Dianati, M., Fallah, S., Oxtoby, D., Mouzakitis, A.: A survey on 3D object detection methods for autonomous driving applications. IEEE Trans. Intell. Transp. Syst. **20**(10), 3782–3795 (2019)

15. Ren, K., Wang, Q., Wang, C., Qin, Z., Lin, X.: The security of autonomous driving: threats, defenses, and future directions. Proc. IEEE **108**(2), 357–372 (2019)

16. Yuan, X., He, P., Zhu, Q., Li, X.: Adversarial examples: attacks and defenses for deep learning. IEEE Trans. Neural Netw. Learn. Syst. **30**(9), 2805–2824 (2019)

17. Naseer, M.M., Ranasinghe, K., Khan, S.H., Hayat, M., Khan, F.S., Yang, M.H.: Intriguing properties of vision transformers. In: Advances in Neural Information Processing Systems, vol. 34, pp. 23296–23308 (2021)

18. Ren, H., Huang, T., Yan, H.: Adversarial examples: attacks and defenses in the physical world. Int. J. Mach. Learn. Cybern. **12**(11), 3325–3336 (2021). https://doi.org/10.1007/s13042-020-01242-z
19. Zhou, H., et al.: Deepbillboard: systematic physical-world testing of autonomous driving systems. In: 2020 IEEE/ACM 42nd International Conference on Software Engineering (ICSE), pp. 347–358. IEEE (2020)
20. Song, D.,et al.: Physical adversarial examples for object detectors. In: 12th USENIX Workshop on Offensive Technologies (WOOT 18) (2018)
21. Feng, R., Chen, J., Fernandes, E., Jha, S., Prakash, A.: Robust physical hard-label attacks on deep learning visual classification. arXiv preprint arXiv:2002.07088 (2020)
22. Lu, J., Sibai, H., Fabry, E.: Adversarial examples that fool detectors. arXiv preprint arXiv:1712.02494 (2017)
23. Yan, Z., Guo, Y., Zhang, C.: Deep defense: Training DNNs with improved adversarial robustness. In: Advances in Neural Information Processing Systems, vol. 31 (2018)
24. Papernot, N., McDaniel, P., Wu, X., Jha, S., Swami, A.: Distillation as a defense to adversarial perturbations against deep neural networks. In: IEEE Symposium on Security and Privacy (SP), pp. 582–597. IEEE (2016)
25. Zheng, Z., Hong, P.: Robust detection of adversarial attacks by modeling the intrinsic properties of deep neural networks. In: Advances in Neural Information Processing Systems, vol. 31 (2018)
26. Lee, K., Lee, K., Lee, H., Shin, J.: A simple unified framework for detecting out-of-distribution samples and adversarial attacks. In: Advances in Neural Information Processing Systems, vol. 31 (2018)
27. Kurakin, A., Goodfellow, I., Bengio, S., et al.: Adversarial examples in the physical world (2016)
28. Szegedy, C., et al.: Intriguing properties of neural networks. arXiv preprint arXiv:1312.6199 (2013)
29. Moosavi-Dezfooli, S.-M., Fawzi, A., Fawzi, O., Frossard, P.: Universal adversarial perturbations. In: Proceedings of the IEEE Conference on Computer Vision and Pattern Recognition, pp. 1765–1773 (2017)
30. Xu, W., Evans, D., Qi, Y.: Feature squeezing: Detecting adversarial examples in deep neural networks. arXiv preprint arXiv:1704.01155 (2017)

Implementation Aspects of Supersingular Isogeny-Based Cryptographic Hash Function

Miraz Uz Zaman$^{(\boxtimes)}$, Aaron Hutchinson, and Manki Min

Louisiana Tech University, 71272 Ruston, LA, USA
{muz001,aaronh,mankimin}@latech.edu

Abstract. Supersingular isogeny-based cryptosystems are considered an attractive candidate for the post-quantum cryptographic world due to their smaller key sizes. Based on the traversal in a supersingular isogeny graph (expander graph), Charles, Goren, and Lauter proposed a cryptographic hash function also known as CGL hash. In this paper, we present our study on the implementation-related aspects of the compact variation of the standard CGL hash function using different forms of elliptic curves (Weierstrass, Montgomery, and Legendre). Moreover, we show that some redundant computations in the original propositions of the CGL hash function can be avoided by utilizing the unique characteristics of the different forms of the elliptic curve. We also compared the running time and the total number of collisions through the experiments with the implemented algorithms.

Keywords: Post-quantum cryptography · Supersingular isogeny · Hash · CGL · Elliptic curves · Weierstrass · Montgomery · Legendre

1 Introduction

The cryptographic secure hash function is one of the widely used cryptographic tools which appears in almost all information security applications. Some long-established applications of secured hash functions are commitment schemes, digital signature schemes, message authentication codes, Blockchain, and password encryption. A cryptographic hash function converts an arbitrary length of input bit string to fixed-size data. One of the fundamental properties of a good hash function is its low computational time. Moreover, a secure hash function should be collision-free and preimage resistant, and the output distribution should be uniform. According to [20], a fully-fledged quantum computer can quickly break the currently standardized hash functions. However, based on a US National Academy report [15], we are roughly a decade away from such a fully-fledged quantum computer. Therefore, a post-quantum secured hash function is required

Supported by Louisiana Board of Regents GR301278.

to resist cryptanalysis for both classical and quantum computers. Moreover, the early deployment of such a post-quantum secured hash function will smooth the transition from pre-quantum to post-quantum cryptography.

In 2016, NIST initiated a process to standardize the post-quantum public-key cryptographic algorithms. After multiple rounds of evaluation and inspection, a handful of algorithms were nominated for the final round. SIKE [6] an Isogeny-based key encapsulation scheme advanced to the final round as an alternative candidate. The SIKE is mainly based on the idea of pseudo-random walks on a supersingular isogeny graph. Charles, Goren, & Lauter et al. first proposed walking on the supersingular isogeny graph (expander graph) to generate a hash function [1] in 2009. The hash function is also known as the acronym *CGL*. In CGL, each bit in the input strings of the hash function is used as the direction to traverse around the graph. Both CGL's and SIKE's security relies on the hardness of finding an isogeny between two supersingular elliptic curves. The best-known attack for both of these cryptosystems have exponential quantum complexity [7, §5]; hence they are quantum secure.

CGL hash function can also be shown as a sequence of 2-isogenies computation on supersingular elliptic curves over the finite field $\mathbb{F}_p^2$. The isogeny computation is mainly carried out through Vélu's [19] formula, where the elliptic curves are expressed in the Weierstrass form. Other than the Weierstrass form, an elliptic curve can also have some other well-known forms [8, §II.B], i.e., Montgomery form, Legendre form, Edward curves, etc. Each form shows a wide variety of computational costs for arithmetic operations and isogeny computations in the prime field. By utilizing unique non-trivial characteristics in the different forms of elliptic curves, some of the redundant computations can be saved from the original proposal of the CGL hash. In this paper, we showed some efficient and compact implementations of CGL on three widely used forms of elliptic curves. To the best of our knowledge, there is one such work [21] on the efficient algorithm of CGL previously. However, the work is only limited to the Weierstrass form. We also compared running times and collisions of our implementations for different prime fields with an extensive number of bit strings.

In Sect. 2 we refresh some basics, i.e., elliptic curve, isogenies, and the CGL hash. Some compact implementations of CGL hash on different forms of elliptic curves are discussed in Sect. 3. We present the theoretical and experimental results in Sect. 4 where we compare the running time and the total number of collisions for a comprehensive number of bit strings.

2   Definitions and Background

2.1   Elliptic Curve and Isogeny

An elliptic curve is a non-singular projective curve of genus 1 over a finite field $\mathbb{F}_q$ of q elements where $q = p^k$ with some prime p. The elliptic curve E over $\mathbb{F}_q$ can be represented as the following affine equation,

$$E/\mathbb{F}_q : y^2 + a_1 xy + a_3 y = x^3 + a_2 x^2 + a_4 x + a_6,$$

where $a_1, a_2, a_3, a_4, a_6 \in \mathbb{F}_q$. If a p-torsion subgroup of an elliptic curve $E[p]$ is non-trivial then the curve is *supersingular* otherwise it's *ordinary* [16, §V.3]. As the CGL is primarily based on supersingular isogeny graphs, in this paper, we interchangeably use the elliptic curve and supersingular elliptic curve. Let E and $\tilde{E}$ be an elliptic curve over $\mathbb{F}_q$. An isogeny $\phi : E \rightarrow \tilde{E}$ is a surjective morphism of curves over $\mathbb{F}_q$ so that $\phi(O_E) = O_{\tilde{E}}$ The rational function ϕ is also a group homomorphism which maps $E(\mathbb{F}_q) \rightarrow \tilde{E}(\mathbb{F}_q)$. Here, the elliptic curves $E/\mathbb{F}_q$ and $\tilde{E}/\mathbb{F}_q$ are isogenous as there exists an isogeny ϕ between them. The existence of ϕ also ensures that there is presence of dual isogeny $\hat{\phi}$ so that $\hat{\phi} : \tilde{E}/\mathbb{F}_q \rightarrow E/\mathbb{F}_q$ [16, §III.6.1]. This also creates an equivalence relation on the finite set of isomorphism classes of elliptic curves defined over $\mathbb{F}_q$. The equivalent class of the elliptic curve under this relation is defined as the isogeny class. For a seperable and non-constant isogeny, the degree of isogeny $deg\phi$ is equal to the cardinality of the kernel i.e.,. $deg\phi = |ker(\phi)|$. Therefore an isogeny can be identified by its kernel. For example, *l-isogeny* would have the kernel of size l. Vélu's formula uses the knowledge of the size of the kernel to compute the isogeny. Two isogenous curves fall into the same isogeny class, i.e., either both are supersingular or both are ordinary.

2.2   Isogeny Graph

In this discussion we will fix field $\mathbb{F}_q = \mathbb{F}_{p^2}$, as all the supersingular elliptic curve in characteristics p are on the same isogeny class and can be defined in either $\mathbb{F}_p$ or $\mathbb{F}_{p^2}$ [11]. The isomorphic classes of the elliptic curve can be represented through j-invariant, which is a unique a priori element of $\mathbb{F}_{p^2}$. A graph of l-isogeny graph can be defined by a set of elliptic curves in $\mathbb{F}_{p^2}$ as the vertices and edges are degrees l-isogeny between them. Such a graph consists of both ordinary and supersingular components. Because of the isogenous relation, supersingular and ordinary components of isogeny graphs are disconnected.

Pizer [12,13] shows that the supersingular component has the property of the Ramanujan graph [10]. Ramanujan graph is a highly connected regular graph also known as expander graph. The details on the Ramanujan graph can be found on [2,10]. Because of the strong connectivity found in Ramanujan graphs, there is only one supersingular component in the isogeny graph which will be the main interest of this paper. The vertices in the isogeny graph are represented as j-invariants, which can be computed from the curve equation, and the total number of vertices is close to $p/12$. CGL hash function employs $l = 2$ isogeny graph.

Figure 1 shows such a 2-isogeny graph $\mathbb{F}_{211^2}$. There are 18 vertices in the graph, which corresponds to supersingular j-invariants, and 2-isogenies refer to the edges between them. All of the 17 vertices show the expected behavior of 2-isogenies except the node with j-invariants of 40. However, it can be shown that as p expands, the total number of nodes with such an exceptional behavior stays small.

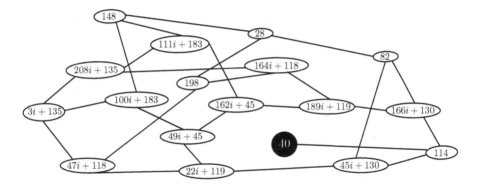

Fig. 1. The 2-isogeny graph for $\mathbb{F}_{211^2}$

2.3   CGL Hash

The rapid mixing property for a random walk in an expander graph showed strong pseudo-random behavior. Such a behavior has been widely used in different cryptographic constructions [4,9]. The principle idea of the CGL hash function is to use the same pseudo-random behavior of supersingular isogeny graph to produce a collision-free hash function. In CGL, the input of the hash function is used as the direction to traverse around the supersingular isogeny graph from the fixed starting vertex with backtracking avoided, and the end vertex is the output of the hash function. As we can see that changing the starting vertex or elliptic curve yields a different hash function, we can define a family of hash functions based on the starting curve. A 2-isogeny supersingular graph is ideally a 3-regular graph. As the CGL hash function avoids backtracking, there are two edges to follow from each vertex to the next vertex. Based on a uniform convention, these two edges will be assigned to the bit 1 and 0 leading to the next vertex.

Let's consider, a starting vertex or an elliptic curve E_1 which is defined as $y^2 = f_1(x)$. Now if we can factor the cubic $f(x)$ into $(x - x_1)(x - x_2)(x - x_3)$, 3 non-trivial 2 torsion points of E_1 can be represented as $\{(x_1, 0), (x_2, 0), (x_3, 0)\}$. Now, consider the computation of an isogeny ϕ that results an isogenous curve E_2 or $y^2 = f_2(x)$ where $ker\phi = \langle(x_1, 0)\rangle$. The other two torsion points $(x_2, 0)$ and $(x_3, 0)$ will map to the same points on curve E_2 i.e., $\phi(x_2, 0) = \phi(x_3, 0)$. The subgroup generated by kernel $\langle(x_2, 0)\rangle$ or $\langle(x_3, 0)\rangle$ on E_2 is the dual isogeny $\hat{\phi}$ return to the curve E_1.

In CGL, the dual isogeny is called the backtracking isogeny. So backtracking can be averted if new cubic $f_2(x)$ can factored out by $(x - \hat{x_2})$ where $\hat{x_2}$ is the x-coordinate of $\phi(x_2, 0)$. The remaining part of the factor is a quadratic term, and the two quadratic roots will be the x-abscissa of the other two torsion points. CGL hash proposes that a convention for ordering the point can be fixed to choose one torsion point with respect to the input bit. The chosen point will determine the next walk in the graph. Consequently, for the n-bit input string, the CGL hash takes a walk of n-steps. The output of the hash function is the j-invariant of the last elliptic curve. The flowchart of the CGL hash function is shown in Fig. 2.

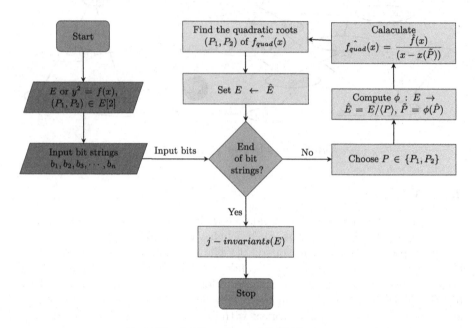

Fig. 2. Flowchart of CGL Hash

3   Compact CGL Hash Algorithms

3.1   Short Weierstrass Form

Any elliptic curve E over a field $\mathbb{F}_{p^2}$ of prime p, with $p > 3$ can be transformed into short Weierstrass form,

$$E : y^2 = x^3 + \alpha x + \beta,$$

where $(\alpha, \beta) \in K$ and $4\alpha^3 + 27\beta^2 \neq 0$. Later condition ensures that there are 3-distinct roots. The j-invariant of the elliptic curve E can be defined by,

$$j(E) = 1728 \frac{4\alpha^3}{4\alpha^3 + 27\beta^2}.$$

2 Isogenies. Let γ be a root of $x^3 + \alpha x^2 + \beta$. An algebric polynomial division by $(x - \gamma)$ shows that,

$$\frac{x^3 + \alpha x + \beta}{(x - \gamma)} = (x^2 + \gamma x + (\alpha + \gamma^2))$$

Therefore, the elliptic curve E can be expressed as,

$$E : y^2 = (x - \gamma)(x^2 + \gamma x + (\alpha + \gamma^2)).$$

So, the 3 torsion points of order 2 are $\{(\gamma, 0), (\frac{-\gamma \pm \sqrt{-4\alpha - 3\gamma^2}}{2}, 0)\}$. According to [18, Theorem 6.13], if $(x_0, 0)$ is a torsion point of order 2 applying 2-isogeny with $ker(\phi) = \langle(x_0, 0)\rangle$ produce the following mapping,

$$\phi : E \to \tilde{E} : y^2 = x^3 + \alpha' x + \beta'$$

$$(x, y) \mapsto \left(\frac{x^2 - x_0 x + t}{x - x_0}, \frac{(x - x_0)^2 - t}{(x - x_0)^2} y \right),$$

where, $t = 3x_0^2 + \alpha$, $\alpha' = \alpha - 5t$, $w = x_0 t$, and $\beta' = \beta - 7w$.

CGL Hash Algorithm for Short Weierstrass Form. The four input parameter of the Algorithm algspswei are α, β, γ over a field of $\mathbb{F}_{p^2}$, and n-bit message $M = (b_1, b_2, \cdots, b_n)$. Here, α, β forms a supersingular elliptic curve E in weierstrass form $y^2 = x^3 + \alpha x + \beta$ over a field of $\mathbb{F}_{p^2}$, γ is one of the root of $x^3 + \alpha x + \beta$. We calculate x-abscissa of other two torsion points (x_0, x_1) in step 2 and step 3 of Algorithm algspswei. From steps 4 to 7, we set a uniform convention to define x_0 and x_1 to navigate the next walk in the graph. The convention is simply to choose the maximum of two values from step 3 as x_0 and the minimum value as x_1 for bit 1 and vice versa for bit 0. Steps 9 and 10 is utilizing Vélu's formula to calculate the next isogenous elliptic curve Weierstrass parameter α and β. The x abscissa of the dual isogeny or the backtracking point in the new isogenous curve is calculated in step 11. The output of the algorithm is the j-invaraint of the last elliptic curve which is calculated in step 13.

Algorithm 1. CGL hashing using Weierstrass Curve

Input: α, β, γ, M
Output: j-invariant
1: **for** bit in M **do**
2:　　$\delta \leftarrow \sqrt{-4\alpha - 3\gamma^2}$
3:　　$(x_0, x_1) \leftarrow (\frac{-\gamma + \delta}{2}, \frac{-\gamma - \delta}{2})$
4:　　**if** $bit \leftarrow 1$ **then**
5:　　　　$(x_0, x_1) \leftarrow \max(x_0, x_1), \min(x_0, x_1)$
6:　　**else** $\{bit \leftarrow 0\}$
7:　　　　$(x_0, x_1) \leftarrow \min(x_0, x_1), \max(x_0, x_1)$
8:　　**end if**
9:　　$t \leftarrow 3x_0^2 + \alpha$, $w \leftarrow x_0 t$
10:　　$\alpha \leftarrow \alpha - 5t$, $\beta \leftarrow \beta - 7w$
11:　　$\gamma \leftarrow \frac{x_1^2 - x_0 x_1 + t}{x_1 - x_0}$
12: **end for**
13: **return** j-invariant $\leftarrow 1728 \frac{4\alpha^3}{4\alpha^3 + 27\beta^2}$

3.2   Montgomery Form

An elliptic curve in Montgomery form over a field $\mathbb{F}_{p^2}$ can be defined by equation

$$E_{(A,B)} : By^2 = x^3 + Ax^2 + x = x(x^2 + Ax + 1),$$

where, $A, B \in \mathbb{F}_{p^2}$ and $B(A^2 - 4) = 0$. The parameter A primarily controls the geometry of $E_{(A,B)}$. The j-invariants of the curve can be expressed as,

$$j(E_{(A,B)}) = \frac{256(A^2 - 3)^3}{A^2 - 4}.$$

2 Isogenies. From the curve equation $E_{(A,B)}$, it can be easily verified that a K-rational point $Q = E(0,0)$ is order of 2. If $P = (x_P, 0)$ is another K-rational point of order 2, then $x_P^2 + Ax_P + 1 = 0$. So, the other two rational points of order 2 are $(\frac{-A \pm \sqrt{A^2 - 4}}{2}, 0)$. According to [14, §4.2], applying 2 isogeny with $ker(\phi) = \langle P \rangle$ generates the following mapping,

$$\phi : E \rightarrow \tilde{E} : by^2 = x^3 + ax^2 + x = x(x^2 + ax + 1)$$

$$(x, y) \mapsto (g(x), yg'(x)),$$

with $b = x_P B$, $a = 2(1 - 2x_P)^2 = 2 - (-A \pm \sqrt{A^2 - 4})^2$, and $g(x) = x\frac{xx_P - 1}{x - x_P}$. Moreover, [14, Corollary 1] shows that kernel of dual of ϕ is $\langle (0,0) \rangle$. Hence, $ker(\hat{\phi}) = \langle (0,0) \rangle$. On the other hand, the authors in [3, Eqs. (18) & (19)] outlines 2-isogeny for $ker(\phi) = \langle (0,0) \rangle$ as, '

$$\phi : E \rightarrow F : By^2 = x^3 + (A + 6)x^2 + 4(2 + A)x$$

$$(x, y) \mapsto \left(\frac{(x - 1)^2}{x}, y(1 - \frac{1}{x^2}) \right).$$

The authors in [14, Remark 6] describes an isomorphism of F with the following mapping,

$$\psi : F \rightarrow G : \frac{B}{\sqrt{A^2 - 4}}y^2 = x^3 - \frac{2A}{\sqrt{A^2 - 4}}x^2 + x$$

$$(x, y) \mapsto \left(\frac{x + A + 2}{\sqrt{A^2 - 4}}, \frac{y}{\sqrt{A^2 - 4}} \right).$$

Now by applying 2-isogeny with kernel of $\langle (0,0) \rangle$ following a simple algebric computation on coefficients of x^2 can be shown that, dual of ψ is also $\langle (0,0) \rangle$.

$$\frac{-2\frac{-2A}{\sqrt{A^2 - 4}}}{\sqrt{\frac{4A^2}{A^2 - 4} - 4}} = \pm A$$

Hence, $ker(\hat{\psi}) = \langle (0,0) \rangle$.

CGL Hash Algorithm for Montgomery Form. The two input parameters of the Algorithm algspsmont are the Montgomery curve parameters $A \in \mathbb{F}_p^2$ so that $y^2 = x^3 + Ax^2 + x$ supersingular elliptic curve and n-bit message M $(b_1, b_2, \cdots, b_n)$. As we know from the previous description, the dual of the kernel is always $\langle (0, 0) \rangle$. So now, for the CGL hashing algorithm $(0, 0)$ is the backtracking point. Hence, we don't need to calculate the backtracking point and other 2 torsion points can be assigned for bit 1 and 0 based on some uniform convention. From step 2 to 8, such a convention have been set to choose the next isogenous curve. The hash function's output will be the j-invariant of the last isogenous curve.

Algorithm 2. CGL hashing algorithm using Montgomery Curve

Input: A, B, M
Output: j-invariant
1: **for** bit in M **do**
2:     $C \leftarrow \sqrt{A^2 - 4}$
3:     $A_0 \leftarrow 2A^2 - 4 + AC$
4:     $A_1 \leftarrow 2A^2 - 4 - AC$
5:     **if** $bit \leftarrow 1$ **then**
6:         $A \leftarrow 2 - \max(A_0, A_1)$
7:     **else** $\{bit \leftarrow 0\}$
8:         $A \leftarrow 2 - \min(A_0, A_1)$
9:     **end if**
10: **end for**
11: **return** j-invariant $\leftarrow \frac{256(A^2-3)^3}{A^2-4}$

3.3   Legendre Form

Another interesting form of elliptic curve is Legendre Form. If $\lambda \in \mathbb{F}_p^2$ and $\lambda \neq 0, 1$, elliptic curve E in Legendre form can be represented as,

$$E_\lambda : y^2 = x(x - 1)(x - \lambda).$$

Here, Legendre coefficient, λ for E is not unique. In fact each of

$$\lambda, \frac{1}{\lambda}, 1 - \lambda, \frac{1}{1 - \lambda}, \frac{\lambda}{\lambda - 1}, \frac{\lambda - 1}{\lambda}$$

yields an Isomorphic E curve. The j-invariant of E_λ is,

$$j(E_\lambda) = 2^8 \frac{(\lambda^2 - \lambda + 1)^3}{\lambda^2 (\lambda - 1)^2}.$$

Considering the fact that most supersingular elliptic curves will have three 2-isogenies, we can infer that those six possible Legendre coefficients for the same j-invariant can be grouped into three pairs where each pair is directly related to each of the three 2-isogenies.

2 Isogenies. The three 2-torsion points are readily available from the elliptic curve expression, E_λ. The points in affine form are $(0,0),(1,0),(\lambda,0)$. From [5, Theorem 4 & 5], it can be shown that applying 2 isogeny when $ker(\phi) \neq (\lambda,0)$ will produce the following mapping,

$$\phi : E \to \tilde{E} : y^2 = x(x-1)(x-\lambda').$$

The relationship between λ and λ' can be shown with the following equation.

$$\lambda = \begin{cases} \frac{(\sqrt{\lambda}+1)^2}{4\sqrt{\lambda}} = \frac{\lambda+1+2\sqrt{\lambda}}{4\sqrt{\lambda}} & \text{if } ker(\phi) = \langle(0,0)\rangle \\ \frac{-(\sqrt{1-\lambda}-1)^2}{4\sqrt{1-\lambda}} = \frac{\lambda-2+2\sqrt{1-\lambda}}{4\sqrt{1-\lambda}} & \text{if } ker(\phi) = \langle(1,0)\rangle \\ \frac{(\sqrt{\lambda}+\sqrt{\lambda-1})^2}{4\sqrt{\lambda}\sqrt{\lambda-1}} = \frac{2\lambda-1+2\sqrt{\lambda}\sqrt{1-\lambda}}{4\sqrt{\lambda}\sqrt{\lambda-1}} & \text{if } ker(\phi) = \langle(\lambda,0)\rangle \end{cases}$$

CGL Hash Algorithm for Legendre Form. The input parameters of the Algorithm algspsleg are Legendre parameter $\lambda \in \mathbb{F}_p^2$ so that $y^2 = x(x-1)(x-\lambda)$ is a supersingular elliptic curve and n-bit message M $(b_1, b_2, \cdots, b_n)$. Similar to the Montgomery form algorithm, the backtracking point is fixed which is $(\lambda,0)$. Therefore, from step 2 to 5, we set kernel point $(1,0)$ for bit 1 and $(0,0)$ for bit 0. The output of the hash function algorithm will be the j-invariant of the last isogenous curve.

Algorithm 3. CGL hashing algorithm using Legendre Curve

Input: λ, M
Output: j-invariant
1: **for** bit in M **do**
2:     **if** $bit \leftarrow 1$ **then**
3:         $\lambda \leftarrow \frac{\lambda+1+2\sqrt{\lambda}}{4\sqrt{\lambda}}$
4:     **else** $\{bit \leftarrow 0\}$
5:         $\lambda \leftarrow \frac{\lambda-2+2\sqrt{1-\lambda}}{4\sqrt{1-\lambda}}$
6:     **end if**
7: **end for**
8: **return** j-invariant $\leftarrow 2^8 \frac{(\lambda^2-\lambda+1)^3}{\lambda^2(\lambda-1)^2}$

3.4 Yoshida et al. Proposed Method for Computing CGL Hash

Yoshida et al. proposed two compact methods for computing CGL hash in [21, §5] for the Weierstrass form of supersingular elliptic curves. Both methods mainly rely on their proposed Theorem [21, Theorem 1] which deduces a relationship between the current and following curve parameters using the non-backtracking torsion point. As both methods theoretically share the exact cost, we implemented their proposed method 1.

4 Result and Discussion

4.1 Algorithmic Cost Comparison

Tables 1 and 2 compare the computational cost for all the three different algorithms described in Sect. sectionspsAlgos. The result in the tables is based on the frequently used assumption that I = 100M, S = 0.67M, and SR = (0.67 log p + 100)M, where I, S, SR, and M represent Inversion, Squaring, Square root, and Multiplication, respectively.

The computational cost measure for calculating 2-isogeny sequences for n-bit input strings and determining the j-invariant of the last isogenous curve. The comparison among the algorithms shows that the algorithm for Montgomery and Legendre form has a lower computational cost than the algorithm for the Weierstrass form. Moreover, simulation result from the implementation of the algorithm in the following subsection also shows the same result.

Table 1. CGL Hash operation counts for different algorithms

Algorithm	Curve Model	Counts			
		Multiplication	Square	Square root	Inversion
1	Weierstrass	$4n + 1$	$3n + 2$	n	$n + 1$
2	Montgomery	$2n + 1$	$n + 1$	n	1
3	Legendre	2	3	n	$n + 1$

Table 2. CGL Hash costs comparison for different algorithms

Algorithm	Curve Model	Costs in M
1	Weierstrass	$(206 + 0.67 \log p)n + 102.33$
2	Montgomery	$(102.67 + 0.67 \log p)n + 101.67$
3	Legendre	$(200 + 0.67 \log p)n + 104$

4.2 Simulation Result

To evaluate the performance of the algorithms algspswei, algspsmont, and algspsleg we wrote a Python script using SageMath [17]. We also implemented the algorithm proposed in [21, §5.3] and compared it with our compact algorithms. All the algorithms are simulated in 64 bit processor Intel®Core™ i5-7500 CPU @ 3.40 GHz x 4 in Ubuntu 18.04.6 LTS operating system. Moreover, we identified the algorithm's running time and the total number of collisions as the comparison criteria as "low computational time" and "collision avoidance" are the two fundamental properties of the hash function. The running time and total collisions have been computed for 2^{20} number of unique 128-bit input strings with different finite (prime) fields. Here, running time means the difference between starting and ending times of the algorithm for each input bit string. To find the central tendency of running time, we took the arithmetic mean of all the 2^{20} unique input bit strings. On the other hand, the total number of collisions is the input bit strings that end up on the same j-invariant. We used the SIKE proposed elliptic curve, or its isomorphic curve over $\mathbb{F}_p^2$, as the starting curve for all the algorithms. The starting elliptic curves are $y^2 = x^3 - 11x + 14$, $y^2 = x^3 + 6x^2 + x$, and $y^2 = x(x-1)(x - 17 + 12\sqrt{2})$ over $\mathbb{F}_p^2$ for Weierstrass, Montgomery, and Legendre forms respectively.

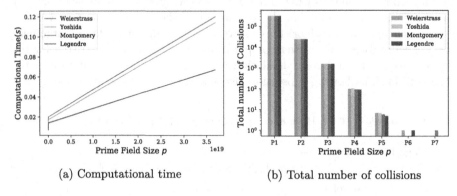

(a) Computational time   (b) Total number of collisions

Fig. 3. Average computation time and total number of collisions for 2^{20} number of 128 input bit strings over different size of finite field $\mathbb{F}_{p^2}$. P1, P2, P3, P4, P5, P6, P7 in Fig. 3b are representing the prime number $2^{24} + 43, 2^{28} + 3, 2^{32} + 15, 2^{36} + 31, 2^{40} + 15, 2^{44} + 7, 2^{48} + 75$ respectively.

Figure 3 shows the simulation result for all four algorithms. The algorithm proposed in [21, §5.3] is designated as Yoshida, and the other three algorithms are represented with the corresponding curve form name. Figure 3a shows that computational time increase with the field size and Algorithm algspsmont, algspsleg have lower computational time than other two algorithms. The total number of collisions decreases exponentially with the increasing prime field sizes shown in Fig. 3b.

In another experiment, we tested the total number of collisions for different sizes of input bit strings on all the implemented algorithms. As we know, for a prime field of size p, there are approximately $\frac{P}{12}$ number of j-invariant or unique isomorphic supersingular elliptic curve. In this experiment, we choose $p \approx 2^{21}$ and checked the collisions for all the combinations of input bit strings up to the length of 18. Figure 4 shows that the number of collisions increases exponentially as the length of the input bit string expands. The more rapid increase of the number of collisions by Montgomery form curves needs more detailed analysis with different starting elliptic curves and prime fields, but one thing clear is that the collision increase like this is not acceptable behavior in a cryptographic hash function. This experiment was designed to choose the proper size of the prime field in the design of a secure hash function.

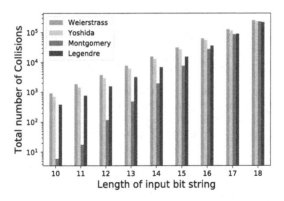

Fig. 4. Total number of collisions for different length of input bit strings

5   Conclusion

In this paper, we presented four different compact implementations of 2-isogeny sequences or a CGL hash function. Out of the four different implementations of the compact CGL function, we found that Legendre and Montgomery forms lead to the best result in computation time. This is the result of the effective use of the fixed backtracking isogeny properties of Montgomery and Legendre form curves which were one of the performance bottlenecks in the standard CGL function. On the other hand, Legendre form-based implementation's collision rates were higher than those for Montgomery form while still lower than those for the other two implementations. We believe that this could be the result of short-length cycles during the computation with Legendre form and we'll dig into the details to find more explanations and solutions.

In future work, we will focus on further reducing the cost of traversal in supersingular isogeny graph as well as the time and collision trade-off study through comparison with other variations of CGL function. We strongly believe a cryptographic hash function's key aspect must be security and a faster hash function with poorer security cannot be accepted.

Our future work also includes the in-depth study of the relation between the six Legendre coefficients and the three 2-isogenies as mentioned in Sect. 3.3 that can lead to a more efficient design of a supersingular isogeny-based cryptographic hash function. If we can use it to avoid or mitigate the calculation of square roots which is an expensive operation in supersingular isogeny graphs, it will provide not only a better way to design a new hash function but also a better way to improve the other cryptographic functions based on supersingular isogeny.

References

1. Charles, D.X., Lauter, K.E., Goren, E.Z.: Cryptographic hash functions from expander graphs. J. Cryptol. **22**(1), 93–113 (2007). https://doi.org/10.1007/s00145-007-9002-x
2. Costache, A., Feigon, B., Lauter, K., Massierer, M., Puskás, A.: Ramanujan graphs in cryptography. In: Balakrishnan, J.S., Folsom, A., Lalín, M., Manes, M. (eds.) Research Directions in Number Theory. AWMS, vol. 19, pp. 1–40. Springer, Cham (2019). https://doi.org/10.1007/978-3-030-19478-9_1
3. Feo, L.D., Jao, D., Plût, J.: Towards quantum-resistant cryptosystems from supersingular elliptic curve isogenies. J. Math. Cryptol. **8**(3), 209–247 (2014). https://www.degruyter.com/document/doi/10.1515/jmc-2012-0015/html. https://doi.org/10.1515/jmc-2012-0015
4. Goldreich, O.: Candidate one-way functions based on expander graphs. In: Goldreich, O. (ed.) Studies in Complexity and Cryptography. Miscellanea on the Interplay between Randomness and Computation. LNCS, vol. 6650, pp. 76–87. Springer, Heidelberg (2011). https://doi.org/10.1007/978-3-642-22670-0_10
5. Hutchinson, A., Elliott, J.: Supersingular isogeny Diffie-Hellman with Legendre form. J. Math. Cryptol. **1**, 19 (2022). https://doi.org/10.1515/JMC.2008.008
6. Jao, D., et al.: Supersingular isogeny key encapsulation. Submission NIST Post-Quantum Standard. Proj. **152**, 154–155 (2017)
7. Jao, D., De Feo, L.: Towards quantum-resistant cryptosystems from supersingular elliptic curve isogenies. In: Yang, B.-Y. (ed.) PQCrypto 2011. LNCS, vol. 7071, pp. 19–34. Springer, Heidelberg (2011). https://doi.org/10.1007/978-3-642-25405-5_2
8. Lara-Nino, C., Díaz-Pérez, A., Morales-Sandoval, M.: Elliptic curve lightweight cryptography: a survey. IEEE Access **6**, 72514–72550 (2018). https://doi.org/10.1109/ACCESS.2018.2881444
9. Lauter, K.E., Charles, D.X., Goren, E.Z.: Pseudorandom number generation with expander graphs (Mar 15 2011), uS Patent 7,907,726
10. Lubotzky, A., Phillips, R., Sarnak, P.: Ramanujan graphs. Combinatorica **8**(3), 261–277 (1988)
11. Mestre, J.F.: La méthode des graphes. Exemples et applications. In: Proceedings of the International Conference on Class Numbers and Fundamental Units of Algebraic Number Fields (Katata), pp. 217–242. CiteSeer (1986)
12. Pizer, A.K.: Ramanujan graphs. Computational perspectives on number theory, Chicago, IL. AMS/IP Stud. Adv, Math **7**, 159–178 (1995)
13. Pizer, A.K.: Ramanujan graphs and Hecke operators. Bull. Am. Math. Soc. **23**(1), 127–137 (1990)
14. Renes, J.: Computing isogenies between montgomery curves using the action of (0, 0). In: Lange, T., Steinwandt, R. (eds.) PQCrypto 2018. LNCS, vol. 10786, pp. 229–247. Springer, Cham (2018). https://doi.org/10.1007/978-3-319-79063-3_11
15. National Academies of Sciences, Engineering Medicine : Quantum computing: progress and prospects (2019). https://doi.org/10.17226/25196
16. Silverman, J.H.: Heights and elliptic curves. In: Cornell, G., Silverman, J.H. (eds.) Arithmetic Geometry, pp. 253–265. Springer (1986). https://doi.org/10.1007/978-1-4613-8655-1_10
17. Stein, W., et al.: Sage Mathematics Software (Version 9.4.0). The Sage Development Team (2021). https://www.sagemath.org/
18. Sutherland, A.: Lecture 6: Isogeny kernels and division polynomials. In: Elliptic Curves–MIT Course No. 18.783. Cambridge MA (2019). https://math.mit.edu/classes/18.783/2019/LectureNotes6.pdf. MIT OpenCourseWare

19. Vélu, J.: Isogénies entre courbes elliptiques. Comptes-Rendus de l'Académie des Sciences, Série I **273**, 238–241 (Juillet 1971)
20. Webber, M., Elfving, V., Weidt, S., Hensinger, W.K.: The impact of hardware specifications on reaching quantum advantage in the fault tolerant regime. AVS Quant. Sci. **4**(1), 013801 (2022)
21. Yoshida, R., Takashima, K.: Simple algorithms for computing a sequence of 2-isogenies. In: Lee, P.J., Cheon, J.H. (eds.) ICISC 2008. LNCS, vol. 5461, pp. 52–65. Springer, Heidelberg (2009). https://doi.org/10.1007/978-3-642-00730-9_4

Trust-Based Communities for Smart Grid Security and Privacy

Seohyun Park, Xiang Li[✉], and Yuhong Liu

Department of Computer Science and Engineering, Santa Clara University,
Santa Clara, CA, USA
{spark4,xli8,yhliu}@scu.edu

Abstract. In smart grids, two-way communication between end-users and the grid allows frequent data exchange, which on one hand enhances users' experience, while on the other hand increase security and privacy risks. In this paper, we propose an efficient system to address security and privacy problems, in contrast to the data aggregation schemes with high cryptographic overheads. In the proposed system, users are grouped into local communities and trust-based blockchains are formed in each community to manage smart grid transactions, such as reporting aggregated meter reading, in a light-weight fashion. We show that the proposed system can meet the key security objectives with a detailed analysis. Also, experiments demonstrated that the proposed system is efficient and can provide satisfactory user experience, and the trust value design can easily distinguish benign users and bad actors.

Keywords: Smart grid · Data aggregation · Blockchain · Security · Privacy

1 Introduction

Smart grid enables sharing information about electricity demand and supply in real time, which improves energy efficiency and provides more features to end-users [1]. With Internet of Things (IoT) applications in smart grids, such as smart meters and IoT appliances, two way communications between end-users and the grid allows frequent meter readings, which leads to more accurate prediction and further optimization of supply and demand. Also, certain tasks, like laundry, can be scheduled at off-peak hours to smooth demand fluctuation and reduce the energy bill of end-users [2].

However, two way communication and high frequency meter reading also raise security and privacy concerns. For example, a cyberattack (e.g. man-in-the-middle attack) may gain access to detailed electricity usage data, such as running laundry or watching television during certain hours of a day, which can be leveraged to infer more sensitive information, such as vacancy in the house [3], and may further lead to security risks like break-ins. Data aggregation at local gateways [4] may mitigate some of the privacy issues, but the computational overhead can be high [5].

© ICST Institute for Computer Sciences, Social Informatics and Telecommunications Engineering 2023
Published by Springer Nature Switzerland AG 2023. All Rights Reserved
Z. J. Haas et al. (Eds.): WiCON 2022, LNICST 464, pp. 28–43, 2023.
https://doi.org/10.1007/978-3-031-27041-3_3

To efficiently address the security and privacy problems, in this paper, we propose a new design, a community based blockchain solution: the end-users are grouped in communities and each community holds a local blockchain, which aggregates electricity usage data of members in the community and reports back to the service provider. Within a community, a time-based trust model is designed to detect bad actors who are not cooperative or having fraudulent behaviors. Compared to cryptography-heavy schemes, the proposed solution is much more lightweight and efficient.

The contributions of this paper are summarized as follows.

- We proposed a community based blockchain solution to address privacy problems in eletricity usage data reporting in smart grids.
- We proposed a time-based trust model, a lightweight solution to security problems in community operations.
- We did extensive analysis on how the proposed system can achieve the security goals and experimentally verified the performance of the proposed system and the effectiveness of the trust value design.

Organization. The rest of this paper is organized as follows. The related works are discussed in Section II. We describe the proposed system in Section III. In Section IV and Section V, the security and the performance aspects of the proposed system are discussed, respectively. Section VI concludes the paper.

2   Related Works

Various security aspects in smart grids are discussed in [3]. Security in smart grid is crucial as a large amount of data is generated, transmitted and possibly exposed. Various cryptographic countermeasures are developed to fight against security threats [6,7].

Privacy in smart grids has been studied from multiple aspects. In [8], a privacy preserving scheme using cryptographic methods was proposed for incentive based demand response in smart grids. In [9], the authors proposed autonomous demand side management based on game theoretic energy consumption scheduling while preserving users' privacy. Multiple privacy preserving data aggregation schemes are also proposed [4,10,11]. At the core of the works, encryption schemes are designed such that only aggregated data can be learned after decryption.

Traditional cryptography-based methods for smart grid security and privacy may impose a large computational overhead [12] to the light-weight IoT devices in smart grids, also, bad actors may circumvent access control to damage the system. Hence, blockchain techniques are studied in smart grids for privacy and security gains [13,14]. For general IoT systems, [15] explored the applicability of blockchain techniques, focusing on hardware specifications and standard, while [16] proposed the implementation of local blockchain in IoT without Proof of Work and coins. For smart grids, blockchain-based applications like anonymous authentication with key management [17] and distributed energy trading [18] were proposed. However, existing works do not provide privacy-preserving electricity usage transmission with awareness of bad actors in the system.

Blockchain-based trust management system for bad actor detection is described in [5], in which the trust is between actors (end-users) in the system. In comparison, we propose to maintain trust at the local community level, which is more suitable for the application we focus on.

3   Time-Based Trust Community System Design

In this section, we first discuss the formation and maintenance of local communities of end-users, the organizational structure of the local community based blockchain, and then introduce detailed operations of data aggregation and the time-based trust system.

3.1   Community Formation and Maintenance

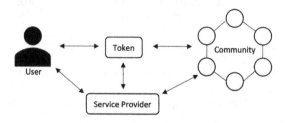

Fig. 1. Registration process

3.1.1   User Registration

Figure 1 shows the registration process when a user signs up with a smart grid service provider. After the user is verified as benign from the service provider, the user generates a pseudo-random number (token) and shares it with the service provider. Once a token is created, user only communicates with the service provider and the community through the token until the account termination is requested. Once the registration is finished, the user is allowed to join a community.

3.1.2   Community Formation

There are two main guidelines when forming communities. 1) Each community should have an appropriate size. If the communities are too small, we may not have the security and privacy guarantees from blockchain and data aggregation. If the communities are too large, it may be too costly for the smart meters to maintain a blockchain due to their limited computing power. 2) Members of a community should be in close proximity. On one hand, it reduces the communication cost within community. On the other hand, users with close proximity may share similar electricity usage patterns, generation patterns (for example, households with solar panels) and policies (for example, different regions may have different baseline utility rates). Hence, having location based communities can help the service provider better optimize energy generation.

We see community formation as an adaptive problem [19]. After initial network setup, the service provider stores the community structure and updates the assignment adaptively based on new users' enrollment/termination and the existing structure, without recomputing the community structure for the whole network from scratch.

Algorithm 1. Community Structure Update

1: **Input:** G, $\Delta G^{(t)}, t = 0, ..., T$, $\Delta E^{(t)}, t = 1, ..., T$
2: $C^{(0)}$=Community-Formation(G, $\Delta G^{(0)}$, $\emptyset$)
3: **for** t=1 to T **do**
4:     $C^{(t)}$=Community-Formation(G, $\Delta G^{(t)}$, $C^{(t-1)}$)
5:     **for** $v \in \Delta E^{(t)}$ **do**
6:         $C^{(t)}$ = User-Termination(G, v, $C^{(t)}$)

Algorithm 2. Scan Community

1: **Input:** d_{max}, communities C, node v
2: $SC = \emptyset$
3: **for** c in C **do**
4:     **if** Distance between c and v is less than d_{max} **then**
5:         add c to SC
6: **Return** SC

Algorithm 3. User-Termination

1: **Input:** M_{min}, set of all communities C, users to terminate V, v's community $c_v, \forall v \in V$. $C_{remove} = \emptyset$
2: **for** $v \in V$ **do**
3:     Remove v from c_v.
4:     **if** c_v.size $< M_{min}$ and c_v not in C_{remove} **then**
5:         Add c_v to C_{remove}
6: $V_{assign} = \cup_{c \in C_{remove}} c$
7: Community-Formation(G, V_{assign}, C)

Algorithm 4. Community-Formation

1: **Input:** d_{max}, M_{max}, set of nodes to assign V, set of communities C.
2: **for** node $v \in V$ **do**
3:     SCs = Scan-Community(C, d_{max})
4:     **if** SCs is empty **then**
5:         Create a new community c and add to C
6:         Add v to c
7:     **else**
8:         $SC_{avail} = \emptyset$
9:         **for** $SC \in SCs$ **do**
10:            **if** $SC.size < M_{max}$ **then**
11:                add SC to SC_{avail}
12:        **if** SC_{avail} is not empty **then**
13:            Find the closest community $c' \in SC_{avail}$ to v
14:            Add v to c'
15:        **else**
16:            Find the closest community $c^* \in SCs$ to v
17:            Split c^* to c^1, c^2 based on proximity, $|c^1| \approx |c^2|$.
18:            add v to the closer of c^1, c^2
19: **Return** C

The overall community formation is described in Algorithm 1. $C^{(t)}$ is the community structure at time t, $\Delta G^{(t)}$ and $\Delta E^{(T)}$ are the user enrollments/terminations at time t respectively and $G^{(0)}$ is the first network snapshot. The community structure at time t is calculated based on the network structure G, updates at time t and the existing community structure. For the base case $t = 0$, there exists no calculated community structure, so we use empty set as an input to Algorithm 4 in this case.

In Algorithm 4, d_{max} is the maximum allowed distance between a node and the center of a community it can join, where the center of a community is the Jordan center [20] of the subgraph formed by nodes in the community. M_{max} is the maximum number of members a community can hold. For each node v, the algorithm first tries to find communities within close proximity of v using Algorithm 2. If no such communities can be found, a new one is created to hold v. Otherwise, the algorithm checks if the communities have open slots for v. If so, v is added to the closest one. If not, the closest community is split to two communities of approximately equal size (depending on whether there's odd or even number of members) and v is added to the closer one of the two new communities. The blockchain of the original community will be forked. A community will not start working until the number of members reaches the minimum threshold M_{min}. Users in such small communities will fall back to traditional reporting methods.

When users V stops service, they will need to be removed from their communities $c_v, \forall v \in V$. As shown in Algorithm 3, the size of communities c_v must be checked to make sure they are still large enough. If the size of c_v falls below the minimum threshold M_{min}, it will be removed from the community structure and Algorithm 4 will be called for all the remaining members of c_v to find their new communities.

Time Complexity. For Algorithm 2, since the max number of communities scanned is n where n denotes the total number of nodes, it's complexity is $O(n)$. Algorithm 4 has time complexity $O(n)$ for each new node to be added, as scan community (line 3), check if communities are within size limit (lines 9–11), community split (lines 16–18) can all be done in $O(n)$ time and the rest operations are $O(1)$. Hence, the overall time complexity of Algorithm 4 is $O(|V|n)$ where V is the set of nodes that need community assignment. For Algorithm 3, the complexity can be $O(n^2)$ in the worst case when community removal is needed for all remaining nodes, but it is a very rare case in practice. In most of the cases, it has $O(|V|)$ complexity. For Algorithm 1, at each time step, we will call Algorithm 4 at most twice for each node, hence the overall time complexity for Algorithm 1 is $O(Tn^2)$ for all T time steps.

3.1.3   Genesis Transaction

Once community formation is completed, the service provider generates a local blockchain for each community and the blocks are not shared with other communities. For each community, a genesis block is created by the service provider, so that members of the community can create blocks following the genesis block.

Figure 2 shows the structure of local blockchain with the genesis block. The service provider shares a key generated using generalized Diffie-Hellman with a new user to join the community and the policy header gets updated to include a new member in the community.

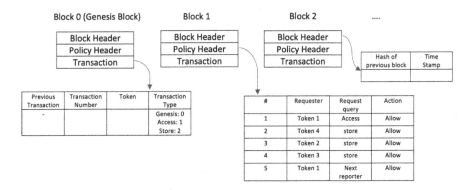

Fig. 2. Local blockchain structure

3.2 Data Aggregation

For a community c with enough members, each time a meter reading is required, a reporter is selected within the community from the latest block to aggregate the electricity usage data and report to the service provider so all members listed in the policy header can participate in the data aggregation. For each report, every member M_i sends encrypted data D_i from their smart meter to the selected reporter.

$$\sigma_i = x_i H(D_i || M_i || t) \tag{1}$$

where σ_i is a signature signed with private key x_i, H is a cryptographic hash function, and t is the time it is generated. In this process, the records are created in the local blockchain in the form of a transaction. Then, the reporter will aggregate the received data in a privacy preserving way [4].

$$D = \sum_{i=1}^{n} D_i \bmod n^2 \tag{2}$$

After data aggregation, it is signed with the private key of the reporter to create a signature σ_r.

$$\sigma_r = x_r H(D || M_r || t) \tag{3}$$

Then, $D || M_r || \sigma_r$ is reported to the service provider.

Communication Costs. During data aggregation, there will be communication costs within each community to reach consensus. For the communication overhead, each user sends a 2048 bit ciphertext to the reporter, so the reporter receives $2048n$ bits of ciphertext in total, then after the data aggregation, the reporter sends a 2048 bit ciphertext to the service provider. Meanwhile, the consensus can be reached with linear communication cost of upper bound $2logloglog(n)$, and lower bound $logloglog(n)$ given that we have m bits of memory where $m > 3logloglog(n)$ [21]. This result shows that the proposed architecture can be implemented to the hardware that lacks high computing power and memory resources.

3.3 Time-Based Trust System

While having blockchain-based local communities in smart grids brings privacy benefits, maintaining benign communities arises as a new issue. Each member has a power in consensus, so compromised members can affect others. A more severe situation is when a compromised member is selected as a reporter. To reduce the impact from compromised members/bad actors in a blockchain, either proof of work (PoW) [22] or trust [5] may be used. We argue that PoW cannot work well in the case of smart grids, since smart meters have computational resource limits and are unlikely to outperform the bad actors. On the other hand, a carefully designed trust system may be suitable for smart grids.

In the system, trust is used to vote and report. When reporting electricity usage data, the aggregated report is generated with the consensus from community members, and members with higher trust value have higher voting power compared to those with lower trust value. Also, members with low trust values may be reported for suspicious activities. We let trust be a numerical value in range $[0, 1]$. At the time of enrollment, all new members are given a relatively high trust value. Then, two factors may change the trust value: time and interaction. Trust has the time-decaying property because it is more likely to have a firmware update overdue from the service provider and old firmware is more prone to the attacks. To formulate this:

$$T(t) \propto T(0) \times e^{\frac{-t}{\tau}} \tag{4}$$

where T(t) is the trust value at time t, $T(0)$ is the initial trust value and τ is the time constant. This equation is derived from Newton's law of cooling. Since trust decreases over time, users have to participate in the community's consensus and update the firmware to slow down the trust loss.

We also associate trust with the participation in community activities. We adapt the idea of reputation management in P2P networks [23] and define the value S_{ic} as:

$$S_{ic} = sat(i, c) - \gamma \times unsat(i, c) \tag{5}$$

where $sat(i, c)$ and $unsat(i, c)$ is the number of satisfactory/unsatisfactory transactions member i had within a community c. Here the unsatisfactory transactions are disagreements to the consensus or simply no participation. $\gamma > 1$ is a tunable parameter to penalize unsatisfactory transactions.

The value is further normalized with a sigmoid function to S'_{ic}, where

$$S'_{ic} = \frac{e^{S_{ic}}}{e^{S_{ic}} + 1} \tag{6}$$

$S'_{ic} \in (0, 1)$ and for newly enrolled users wiht $S_{ic} = 0$, $S'_{ic} = 0.5$. Denote

$$\Delta v = \begin{cases} 0 & \text{latest security update is installed} \\ t - t^r_{v_i+1} & \text{latest security update is not installed} \end{cases}$$

where t is the current time and $t^r_{v_i+1}$ is the release time of the oldest security update that i have not installed. Also denote f as the security update frequency, the trust value can be represented as

$$T_{ic}(t) = T_{ic}(0) \times e^{\frac{-t}{\tau} \times (1 - \frac{S'_{ic}}{1+\Delta v/f})} \tag{7}$$

Hence, when a member i has a lot of satisfactory transactions ($S'_{ic} \approx 1$) and always keep the security software up-to-date ($\Delta v = 0$), its trust value will be close to 1.

When a community c is split, members of c will carry their trust value in c to their new communities. When a community c is removed, members of c will join new communities as new members. If their original trust value is lower than a threshold, they may need to be re-authenticated before joining.

4   Security Analysis

Confidentiality, Integrity, and Availability (CIA) are the key objectives in the security requirements [24]. In this section, we will first discuss how these three objectives are achieved with the proposed design. Next, we will describe the replay attack scenario and how the proposed design can prevent such attacks. Then, we will run a simulation to demonstrate how the trust system can detect bad actors in the smart grid.

4.1   CIA Analysis

4.1.1   Confidentiality

As maintaining the trust value is required for the members, it provides assurance to benign members that they can trust each other for the data transmission. Moreover, the data that they transmit is encrypted and the reporter does not have the private key for other members to decrypt and access the contents. From the outside of the community, an adversary may obtain the data. However, since the data is aggregated, though the adversary may gain the accesses to the data, the data won't be linked to the individual usage.

4.1.2 Integrity

Data integrity is a key part in the smart grid both for billing and rewards and for the correct and accurate demand prediction. As each local blockchain generates blocks for each of their reports to the service provider, the integrity can be traced back and validated through the generated blocks. As the blockchain blocks are tamper proof, the data integrity can be maintained.

4.1.3 Availability

The design with randomized reporters in local communities mitigates the possible unavailability of centralized aggregators like local gateways [4]. In the cases that an attacker tries to steal the aggregated data in the middle of the transmission or to simply block the transmission to achieve denial of service, it will be harder for the attacker to track and steal or make the data unavailable as the reporter changes every time.

   If any attempt of an attack is made, instead of the service provider observing the anomaly, it can be enabled with rule based anomaly detection system by allowing community members to report other participants within the community. We propose five specific rules, summarized in Table 1, to detect bad behaviors. For example, if a member failed to participate in community activities for certain period of time or denied most of the consensus, its trust value can be lower than a threshold and the other members can report to the service provider to re-authenticate the member. In addition, time-dependent price (TDP) refers to the dynamic pricing the service provider places on the electricity rate to control the demand. Smart appliances are capable of receiving the TDP and run the task when the price is low in the day, which opens up the vulnerability of False Data Injection (FDI) attack. In FDI attacks, malicious users may report data mismatching the TDP. However, those users will have low trust values as they violate the rules, hence the attack can be greatly mitigated.

   If there are no threats initiated from attackers, anomaly detection system can be applied to regular operations to remind the members to update their firmware to restore trust, as it naturally decays over time.

Table 1. Behavior rules for monitoring members

	Rule Descriptions
1	Report a member who does not participate in the consensus.
2	Report a member who falls below the threshold of trust value.
3	Report a reporter who does not agree with the consensus.
4	Share time-dependent price (TDP) with members and report if mismatch occurs.
5	Compare the TDP with previous date and report if mismatch occurs above the threshold.

4.2   Replay Attack Prevention

In this section, we discuss how the proposed system can prevent the replay attack.

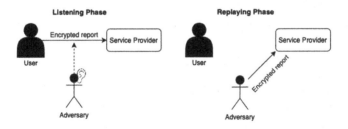

Fig. 3. Replay attack procedure

4.2.1   Attack Scenario

Replay attack is an eavesdropping attack where an adversary intercepts the conversation between two parties and use the replay of the message in favor of the adversary. Typical replay attack has two phases shown in Fig. 3. First phase is listening to the user's communication and storing the encrypted message with the signature, in our case, the aggregated report. The second phase is replaying or re-sending the exact message without decrypting to the service provider from the adversary. When the encrypted communication occurs with the timestamp included, two parties negotiate the discrepancy interval Δt to accept the valid messages [25] and the replay attack can still occur if the adversary can replay the recorded message within the negotiated discrepancy time period. Suppose Δt is static throughout the communication, the adversary can record the valid message in t_r where t_r is the time spent to record the valid message and replay to the service provider within $\Delta t - t_r$ to be treated as valid messages. A replay attack may prevent a proper connection between two benign parties, resulting in unavailability. It can be significantly harmful to smart grid users as they may lose their service.

4.2.2   Protection Scenario

Conventional approach to prevent replay attacks attaches the timestamp with a prefixed discrepancy [8,26]. However, as discussed above, a replayed message with small delay may still be treated as valid. To be more resistant against replay attack, we show that randomly changing the reporter within the community can be helpful, since it gives an extra verification step for the service provider along with the timestamp. Even if the adversary eavesdrops and replay the report within the negotiated discrepancy, the service provider will expect next report from another user, invalidating the duplicate report and flagging the anomaly.

Randomized reporter also prevents specific nodes in the community from becoming special target to the adversary as well as becoming overloaded both in communication and computational costs. Even if a reporter is attacked, e.g. by a denial-of-service attack, the overall operation can continue with another reporter, and an anomaly report will be sent by other members in the community due to lack of participation.

5   Performance Analysis

5.1   Experiment Setup

Data Set. In this experiment, we use the Pegase 9241 node network from Pandapower [27]. Since we want to simulate a set of smart grid consumers, only the loads and their geographic locations are extracted from the data set. In total, we have 4,461 nodes.

Simulation Method. To simulate a real smart grid with user enrollment and termination, we start the smart grid with 3,000 random users and simulate 100 time steps. At each step, we randomly terminate 1–2 smart grid users and randomly enroll 1–2 non-smart grid users. In each experiment below, we ran the simulation 1,000 times and report the average numbers.

Metrics Considered. We consider both the efficiency of community formation and user experience, with the following metrics:

- **Number of community splits.** Throughout the simulation, how many communities are split. Community split may increase operational burden and may be bad for users in them. As splitting a community requires communicating with every member in the community, forking the blockchain, and assigning members to new communities.
- **Number of community removals.** Throughout the simulation, how many communities are removed due to size smaller than minimum after user termination. Community removal causes disturbance to members of the removed communities.
- **Number of non-community users.** The average number of users who can not join a community with adequate size in each time step. Those users may be distant from the existing communities and may have to report to the service provider on their own, resulting in a higher security risk.
- **Running time.** Total time taken for community formation simulation.

5.2   Simulation Results

We observe the change in the above four metrics varying the maximum community size and the maximum allowed distance between a member and the community center. The max community size varies between $[100, 300]$ and max allowed distance varies between $D/5$ to D, where D is the maximum distance between any two nodes. Min community size is set to be $1/4$ of max community size.

Since there are two variables, we use heat maps to illustrate the experiment results in Figs. 4, 5, 6 and 7.

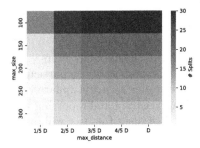

Fig. 4. Number of community splits

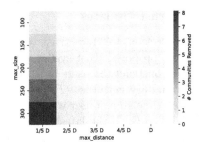

Fig. 5. Number of community removals

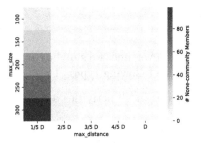

Fig. 6. Number of non-community users

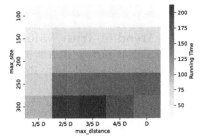

Fig. 7. Running time (seconds)

From Fig. 4, we can see that more splits may happen when the maximum community size is smaller and the max allowed distance is larger. Figure 5 and Fig. 6 shows similar trends for the number of non-community users and the number of community removals. Both values are small when max distance is at least $2/5D$. For non-community users, it is expected, since a large enough max distance grants the users to find suitable communities to join. For number of community removals, when max distance is small, the members in a community must be closer to each other, so when some of the members terminated service, it is harder to find new members to join. As for running time, we can see in Fig. 7 that the time taken for community formation is longer when max community size is larger, since more updates are needed within a community when a new member joins. In general, the algorithms can finish initial community setup and all updates efficiently, as the total running time never exceeds 200 s in all cases. It is notable that the running time does not always grow monotonically with max distance, as in the case when max community size is 300. It is possibly due to large time consumption from rare community removal cases for max distances $2/5D$ and $3/5D$, since there tend to be more communities to choose from when enrolling members from a removed community. While for larger max distance, community removal will not happen at all.

5.3   Trust Updates

In this section, we track trust value updates for different types of users to show that the proposed trust system can easily differentiate the anomaly users.

We construct the users by varying two parameters: probability to participate in community activities (P_a) and probability to install a security update (P_s). At each time step, a user will participate in data aggregation and reporting with probability P_a. If the latest security update is not installed, the user will install it with probability P_s.

Throughout this experiment, we set the trust parameters as follows: time constant $\tau = 2$, unsatisfactory transaction penalty constant $\gamma = 3$. Also, we assume a report is sent for every time step and a security update happens every 24 time steps $(f = 24)$.

5.3.1   Trend of Trust Value

To have a clear picture of how trust value changes overtime, we simulate reporting and security updates for 100 time steps for the following types of users:

- **Ideal User:** $P_a = P_s = 1$, the user participates in all activities and always install updates as soon as possible.
- **Normal Benign User:** $P_a = P_s = 0.9$, the user is generally cooperative but may forgot to participate or update time-to-time.
- **Benign User Slow Update:** $P_a = 0.9, P_s = 0.3$, the user is generally cooperative but is slow on keeping software up-to-date.
- **Updated but not Too Active:** $P_a = 0.6, P_s = 0.9$, the user is generally up-to-date for software but often ignores community activities.
- **Inactive:** $P_a = 0.2, P_s = 0.2$. The user is mostly inactive.

From Fig. 8, we can see that users with high P_a value generally have high trust. If they do not always install security update on time, their trust value may have certain dips, but the trust value can recover. However, for users with low P_a, their trust value will soon become very low, the lower the P_a value, the faster the drop. Even high P_s won't help.

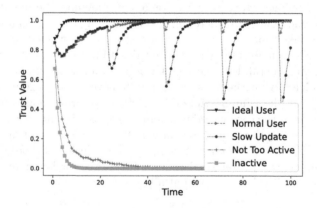

Fig. 8. Trust changes for different types of users

5.3.2   Time to Become Untrusted

To better understand the impact of P_a and P_s to how soon the user becomes "untrusted" (trust value below a threshold, we vary P_a, P_s and log the first time step that the average trust value drops below 0.1. For each pair of P_a, P_s, we run simulation for $1,000$ time steps. The result is illustrated in Fig. 9. It is clear that users will never become untrusted as long as they are relatively active ($P_a >= 0.8$) and will eventually install security updates ($P_s >= 0.2$). Otherwise, the user will soon become untrusted. It is expected since we do want the system to penalize unsatisfactory transactions more. For security updates, it is fine to install them with a delay.

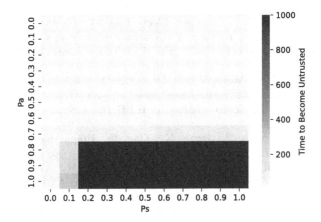

Fig. 9. Time for a user to become untrusted

6   Conclusion

In this paper, we designed a trust-based community system with local blockchains to address security and privacy issues in smart grid, with a focus on problems in frequent meter readings. The proposed trust manage system helped with efficient data aggregation and can also be used to detect bad actors. We conducted detailed security analysis to show that the proposed system meets the key security objectives. Also, we demonstrated the performance of the proposed system through experiments.

Acknowledgement. This work was supported by NSF CNS-1948550.

References

1. Fang, X., Misra, S., Xue, G., Yang, D.: Smart grid-the new and improved power grid: a survey. IEEE Commun. Surv. Tutorials **14**(4), 944–980 (2011)
2. Jordehi, A.R.: Optimisation of demand response in electric power systems, a review. Renew. Sustain. Energy Rev. **103**, 308–319 (2019)

3. Kumar, P., Lin, Y., Bai, G., Paverd, A., Dong, J.S., Martin, A.: Smart grid metering networks: a survey on security, privacy and open research issues. IEEE Commun. Surv. Tutorials **21**(3), 2886–2927 (2019)
4. Rongxing, L., Xiaohui Liang, X., Li, X.L., Shen, X.: EPPA: an efficient and privacy-preserving aggregation scheme for secure smart grid communications. IEEE Trans. Parallel Distrib. Syst. **23**(9), 1621–1631 (2012)
5. Samuel, O., Javaid, N., Khalid, A., Imrarn, M., Nasser, N.: A trust management system for multi-agent system in smart grids using blockchain technology. In: GLOBECOM 2020–2020 IEEE Global Communications Conference, pp. 1–6. IEEE (2020)
6. Wang, W., Zhuo, L.: Cyber security in the smart grid: survey and challenges. Comput. Netw. **57**(5), 1344–1371 (2013)
7. El Mrabet, Z., Kaabouch, N., El Ghazi, H., El Ghazi, H.: Cyber-security in smart grid: survey and challenges. Comput. Electr. Eng. **67**, 469–482 (2018)
8. Gong, Y., Cai, Y., Guo, Y., Fang, Y.: A privacy-preserving scheme for incentive-based demand response in the smart grid. IEEE Trans. Smart Grid **7**(3), 1304–1313 (2015)
9. Mohsenian-Rad, A.-H., Wong, V.WS., Jatskevich, J., Schober, R., Leon-Garcia, A.: Autonomous demand-side management based on game-theoretic energy consumption scheduling for the future smart grid. IEEE Trans. Smart Grid **1**(3), 320–331 (2010)
10. Jia, W., Zhu, H., Cao, Z., Dong, X., Xiao, C.: Human-factor-aware privacy-preserving aggregation in smart grid. IEEE Syst. J. **8**(2), 598–607 (2013)
11. Mohammed, H., Tonyali, S., Rabieh, K., Mahmoud, M., Akkaya, K.: Efficient privacy-preserving data collection scheme for smart grid AMI networks. In: 2016 IEEE Global Communications Conference (GLOBECOM), pp. 1–6. IEEE (2016)
12. Khurana, H., Hadley, M., Lu, N., Frincke, D.A.: Smart-grid security issues. IEEE Secur. Priv. **8**(1), 81–85 (2010)
13. Goranović, A., Meisel, M., Fotiadis, L., Wilker, S., Treytl, A., Sauter, T.: Blockchain applications in microgrids an overview of current projects and concepts. In: IECON 2017–43rd Annual Conference of the IEEE Industrial Electronics Society, pp. 6153–6158. IEEE (2017)
14. Mollah, M.B., et al.: Blockchain for future smart grid: a comprehensive survey. IEEE Internet of Things J. **8**(1), 18–43 (2020)
15. Christidis, K., Devetsikiotis, M.: Blockchains and smart contracts for the Internet of Things. IEEE Access **4**, 2292–2303 (2016)
16. Dorri, A., Kanhere, S.S., Jurdak, R., Gauravaram, P.: Blockchain for IoT security and privacy: the case study of a smart home. In: 2017 IEEE International Conference on Pervasive Computing and Communications Workshops (PerCom workshops), pp. 618–623. IEEE (2017)
17. Wang, J., Wu, L., Choo, K.-K.R., He, D.: Blockchain-based anonymous authentication with key management for smart grid edge computing infrastructure. IEEE Trans. Ind. Inf. **16**(3), 1984–1992 (2019)
18. Wang, N., et al.: When energy trading meets blockchain in electrical power system: the state of the art. Appl. Sci. **9**(8), 1561 (2019)
19. Dinh, T.N., Nguyen, N.P., Alim, M.A., Thai, M.T.: A near-optimal adaptive algorithm for maximizing modularity in dynamic scale-free networks. J. Comb. Optim. **30**(3), 747–767 (2015)
20. Hedetniemi, S.M., Cockayne, E., Hedetniemi, S.: Linear algorithms for finding the jordan center and path center of a tree. Transp. Sci. **15**(2), 98–114 (1981)

21. Fanti, G., Holden, N., Peres, Y., Ranade, G.: Communication cost of consensus for nodes with limited memory. Proc. Nat. Acad. Sci. **117**(11), 5624–5630 (2020)
22. Jakobsson, M., Juels, A.: Proofs of work and bread pudding protocols (Extended Abstract). In: Preneel, B. (ed.) Secure Information Networks. ITIFIP, vol. 23, pp. 258–272. Springer, Boston, MA (1999). https://doi.org/10.1007/978-0-387-35568-9_18
23. Kamvar, S.D., Schlosser, M.T., Garcia-Molina, H.: The eigentrust algorithm for reputation management in P2P networks. In: Proceedings of the 12th International Conference on World Wide Web, pp. 640–651 (2003)
24. Komninos, N., Philippou, E., Pitsillides, A.: Survey in smart grid and smart home security: issues, challenges and countermeasures. IEEE Commun. Surv. Tutorials **16**(4), 1933–1954 (2014)
25. Denning, D.E., Sacco, G.M.: Timestamps in key distribution protocols. Commun. ACM **24**(8), 533–536 (1981)
26. Guan, Z., Zhang, Y., Zhu, L., Longfei, W., Shui, Yu.: Effect: an efficient flexible privacy-preserving data aggregation scheme with authentication in smart grid. Sci. China Inf. Sci. **62**(3), 1–14 (2019)
27. Thurner, L., et al.: pandapower-an open-source python tool for convenient modeling, analysis, and optimization of electric power systems. IEEE Trans. Power Syst. **33**(6), 6510–6521 (2018)

Decentralized Federated Learning: A Defense Against Gradient Inversion Attack

Guangxi Lu[1], Zuobin Xiong[1], Ruinian Li[2], and Wei Li[1(✉)]

[1] Department of Computer Science, Georgia State University, Atlanta, GA, USA
{glu3,zxiong2}@student.gsu.edu, wli28@gsu.edu
[2] Department of Computer Science, Bowling Green State University,
Bowling Green, OH, USA
lir@bgsu.edu

Abstract. Federated learning (FL) is a machine learning technique that enables data to be stored and calculated on geographically distributed local clients. In centralized FL, there is an orchestrating system server responsible for aggregating local client parameters. Such a design is vulnerable to gradient inversion attacks where a malicious central server can restore the client's data through the model gradients. This paper proposes a Decentralized Federated Learning (DFL) method to mitigate the gradient inversion attack. We design a federated learning framework in a decentralized structure, where only peer-to-peer communication is adopted to transfer model parameters for aggregating and updating local models. Extensive experiments and detailed case studies are conducted on a real dataset, through which we demonstrate that the proposed DFL mechanism has excellent performance and is resistant to gradient inversion attack.

Keywords: Federated learning · Peer to peer network · Privacy protection

1 Introduction

Training machine learning model requires massive date, but the required training data is often stored at different silos or devices, making it difficulty for aggregation. Federated Learning (FL), as a prevalent distributed machine learning framework, can effectively solve the data island problems by hiring a central server to help multiple silos/devices train the model collaboratively. By training a global model without sharing local data, FL achieves privacy protection compared to traditional machine learning methods. Following this idea, FL has been applied in various fields, such as Electronic Finance [1], Recommendation System [2], and Biomedicine [3].

Recent research has shown that federated learning does not perfectly protect local data [4–6]. Although all data are stored locally during federated learning,

Z. J. Haas et al. (Eds.): WiCON 2022, LNICST 464, pp. 44–56, 2023.
https://doi.org/10.1007/978-3-031-27041-3_4

the transmission of model parameters during training can still leak important private information. Specifically, an attack known as gradient inversion attacks threatens the private data in federated learning. Since the central server holds all the model parameters in the training process, it can obtain exact training gradients from the parameters change and rely on these gradients to restore the private data maliciously.

Removing the central server is an intuitive way to resist gradient inversion attacks. Following this idea, we proposed privacy-preserving decentralized federated learning method(DFL) to resist this gradient inversion attack by removing the central server and hide the gradients from the attacker. In DFL, no centralized parameter server is required to maintain a global model over the local clients. Instead, all clients in the system are directly connected to their neighboring clients, forming a peer-to-peer (P2P) network/graph structure where they only communicate with their one-hop neighbors. In this DFL method, the clients trains their model locally with their own data, transmit the model to one-hop neighbors through the peer-to-peer network, and then update the new model by aggregating received model parameters. As a result, the mighty global model does not exist during model training. Therefore, a malicious attacker cannot obtain accurate model gradients, and the private data of clients is protected.

To validate the privacy-preserving capability and training efficiency of DFL, we conduct extensive experiments on the FASHION-MNIST dataset for image classification tasks. The experiments show that DFL guarantees that parameter transmitted in P2P communication manner does not compromise the privacy of local data. The contributions of this paper are summarized as follows:

- A Decentralized Federated Learning method (DFL) is proposed. Instead of using a central server to aggregate client model parameters, the DFL uses a peer-to-peer network to train models by aggregating parameters from neighboring clients.
- We investigate the problem of privacy leakage in FL and demonstrate that DFL can prevent local data feature leakage by comparing and analyzing the gradient inversion attacks on centralized and decentralized federated learning frameworks.
- Extensive experiments are performed to evaluate the performance of the proposed DFL. In addition, the privacy-preserving capability of the DFL is verified by performing the gradient inversion attacks on the trained DFL model.

The rest of this paper is organized as follows. The current studies in related fields are introduced in Sect. 2. The preliminary is introduced in Sect. 3, following which we propose our DFL method in Sect. 4. The experimental results and analysis are provided in Sect. 5. Finally, we summarize this article in Sect. 6.

2 Related Work

In this section, we present related work of gradient inversion attack and introduce the development of Decentralized Federated Learning at the current stage.

2.1 Gradient Inversion Attack

The training process of federated learning is considered as a privacy-preserving process because the local dataset never leaves local clients. However, recent studies have shown that attackers can effectively restore local data through gradient inversion attack, which significantly affects the privacy-preserving capability of federated learning. Le *et al.* [7] first proposed that model gradients may leak private information about the training data. Hitaj *et al.* [8] proposed a Generative Adversarial Network (GAN) based gradient inversion attack model. This GAN-based framework uses the global model parameters as discriminators, generates false data through generators, and makes the generated data with the same distribution as the private training data. Zhu *et al.* [4] proposed a deep leakage of gradient (DLG) framework. The DLG method first generates dummy gradients by inputting dummy data and dummy labels into a model. Then, the distance between the dummy gradients and the true gradients is optimized so that the dummy data and labels are approximately equal to the private training data and labels. Zhao *et al.* [9] proposed an improved DLG model, which adds a label prediction module to the original DLG. This improved DLG model only needs to optimize the dummy data, which significantly improves the inference efficiency and accuracy of the model. In the work of [5], authors proposed a gradient inversion attack model for multi-batch federated learning. This attack model is able to restore the original image from the model gradient even if the batch size is up to 100. Yin *et al.* [6] proposed the GradInversion method, which can effectively recover the original hidden image from random noise by inverting the given batch-averaged gradients.

The above attacks significantly threaten the security and privacy of federated learning. Although some methods can protect gradients of a trained model, such as differential privacy or homomorphic encryption, they cannot essentially solve the problem of privacy leakage.

2.2 Decentralized Federated Learning

Research on decentralized federated learning is still at the early stage. Currently, there are two general schemes for decentralized federated learning. The first type of schemes select a node from a peer-to-peer network as a temporary central parameter server through some election mechanism, thus ensuring the fairness and security of the network. Behera *et al.* [10] proposed a decentralized federated learning method based on the Raft consensus algorithm. This method does not have a constant central server but achieves aggregation of models by continuously selecting temporary nodes as central servers. Wang *et al.* [11] proposed a novel federated framework called "swarm learning", in which the model selects a central server in the network through the blockchain to enable the secure aggregation of model parameters.

The other type of schemes obtain global consensus through the peer-to-peer network and train the model. Lalitha *et al.* [12] proposed a fully decentralized federated learning method. This method introduces the concept of data distribution beliefs and uses a Bayesian-like approach to allow all clients to train a global model jointly. Based on this work, Lalitha *et al.* [13] proposed an improvement method. In the improved method, each client obtains a local belief, and a global belief among all nodes is obtained through communication. Then, all clients jointly train a global model with this global belief. Hu *et al.* [14] proposed a decentralized federated learning training method based on gossip communication protocol. This model achieves convergence of the federated learning by passing the model parameters in the segment.

For the above methods, a malicious client can still restore the private data of the target victim by inputting the neighboring model parameters and the global model parameters. There still does not exist a decentralized federated learning method that can defend against gradient inversion attack effectively.

3   Preliminaries

Federated learning is proposed to protect data privacy in participating local clients. The most commonly used federated learning algorithm is the FedAvg [15]. Assume that there are K clients and one parameter server involved in the system. The core idea of FedAvg is to train the model on each client i, $i \in \{1, 2, \cdots, K\}$ and upload these local models to the server. The server, then, performs global model aggregation based on these uploaded models by FedAvg. Specifically, for each training round t, the central server first distributes the global model w_{global}^t to each client for local training. The initial model of each local client i in round t is $w_i^{t_0} = w_{global}^t$. Then, local training is performed on each client for E epochs, producing an updated local model $w_i^{t_E}$. In each local training epoch $e \in \{0, 1, \ldots, E-1\}$, the client picks a local data point (x_i, y_i) to obtain a local model gradient:

$$\nabla w_i^{t_e} = \frac{\partial \ell \left(F\left(x_i, w_i^{t_e}\right), y_i\right)}{\partial w_i^{t_e}}, \tag{1}$$

where $F(\cdot)$ is the predicted value of the model for the input data x_i, $w_i^{t_e}$ is the local model in the t-th training round after e local epochs.

Then, the local client model is updated by stochastic gradient descent (SGD):

$$w_i^{t_e+1} = w_i^{t_e} - \eta \nabla w_i^{t_e}, \tag{2}$$

where η is the learning rate. After E epochs of local training, the final local model on client i is $w_i^{t_E}$, which can be represented as w_i^{t+1} (*i.e.*, $w_i^{t+1} = w_i^{t_E}$). Then, the local client uploads this local model w_i^{t+1} to the central server for aggregation. In the server aggregation, the server averages all the local models to obtain the global model w_{global}^{t+1} as Eq. (3),

$$w_{global}^{t+1} = \sum_{i=1}^{K} \frac{n_i}{n} w_i^{t+1}, \tag{3}$$

where n_i is the size of dataset in client i, and $n = \sum_{i=1}^{K} n_i$. Once w_{global}^{t+1} is obtained, the server sends this global model to each client to start the next round of local training.

During the FedAvg process, only the local model and global model parameters are transmitted between the server and clients, achieving the joint training of multiple clients without sharing local data. However, these model parameters can still leak private information as pointed out by recent research in Sect. 2. Among those gradient inversion attacks, Deep Leakage from Gradients (DLG) model [4] expresses the severest threat to federated learning. This attack can be used to infer the possible labels and perfectly restore the data of a target client by the gradients. Specifically, the DLG model first randomly initializes a dummy data point (x_i', y_i') for the target client i. Then, a dummy gradient $\nabla w_i'^t$ at the t-th training round is calculated by feeding the data into the global model w_{global}^t as Eq. (4):

$$\nabla w_i'^t = \frac{\partial \ell \left(F\left(x_i', w_{global}^t\right), y_i'\right)}{\partial w_{global}^t}. \tag{4}$$

By minimizing the distance between the dummy gradient $\nabla w_i'^t$ and the true local gradient ∇w_i^t, the DLG method can optimize the dummy data and labels (x_i', y_i') to true data and labels (x_i, y_i). The objective function of the DLG model is as follows:

$$x_i'^*, y_i'^* = \arg\min_{x_i', y_i'} \left\| \nabla w_i'^t - \nabla w_i^t \right\|^2$$

$$= \arg\min_{x_i', y_i'} \left\| \frac{\partial \ell \left(F\left(x_i', w_{global}^t\right), y_i'\right)}{\partial w_{global}^t} - \frac{w_i^{t_0} - w_i^{t_E}}{\eta} \right\|^2 \tag{5}$$

where $x_i'^*, y_i'^*$ are the recovered data and label. Since the server controls the global model $w_{global}^t = w_i^{t_0}$ and all local models $w_i^{t+1} = w_i^{t_E}$ in FedAvg method, it is possible that the malicious server can perform data restoration for all target clients via Eq. (5). It should be noticed that the objective function of DLG is the distance between gradients, and it is necessary to calculate gradient to optimize this function. Therefore, the prediction function $F(\cdot)$ should be second-order derivable. Fortunately, most machine learning models are second-order derivable.

4   Methodology

4.1   Peer to Peer Network

Our proposed DFL adopts peer-to-peer (P2P) communication to build a fully decentralized federated learning framework. We denote the peer-to-peer communication network with an undirected graph $G = (V, A)$, where V is the set of nodes (i.e., clients), and A is the adjacency matrix of this graph. For any node $i \in V$, we define the neighboring node set as $N(i)$. So, the value $A_{ij} \in \{0, 1\}$ is equal to 1 if and only if $j \in N(i)$. We assume that this network is a strongly connected aperiodic graph, which makes the matrix A aperiodic and irreducible.

In the setting of our DFL, the client i periodically communicates to its neighboring nodes $N(i)$ for model training. Thus node i can only get information

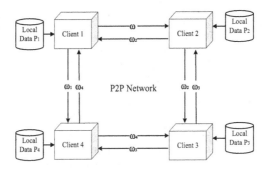

Fig. 1. Decentralized federated learning framework structure

about the neighboring nodes $N(i)$ in each communication round. Therefore, if the client i wants to get the information of a node q-th hop away, it needs to make q rounds of communication. The theory of six degrees of separation [16] provides the relation between the average path length and the number of neighboring clients, which is expressed in Eq. (6):

$$Q = \frac{\log(K)}{\log(R)}, \tag{6}$$

where K is the number of clients in this network, R is the average number of neighbors per node, and Q is the average path length of any two nodes in this network. The balance between the number of neighboring nodes R and the average path length Q is crucial when building this peer-to-peer network. Too many neighboring nodes will lead to the overhead of single node communications, while too large average path length means that each node needs more communication rounds to obtain information from further clients.

4.2 Decentralized Federated Learning Algorithm

The Decentralized Federated Learning (DFL) framework is shown in Fig. 1. Each client i stores the local datasets P_i, and connects to the assigned clients through the P2P network.

The DFL framework is divided into three states: Initialization, Local Training, and Parameter Aggregation. The Initialization state is to initialize client models and peer-to-peer networks at the beginning of training. Then, each client performs Local Training and Parameter Aggregation to update their models. We also refer to the execution of these two states (*i.e.*, Local Training and Parameter Aggregation) as one training round of the DFL.

Initialization. We need to build the P2P network structure and initialize the local model parameters in the initialization state. We use a server to assist with this state. Note that the server is only used to initialize the DFL framework instead of being a part of the training process. Thus, this framework remains a decentralized federated learning framework. Specifically, the server generates a graph structure with specific settings and assigns each client with its neighboring clients. Then, each client establishes communications with the neighboring clients according to the server information. At the same time, the initialized parameters of the model are sent to each client, thus ensuring the consistency of the client initialization parameters.

Local Training. In the local training state, a client i takes the local model w_i^t in training round t as the input model and local dataset P_i as the input data to train an updated model $\overline{w}_i^{t_0}$. The local training is set to train E local epochs with local minibatch B. In particular, the local model w_i^t is optimized by stochastic gradient descent (SGD) via Eq. (1) and Eq. (2). When E local training epochs are completed, the updated model parameters $\overline{w}_i^{t_0}$ is equal to the final local model, $i.e.$, $\overline{w}_i^{t_0} = w_i^{t_E}$.

Parameter Aggregation. After the local training state, all clients start the Parameter Aggregation state. There are $D(D \geq 1)$ communication rounds in this parameter aggregation state. For each communication round, client i sends updated model parameters $\overline{w}_i^{t_d}, d \in \{0, 1, \ldots, D-1\}$ to all its neighboring clients $N(i)$. For convenience, the client only receives data without any feedback. The model aggregates all the received updated models to form newly updated parameters. The parameter aggregation can be described as:

$$\overline{w}_i^{t_{d+1}} \leftarrow \frac{1}{M} \sum_{j=1}^{M} \overline{w}_j^{t_d}, \tag{7}$$

where $j \in N(i)$ is the neighboring client of client i, d is the current communication round, and $M = |N(i)|$ is the number of neighbors for client i. When D communication rounds are completed, the newly obtained local model in $t+1$ round w_i^{t+1} is equal to final updated model, where $w_i^{t+1} = \overline{w}_i^{t_D}$.

The complete DFL algorithm is shown in Algorithm 1.

4.3   Training Scheme

Considering the uncertainty of the convergence for decentralized federated learning, we design various training schemes for the proposed DFL with different D values. In the individual scheme (DFL-I), the communication rounds D is set to 1, and the client can only communicate with neighboring nodes within one-hop. As a result, it is more difficult to obtain a global consensus. Therefore, the trained model is prone to oscillation, converging relatively slowly. However, the advantage of DFL-I is that the communication cost for each node is relatively small. In the global scheme (DFL-G), the communication rounds D is set to $\lceil Q \rceil$, in which the model can reach the global consensus in each training round. Consequently, DFL-G tends to train the same model, which requires fewer training rounds for a single client to reach convergence. However, the communication costs for each node are relatively high.

5 Experiments

5.1 Datasets

In this paper, Fashion-MNIST [17] is used as an experimental dataset. Fashion-MNIST contains 60,000 images for training and 10,000 images for testing. In our experimental setting, the Fashion-MNIST dataset is divided in three ways to represent the different sets of clients. (i) Average division. The dataset is randomly divided into K shards, where each shard has the same amount of data. (ii) Not identically and independently distributed with balanced amount(Non-I.I.D balanced). The dataset is divided into K shards, where each shard has the same amount of data but different labels. (iii) Not identically and independently distributed with imbalanced amount(Non-I.I.D imbalanced). The dataset is divided into K shards, where each shard has a different amount of data and labels.

Algorithm 1. Decentralized Federated Learning Algorithm.

Inputs: Dataset P_i from each client $i \in V$.

Outputs: K well trained models ω_i^T for each client $i \in V$.

Initialization:

The server forms a P2P network and initialize the model parameters of each client ω_i^0.

for DFL training round t from 0 to T **do**

    Local Training:

    $\beta \leftarrow$(split P_i into batches of size B)

    for each local epoch e from 0 to E **do**

        for batch $b \in \beta$ **do**

            $\omega_i^{t_{e+1}} = \omega_i^{t_e} - \eta \nabla \omega_i^{t_e}$

        end for

    end for

    $\overline{\omega}_i^{t_0} = \omega_i^{t_E}$

    Parameter Aggregation:

    for Communication round d from 1 to D **do**

        Send $\overline{\omega}_i^{t_d}$ to all neighborhood node $j \in N(i)$

        Receive $M = |N(i)|$ data parameters

        Updata local model:

        $\overline{\omega}_i^{t_{d+1}} \leftarrow \frac{1}{M} \sum_{j=1}^{M} \overline{\omega}_j^{t_d}$

    end for

    $\omega_i^{t+1} = \overline{\omega}_i^{t_D}$

end for

5.2 Experiment Setting

In order to evaluate the performance of the decentralized federated learning method, we compare the accuracy and convergence efficiency of model training between four baselines and our proposed DFL.

- Centralized machine learning method (CML): The model structure is a four-layer CNN (1*28*28–32*28*28–32*14*14–64*14*14–64*7*7).
- Centralized federated learning method (CFL): We use FedAvg [15] algorithm with the same CNN model structure.
- Decentralized federated learning baseline: We use a Gossip-based (SGossip) [14] and Global Belief-based decentralized federated learning method (GB) [13] with the same CNN model structure.

Table 1. The accuracy of image classification on the fashin-MNIST datasets.

	Average division	Non-I.I.D balanced	Non-I.I.D Imbalanced
CML	92.98%		
CFL	90.54%	88.56%	88.32%
SGossip	89.21%	88.18%	87.62%
GB	87.44%	86.36%	86.19%
DFL-I	84.67%	82.54%	80.66%
DFL-G	85.55%	84.48%	82.26%

Table 2. The accuracy of label restoration attack by DLG.

Batchsize	1	5	10	16	32
CFL	100%	97.42%	95.74%	94.32%	88.53%
SGossip	100%	95.33%	92.31%	90.76%	85.44%
GB	100%	87.48%	84.55%	81.82%	74.64%
DFL-I	100%	54.42%	48.78%	41.71%	27.54%
DFL-G	100%	64.88%	60.14%	53.87%	45.67%

The initial learning rate of all baselines is set at 0.01. For all federated learning methods, the training rounds are set to 500. We analyze the performance by comparing the classification accuracy and restoration result after DLG attack.

5.3 Performance Evaluation

Table 1 shows the accuracy of each method for the image classification task. According to the results, the centralized machine learning (CML) method has the best image classification accuracy. For decentralized federated learning, the accuracy of gossip-based method (SGossip) is relatively high. This is because the SGossip method consumes high communication costs to enable all clients to jointly train the same global model. Essentially, the training effect of gossip-based decentralized federation learning is similar to CFL. For our DFL structure, the accuracy of DFL-G is higher than DFL-I. Compared to DFL-I where a training round only trains with one-hop neighboring, each DFL-G training round

Table 3. The results of image restoration attack by DLG.

	FFT	PSNR
CFL	0.165	12.82
SGossip	0.276	12.02
GB	0.506	9.96
DFL-I	1.301	3.22
DFL-G	0.952	4.98

trains with more clients and more datas. Therefore, DFL-G can train a more accurate model for image classification. In addition, when the data distribution is Non-I.I.D and imbalanced, the accuracy of centralized federated learning decreases slowly. However, our DFL leads to more degradation in accuracy under the Non-I.I.D and imbalanced distribution. When the data distribution is Non-I.I.D, especially when the local distribution is not consistent with the global distribution, the gap between the local model and the theoretical global optimal model will be more significant, leading to a large classification error. Table 2 shows the results of the label inference attack under the Deep Leakage from Gradients (DLG) attack. The accuracy of label prediction decreases as the batch size increases because the data with batch size N has $N!$ different permutations [4], which makes label inference attacks harder. The label restoration accuracy of DLG for the GB method is lower than that of the SGossip and CFL method, while the label restoration accuracy of the DFL method is much lower than that of the GB method. This is because in our DFL, the attacker cannot obtain the exact training gradient by global model, thus causing errors when optimizing the dummy labels in Eq. (5). Furthermore, the label inference attacks perform worse when DFL-I is used than DFL-G. In the DFL-I scheme, each client is trained jointly with the one-hop neighbor, so each training model has differences based on localization. In the DFL-G scheme, each client is trained jointly with more clients through more communication, reducing the localization of model training and making each training model the same. Therefore, the attacker's model parameters can approximate the victim's model parameters to obtain a more accurate gradient, which increases the accuracy of the label restoration.

We also compare the performance of DLG for image restoration under different federated learning methods. We use two metrics to determine the restoration results of the images. The first is the cosine distance between the original and restored images after the 2-dimensional Fast Fourier Transform (FFT). A higher FFT value represents a worse restoration result and better privacy-preserving ability of the method. The other metric is the Peak Signal-to-Noise Ratio (PSNR) between the original image and the restored image. A higher value of PSNR means a better restoration result and a worse privacy-preserving ability of the method. Based on the results shown in Table 3, the DFL model achieves higher FFT and lower PSNR values, which implies better privacy protection compared to the baseline model. This result is similar to the results we obtained from label inference attack. This is because other federated learning methods tend to train a global model, whereas the DFL method trains different local models suitable for their local dataset. As a result, the attacker does not have access to the local model of the target client, and therefore, cannot obtain an accurate gradient inversion attack for image restoration.

Table 4 shows the required communication rounds for each method. The centralized federated learning method (CFL) requires a small number of communication rounds. The decentralized federated Learning methods with individual training scheme (GB and DFL-I) require more communication rounds, because decentralized methods are more prone to parameter oscillations during model training process compared with centralized methods. The decentralized federated learning methods with global training schemes (SGossip and DFL-G) require the most communication rounds, because the global schemes consume more communication rounds to reach global consensus. There are more clients involved in training process, thus more communication rounds are needed to train a more accurate model rather than those individual training schemes.

Table 4. Communication round of each model.

	Average division	Non-I.I.D balanced	Non-I.I.D imbalanced
CFL	62	82	93
SGossip	972	1104	1152
GB	193	231	241
DFL-I	437	477	492
DFL-G	1173	1266	1320

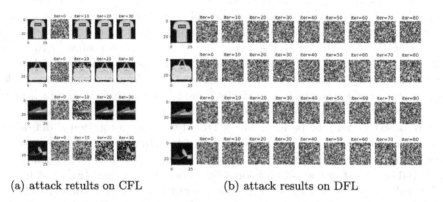

(a) attack retults on CFL   (b) attack results on DFL

Fig. 2. Case study of image restoration attack on fashion-MNIST dataset.

Figure 2 shows the image restoration result of DLG on CFL and DFL. Here, the attacker restores four images of the target t-shirt, bag, sneaker, and sandal. In each subfigure, the first column represents the original images, followed by the images restored by the DLG model as the number of DLG training rounds increases. From Fig. 2, it can be found that the CFL method is vulnerable to DLG attack, where the training data is recovered clearly within 30 rounds. By comparison, the DFL method can resist the image restoration attack by DLG much better. Figure 2 shows that the original image is still not restored after 80 rounds with the DFL model. The case study demonstrates that our DFL method achieves better privacy against DLG attacks.

6   Conclusion

This paper proposes a decentralized federated learning method (DFL), in which local clients can transfer model parameters through a peer-to-peer network to their neighboring client and thus train a model jointly without a central parameter server. Through extensive experiments, we compare our proposed DFL with other DFL designs and demonstrate that our DFL method effectively defend against gradient inversion attacks and maintain excellent model performance.

References

1. Yang, W., Zhang, Y., Ye, K., Li, L., Xu, C.-Z.: FFD: a federated learning based method for credit card fraud detection. In: Chen, K., Seshadri, S., Zhang, L.-J. (eds.) BIGDATA 2019. LNCS, vol. 11514, pp. 18–32. Springer, Cham (2019). https://doi.org/10.1007/978-3-030-23551-2_2
2. Tan, B., Liu, B., Zheng, V., Yang, Q.: A federated recommender system for online services. In: Fourteenth ACM Conference on Recommender Systems, pp. 579–581 (2020)
3. Xu, J., Glicksberg, B.S., Su, C., Walker, P., Bian, J., Wang, F.: Federated learning for healthcare informatics. J. Healthcare Inform. Res. 5(1), 1–19 (2021)
4. Zhu, L., Liu, Z., Han, S.: Deep leakage from gradients. In: Advances in Neural Information Processing Systems, vol. 32 (2019)
5. Geiping, J., Bauermeister, H., Dröge, H., Moeller, M.: Inverting gradients-how easy is it to break privacy in federated learning? Adv. Neural Inform. Process. Syst. 33, 16937–16947 (2020)
6. Yin, H. .,Mallya, A., Vahdat, A., Alvarez, J.M., Kautz, J.: See through gradients: Image batch recovery via gradinversion. In: Proceedings of the IEEE/CVF Conference on Computer Vision and Pattern Recognition, pp. 16337–16346 (2021)
7. Phong, L.T., Aono, Y., Hayashi, T., Wang, L., Moriai, S.: Privacy-preserving deep learning: revisited and enhanced. In: Batten, L., Kim, D.S., Zhang, X., Li, G. (eds.) ATIS 2017. CCIS, vol. 719, pp. 100–110. Springer, Singapore (2017). https://doi.org/10.1007/978-981-10-5421-1_9
8. Hitaj, B., Ateniese, G., Perez-Cruz, F.: Deep models under the gan: information leakage from collaborative deep learning. In: Proceedings of the 2017 ACM SIGSAC Conference on Computer and Communications Security, pp. 603–618 (2017)
9. Zhao, B., Mopuri, K. R., Bilen, H.: idlg: Improved deep leakage from gradients. arXiv preprint arXiv:2001.02610 (2020)
10. Behera, M.R., Shetty, S., Otter, R., et al.: Federated learning using peer-to-peer network for decentralized orchestration of model weights (2021)

11. Warnat-Herresthal, S., Schultze, H., Shastry, K.L., Manamohan, S., Mukherjee, S., Garg, V., et al.: Swarm learning for decentralized and confidential clinical machine learning. Nature **594**(7862), 265–270 (2021)

12. Lalitha, A., Shekhar, S., Javidi, T., Koushanfar, F.: Fully decentralized federated learning. In: Third workshop on Bayesian Deep Learning (NeurIPS) 2018

13. Lalitha, A., Kilinc, O.C., Javidi, T., Koushanfar, F.: Peer-to-peer federated learning on graphs. arXiv preprint arXiv:1901.11173 (2019)

14. Hu, C., Jiang, J., Wang, Z.: Decentralized federated learning: A segmented gossip approach. arXiv preprint arXiv:1908.07782 (2019)

15. McMahan, B., Moore, E., Ramage, D., Hampson, S., y Arcas, B.A.: Communication-efficient learning of deep networks from decentralized data. In: Artificial intelligence and statistics. PMLR, pp. 1273–1282 (2017)

16. Watts, D.J., Strogatz, S.H.: Collective dynamics of 'small-world' networks". Nature **393**(6684), 440–442 (1998)

17. Xiao, H., Rasul, K., Vollgraf, R.: Fashion-mnist: a novel image dataset for benchmarking machine learning algorithms. arXiv:1708.07747 (2017)

Blockchain and Wireless Networks

A Framework for a Blockchain-Based Decentralized Data Marketplace

Meshari Aljohani$^{(\boxtimes)}$ ⓘ, Ravi Mukkamala ⓘ, and Stephan Olariu ⓘ

Department of Computer Science, Old Dominion University, Norfolk, VA 23529, USA
{maljo001,rmukkamag,solariu}@odu.edu

Abstract. Data is critical for improving an individual's quality of life. Its value provides opportunities for users to profit from data sales and purchases. Data marketplace users, on the other hand, must share and trade data in a secure and trusted environment while maintaining their privacy. The paper's first major contribution is to identify enabling technologies and challenges to the development of decentralized data marketplaces. The second major contribution is the proposal of a blockchain-based decentralized data marketplace framework. The proposed framework allows sellers and buyers to transact with greater confidence. The system employs a novel approach to enforcing honesty in data exchange among anonymous individuals by requiring a security deposit. The system has a time frame before the transaction is considered complete.

Keywords: Blockchain · Data · Data marketplace · Smart contract · Reputation

1 Introduction

Data is considered one of the most valuable assets for modern businesses. Companies like Google and Facebook provide free services in return for users' data [18]. So, the importance of data creates opportunities for users to make profits from selling and buying data. As a result, data marketplace is being the conventional framework that enables participants to trade their data. In a centralized marketplace, all transactions are directed through one central exchange. While data marketplaces enable individuals and companies to monetize their data, centralized data marketplaces suffer from several shortcomings. Single points of failure, data privacy, and security are examples of these shortcomings. Blockchains offer a potential answer to such problems. They help build a decentralized data marketplace. A decentralized data marketplace is one in which there is no central authority or server and where data owners retain control of their data and store it on their own devices [19].

Dealing with unknown sellers without a trusted third party (e.g., Amazon, eBay) could lead to cheating [11]. A reputation system is a solution for this kind of issue, allowing buyers and sellers to minimize their risks by selecting carefully

Z. J. Haas et al. (Eds.): WiCON 2022, LNICST 464, pp. 59–75, 2023.
https://doi.org/10.1007/978-3-031-27041-3_5

their transaction partners. Nevertheless, sellers with bad reputations try to avoid this by implementing different methods to make buyers believe they are good sellers [3].

Enforcing terms and conditions is challenging in a decentralized marketplace because there is no trusted authority or intermediary who could intervene into event of a dispute. So, once the transaction is submitted, there is no way for the buyer to get a refund. However, users are required to accept the terms and conditions of centralized marketplaces such as Amazon and eBay. Buyers can file a claim and request for a refund. Issues such as these have motivated us to propose a novel solution based on blockchains.

1.1 Contributions

In this paper, a data marketplace framework is proposed based on a novel idea of using a Dispute Resolution Center (DRC) and enforcing security deposits using smart contracts based on blockchains such as the Ethereum Blockchain.

The contribution includes the following:

1. Identifying challenges ahead;
2. Identify enabling technologies for decentralized data marketplaces;
3. Providing a framework for a decentralized data marketplace;

This paper is organized as follows: Sect. 2 summarizes the related work. Data Marketplace challenges and enabling technology are identified in Sect. 3 and 4, respectively. In Sect. 5, use cases are explained. In Sect. 6, the proposed Decentralized Data Marketplace Framework is described. In Sect. 7, the Global Data Marketplace is clarified. Finally, Sect. 8 summarizes and concludes the paper.

2   Related Work

In this section, various related work that used blockchain in data marketplace is presented. The main motivation of implementing blockchain in data marketplace is to provide a trust worthy environment while preserving the users privacy. Trust plays a significant role in marketplaces. Buyers are concerned when dealing with unknown sellers which affects their decisions on purchasing from that market [8]. Distributed Ledger Technology (DLT) was employed by [16] to establish a decentralized anonymous marketplace with a Sybil-attack resistant design. The system was implemented by utilizing existing blockchains and anonymous payment systems, such as Zerocash. Different approach was introduced by [6] to demonstrated a decentralized marketplace for private data. The system uses a smart contract for privacy-preserving of data, and enables data providers to impose their term of use, or constrain the use on their data. However, the system lacks a reputation system as well as a method for the buyer to dispute a transaction. Similarly, [21] proposed a solution that provides a reliable search and purchase method using Name Data Networking (NDN). However, the proposed system does not include a dispute system. The authors in [15] offered a semi-decentralized data marketplace that provides micro services. Payment choices, storage options, and a metadata generator are available through the proposed system, which is implemented on local servers. For trading and valuing transactions, the smart contract-based blockchain is used.

Moreover, [19] proposed a decentralized data marketplace with three participants: sellers, buyers, and notaries. The buyer initiates the transaction by creating a data order and forwarding it to notaries to receive their fees and terms and conditions. The buyer then adds the list of notaries to the data order, together with their fees, terms of service, and signatures, and submits it to the smart contract. Sellers receive the data order, which contains the requested data, the suggested notary (just one), data price, and the terms and conditions of data use. The data response is then sent to the seller. When the buyer receives the sellers' data response, she selects a group of sellers and adds them to the contract. The data is then uploaded by the selected sellers to the specified address, which was sent by the buyer. The transaction is completed, and the payments are delivered after the buyer has the personal information. Nevertheless, the data buyer should verify with notaries to obtain their signed certificates before completing the data order. The limitation of this mechanism is that the notaries are paid whether the data is notarized or not, which adds an additional cost to the transaction.

3 Data Marketplace Challenges

Existing data marketplace frameworks are provided in the form of a centralized or decentralized systems. Centralized data marketplaces have many challenges that are addressed in decentralized data marketplaces. In this section, we present the most common challenges in centralized marketplaces.

3.1 Availability

Data availability refers to the ability to access a system's data when it is needed. Data marketplace systems store the required data to provide services for their users. Hence, it is important to ensure their availability to provide the needed data once it is requested. System updates, network breakdowns, and unpredictable faults are events prevent data from being accessed in a timely manner. More importantly, centralized data marketplaces are vulnerable to Single Point of Failure SPOF which is a feature in centralized systems that reduces its availability. SPOF means that the entire system becomes unavailable if the central node fails. Decentralized marketplaces, on the other hand, are designed to avoid the SPOF to provides higher availability since the other nodes are still available to access even if one of the other nodes fail.

3.2   Scalability

Scalability is one of the a main features in marketplaces to ensure that a marketplace is able to accommodate a large number of users. Centralized marketplaces, however, as any centralized system only scale at the server level, implying that only the central server scalability determines the number of users. Decentralized marketplace, on the other hand, incorporate additional number of servers in which each of them can serve additional number of users.

3.3   Privacy

The operators of centralized marketplaces may compromise the privacy of their users by knowing their real identities. Users on-site activities such as selling, buying, preferences, searching, etc. may be stored with their real identities and used for many purposes without user's knowledge. They also may reveal users' identities and personal information to a third party. In contrary, decentralized marketplaces identify their users with public keys that makes the users identity is anonymous. Hence, users data and information are not related to their real identities.

3.4   Security

Security is one of the most important requirements in data marketplace transactions. In centralized marketplaces, users share personal information such as real names, addresses, and sensitive data such as bank accounts and credit cards. A data breach can expose this information to malicious sources, putting them at risk. Moreover, data stored on the server could be stolen by attackers. On top of that, a single point of failure is one of the security issues for such systems, which are often exposed to malicious attempts such as DDoS attacks. Decentralized marketplaces, on the contrary, do not require users' information. Users can send and receive money under anonymous identities using public and private keys. The only concern is if the users share or lose their private keys.

4   Enabling Technologies

The purpose of this section is to highlight existing technologies that assist data marketplaces in overcoming the aforementioned issues.

4.1   Blockchain Technology

Blockchain technology is one of the important aspects that empowers marketplaces. It helps eliminate middlemen who are operating the system by implementing a decentralized system. Multiple decentralized nodes verify transactions on a blockchain, and anyone can join or leave the network at any time without affecting the network's capacity to achieve a consensus on transactions. Decentralization is a key to the technology that enables peer-to-peer exchange on the

Blockchain. It is a distributed, immutable ledger that supports the process of recording and tracking transactions. It is formed of connected blocks that are linked securely by using hard mathematical calculation and cryptographic hash function. Each participant has a private key and a public key, so any transaction is encrypted by using the public key and only decrypted by the accompanying private key [18].

In addition, data on the blockchain is immutable, so it can't be deleted or changed because it needs validation by the network. Also, marketplaces based on blockchain are more tolerant to the Single Point of Failure SPOF since data are distributed among the network nodes. They do not rely on a single entity; every member on the network has a copy of the ledger. Therefore, the risks of attacks like DDoS attacks can be avoided. Moreover, marketplaces based on the blockchain do not require intermediaries; the smart contract can be executed automatically. Also, payments do not need a third party, and they are instant.

IOTA is another blockchain technology that is a cryptocurrency and open-source distributed ledger built for the Internet of Things (IoT). It stores transactions in its ledger using a directed acyclic graph, which has the potential to be more scalable than blockchain-based distributed ledgers. The scalability of this system is achieved by removing the need for miners to confirm transactions and replacing them with nodes that want to add a new transaction but must first validate two previous transactions [16]. Therefore, transactions requiring micro-payments can be done easily and without cost [16]. The network obtains consensus through the IOTA Foundation's coordinator node which means it is currently centralized. Coordicide-IOTA 2.0, a new follow-up update, aims to eliminate the need for the coordinator for consensus [12]. IOTA has a number of benefits over Blockchains, including fee-free transactions, micro-transactions, and energy efficiency [10].

4.2   Artificial Intelligence (AI)

With the improvement of machine processing and the growth of data, artificial intelligence (AI) (computer vision, natural language, virtual assistants, robotic process automation, and advanced machine learning) has come to the surface. 70% of companies might have implemented at least one type of AI technology, but less than half will adopt all five types by 2030 as anticipated by [4].

Many researchers have proposed solutions related to reputation systems on marketplaces using machine learning. [7] provided a solution for the "all positive reputation" problem in the marketplace reputation system, where the average reputation score is 99 percent. They derive criteria based on opinion expressions using Natural Language Processing algorithms. They also present an approach that uses dependency relation analysis and the Latent Dirichlet Allocation (LDA) topic modeling technique to cluster these phrases into criteria and generate reputation rating and weight. Their research tries to eliminate positive bias in seller raking. The research was carried out in Hindi on eBay and TripAdvisor databases. LSTM Neural Network (NN) was used in [12] to analyze data collected from a Facebook page of AliExpress, a well-known marketplace to classify positive and negative reviews.

Similarly, machine learning was used to predict users' reliability. [1] proposed a reputation model using from their profiles. They extracted users' ratings and feed them to the machine learning algorithms to calculate users' weight. Then they used it with a weighted average method to compute the final product quality score. They utilized multiple machine learning algorithms: linear regression (LR), support vector regression (SVR), K-nearest neighbor (KNN), and regression tree (RT).

5   Use Cases

In this section, various use cases are presented to demonstrate how the afore-mentioned enabling technologies alleviate data marketplace challenges. The use cases are categorised based on the data nature into two main types: static data use cases and real-time use cases to show how solutions tackle the challenges considering the data nature.

5.1   Static Data Use Cases

Static data refers to the fixed datasets or data that never changes after collecting. In data marketplace, static data is a one-time payment model. Customers purchase the static data as a single unit at once. The following two cases deal with static data.

Use Case A1: Healthcare Data

Consider the following scenario: a data marketplace selling healthcare datasets of diabetes patients. When a buyer wants to buy a dataset from the data marketplace, she looks for a seller with a good reputation and reasonable data pricing. The buyer negotiates the requirements with the seller. The seller wants to control her data by not uploading it to a third-party server. Instead, she will send it directly to the prospective buyer. As part of the negotiation, the seller provides metadata to the buyer, which is information about the data such as data description, number of records, file size, etc. Once they have reached an agreement, they both hash the offer and submit it to the smart contract, which acts as a middleman. In addition, the seller submits a security deposit, the URL of the encrypted data, and the decryption key, and the buyer submits payment and a security deposit.

Furthermore, this case has a privacy issue both parties desire to maintain their privacy. In this situation, technology like blockchain aids in the protection of the user's privacy and anonymity. Furthermore, because it compensates for the lack of authority, consumers can trade with confidence.

Use Case A2: Data Provenance

Many buyers are interested in purchasing data from well-known data providers. However, these providers usually don't sell data directly to buyers.

Instated, a third party collects data from these sources and resells it to buyers. For example a case as in Use Case A1, the buyer wants to buy diabetic patients data from a seller. The seller offers a dataset from Sentara Healthcare, which is a well-known healthcare provider. After the buyer received the data, she decides to dispute it and claim that the data was fake. Without relying on centralized authority, blockchain-based smart contracts serve as a trusted intermediary for data and payment exchange. Furthermore, artificial intelligence AI technologies such as deep learning and machine learning are possible solutions for such issues. In [9] and [17], authors leveraged AI technologies as solutions for data provenance.

5.2 Real-Time Data Use Cases

Real-time data is information that is available at the time it is generated. As soon as it is collected, the data is sent to users. In the interim, the data could be stored on the owner's server for later use. However, real-time data is a subscription model in which customers pay for services for some time. We provide two scenarios based on the data type. Real-time data is critical, and its value varies depending on the industry. Some businesses can tolerate a few seconds of delay, while others cannot. COVID-19 maps, which show the COVID-19 status for a specific location, are one example of this data.

It is difficult to exclude third parties when selling real-time data, especially when dealing with anonymous participants who want to maintain their anonymity. Furthermore, sellers want to be paid in full, whereas buyers require data for a specific time period. Users can meet these conditions with the help of a blockchain-based smart contract.

Use-Case B1: Weather Temperatures

Consider the case of a buyer looking to purchase real-time streaming data. If a buyer wishes to purchase weather temperatures from several locations, for example, she will choose a seller based on his reputation score and price. They then begin to negotiate over the requirements. The buyer, for example, specifies requirements such as acceptable latency, packet loss percentage, and service unavailability. They then submit the smart contract if they have reached an agreement as to the proposed framework. Until the contract expires, the seller begins transmitting data to the buyer.

If all goes well, the buyer will get his data and the seller will get his money. If, on the other hand, the buyer decides to be dishonest and claims that he did not receive the data for the time period specified in the contract, she will file a claim asking for a refund to a mediator, who is a person who works to reach an agreement amongst those who are involved in a dispute.

To eliminate the cost of engaging a third party and preserve privacy, blockchain is a solution where participants can ensure transact with each other safely. Also, it can track generated data by saving hash value as a footprint. So, the mediator, who is only needed when the buyer raises a dispute, can check on the recorded hash value. A smart contract can be implemented as proposed in section in this paper (Sect. 6) provides a trusted environment where both participants can exchange transactions without the involvement of the mediator.

Use-Case B2: Stock Market

Real-time data is extensively used in many trading applications, such as the stock market. Users can find different services in these applications, like stock quotes, last sales, best bid, and other services. Most of these services are free, but they do not provide real-time data. According to Reuters [13], all quotes are delayed by a minimum of 15 min.

Stock prices go up or go down second by second, which presents a fluctuation. That is why the current price is very important for users. It allows them to make decisions on price moves. On the contrary, trading on old data could cost a lot for users if they failed to detect an uptrend or downtrend within a stock.

In this case, a user is interested in real-time stock quotes. So, she subscribes to a service. She starts to use the service by selling, buying, or bidding based on the price. Since the service is subscription-based, if the user does not file a complaint by the end of the day, which means the transaction is completed and considered successful. If the trader files a complaint, it will go to a mediator for check.

For example, if the user placed an order to sell his stock based on the current price. Let us assume a company's stock price was $75 at 10:20 am based on the information sent by the provider. The user sold his stocks based on that price. Because of the delay, the order was executed at the price of $65 since the correct price at 10:20 was $65. Therefore, she filed a claim and asked for a refund.

In this case, the provider should feed the system and the smart contract with a time-stamp along with the price. So the mediator will check and compare it with the current information. Eliminating third parties and exchanging transactions can be achieved using technologies, such as blockchain and smart contracts, which are described in the proposed system in Sect. 6.

6 Proposed Framework for a Decentralized Data Marketplace

With the use of decentralized data marketplaces, users can communicate with one another directly. Without the assistance of a middleman, payments and data are transferred and received simultaneously between the buyer and the seller. Figure 1 demonstrates the data marketplace's architecture. In this section, we are going to illustrate the proposed design.

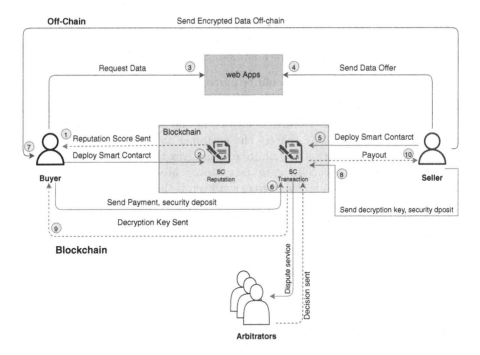

Fig. 1. A decentralized data marketplace framework

6.1   System Architecture

In this part, the component of the proposed decentralized data marketplace is presented.

Users: the marketplace has three main players listed below:

1. **Buyers** are a person or an entity who is willing to buy data from a seller.
2. **Sellers** are a person or an entity who owns data and willing to sell it to a buyer.
3. **Arbitrators** are an independent person who has been officially appointed to resolve a dispute.

Buyers could report to the authorities about any product in a centralized marketplace depending on the terms and conditions. As a result, they were able to return the things they had bought and get a refund. However, since there is no middleman between the buyer and the seller in a decentralized marketplace, this scenario is not applicable. Furthermore, it is impossible to return the data due to its nature. The buyer has the right to a refund in this situation if the requested data does not satisfy the contractual obligations of the buyer, but who would make that decision? Engaging arbitrators who can settle business conflicts in return for remuneration is one way to address this problem. Arbitrators' main duty is to receive buyer disputes and settle them by looking into the contract. The smart contract is then informed of the outcome. Choosing arbitrators in a decentralized market is difficult for a number of reasons, including:

1. The selection of arbitrators should be agreed upon by both parties.
2. The arbitrators must be qualified and well-known.

Authors in [19] provide the Notaries approach as one way to choose arbitrators. They provide a system that enables the customer to pick a member from a list and extend an invitation to join. She then gives the vendors the list, who must select one before returning it to the customer after they have agreed. The notaries are to be paid under this agreement even if there is no dispute.

As an alternative, we choose arbitrators based on how well-known they are. Only when a dispute occurs using this method is the need for arbitrators present. In other words, the transaction is final if the buyer doesn't submit a claim. Thus, the arbitrators will only be compensated if a conflict arises. Both participants can select one arbitrator, and the smart contract will select one at random as a casting vote.

One problem that can arise is that if the cost of the data is low, consumers might decide not to file a complaint due to the high expense of doing so. We, therefore, have two categories of arbitrators to address this issue. Arbitrators who have more tokens than the minimum required by the data marketplace fall under the first type. These arbitrators will be given the security deposit that one of the parties would lose it. The second group of arbitrators has tokens below the threshold. These arbitrators will be encouraged to sign up as arbitrators so they may accumulate more tokens and reach the necessary level to start receiving payments.

In term of data price, the system selects arbitrators from the marketplace, assuming they are expert in the area.

– High price data– The system selects users randomly if their tokens are more than the $threshold_2$
– Low Price Data– The system selects users randomly no matter their tokens.

Web-Based Portal: the marketplace's front end is the web-based interface. A web or mobile application should be used by both sellers and buyers to submit their offers and requests. They may search, sell, and buy their data through the portal as well. Although the front-end is an off-chain marketplace component, it operates in conjunction with the blockchain components to carry out buyer and seller transactions.

Contract: is an agreements between two users (entities) that, when signing, creates commitments on each party. In the data marketplace, both users sign the contract using their private keys and hash it so they can check it. The contract must then be converted into a smart contract as the next step. Figure 2 shows the process of the contract before converted into a smart contract.

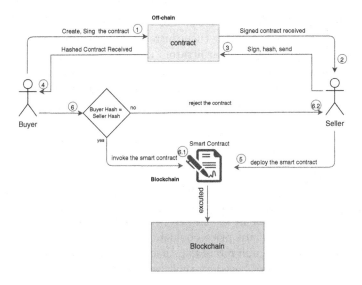

Fig. 2. The process of converting a contract to a smart contract

Smart Contract: because they are composed of rules defined in code, smart contracts are similar to conventional contracts in that regard. In other words, smart contracts are computer programs that run and exist at specified addresses on the Ethereum blockchain. So that they can transfer transactions throughout the network and maintain track of their money. But rather than being controlled by a person, they are placed on a network and executed as a program [5].

A smart contract serves as a trusted third party in the suggested system. Both buyers and sellers may rely on one another to execute transactions quickly and without additional costs. While exchanging data with the participants, it has the capacity to hold paid money. Additionally, the smart contract will use arbitrators to settle any disputes that could arise. Based on the arbitrator's decision, the smart contract completes the transaction. Additionally, the use of smart contracts aims to improve participant trust. Therefore, it's crucial to impose additional restrictions in order to stop people from misbehaving. To complete any transaction in this system, a security deposit is needed from both participants, which is a small payment known as a security deposit, made based on the users' agreement.

The purpose of the smart contract, as previously indicated, is to ensure that the buyer and seller are qualified to complete transactions. The smart contract guarantees that the buyer and seller fulfill the necessary conditions before the transaction can begin. In particular, the smart contract initiates the transaction and delivers the buyer the decryption key if the two hash values are equal. The smart contract starts a countdown timer *timer* after sending the URL to determine how much longer the transaction will take to finish in 24 h. Up until the timer's expiration, the dispute option is available. The buyer can begin and decrypt it after receiving the URL of the encrypted data and the decryption key. The smart contract begins choosing the arbitrators if a dispute arises during the first 24 h of the transaction. The arbitrators then decide whether to accept or reject the dispute. Based on the transaction status, the transaction is considered successful if there is no dispute. Thus, the number of successful and total transactions is increased for both users.

Reputation System: authors in [20] define reputation as a measure of a participant's honesty based on past behavior. The reputation system in the data marketplace helps to build trust among participants by tracking their behavior and forcing them to behave honestly. Sellers with higher reputation scores may be able to sell their data at a higher price. Lower reputation score sellers, on the other hand, may find it difficult to compete with higher reputation score sellers. As a result, lowering the data price could be a solution to attracting buyers' attention and assisting them in rebuilding their reputation. In short, honest participants have market power based on their reputation score, whereas dishonest participants do not.

Reputation systems, on the other hand, have numerous flaws. One of the issues is that rating scores are exposed to other users, which discourages users from submitting negative ratings due to revenge [2]. Furthermore, users may choose not to provide feedback at all, or dishonest users may provide incorrect ratings.

As a result, a rating system based on user performance is one approach that can be derived from the proposed framework. In the proposed system, we can use transaction status to compute users' reputation scores based on their performance. The system provides an objective view of user performance in terms of the number of successful transactions and total transactions. To acquire a user's performance, reputation engines based on binary events or methods for rating aggregation based on simple mean and normal distribution can be implemented using a smart contract.

6.2   System Workflow

In this section, the framework workflow is presented. Figure 3 shows a successful transaction scenario where there is no dispute, ends with both the buyer and the seller total transaction increased by one transaction. Also, the total successful transaction increased by one transaction.

Figure 4 shows an unsuccessful transaction scenario where the buyer rises a dispute and it is accepted, ends with the seller's total and unsuccessful transaction increased by one.

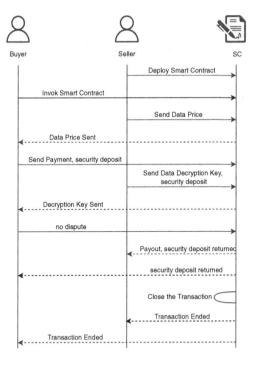

Fig. 3. A scenario for a successful data transaction in decentralized marketplace

In the following, a sequence of events and interactions flow for the proposed system:

1. The Buyer B request data $D_{is} = [DR, PK_B]$ and send it to Seller S to obtain
   (a) Data Requested DR
   (b) Buyer PK_s
2. The Seller S accept the request and send his data offer DO = P, MD, DH, EDU, TC, OH, D_{is} that include:
   (a) Data price P
   (b) Meta data MD
   (c) Data hash DH
   (d) URL Encrypted Data EDU
   (e) Terms and Conditions TC
   (f) Offer Hash OH
   (g) Data D_{is}
3. The buyer B accept the offer DO and send the following to the smart contract:
   (a) Data price P
   (b) Offer hash OH
   (c) Security Deposit SD_B

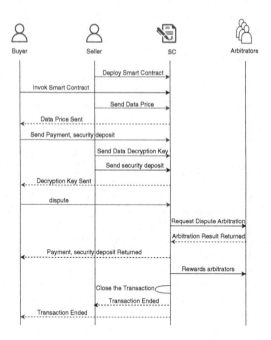

Buyer   Seller   SC   Arbitrators

Fig. 4. A scenario for a unsuccessful data transaction in decentralized marketplace

4. The Seller S send the following to the Smart Contract:
   (a) Security Deposit SD_S
   (b) Data decrypted key DK
   (c) Offer hash OH
5. Smart Contract sends the following to the Buyer B
   (a) Data decrypted key DK
6. Smart Contract after Time T:
   (a) *CaseOne* (NO dispute):
       i. Send the data Payment DP to the Seller S
       ii. Send the Security Deposit SD_S to the Seller S
       iii. Send the Security Deposit SD_B to the Buyer B
       iv. Submit Transaction Status for Seller S = Successful, Buyer B = Successful
   (b) *CaseTwo* (dispute):
       i. Decision D = True, where buyer is right
          A. Send the data Payment to the Buyer B
          B. Send the Security Deposit SD_B to the Buyer B
          C. Send the Security Deposit SD_S to the Arbitrators
          D. Submit Transaction Status for Seller S = Unsuccessful, Buyer B = Successful
       ii. Decision D = False, where buyer is wrong
          A. Send the data Payment to the Seller S
          B. Send the Security Deposit SD_S to the Seller S

      C. Send the Security Deposit SD_B to the Arbitrators

      D. Submit Transaction Status for Seller S = Successful, Buyer B = Unsuccessful

7. Arbitrators receives the dispute from Buyer B and does the following:
   (a) Check on the dispute
   (b) Send the decision to the Smart Contract:
       i. Decision D = F, if the Buyer B is wrong
       ii. Decision D = T, if the Buyer B is correct

7 Towards a Global Data Marketplace

In e-commerce, such as data marketplaces, participants' locations could not be known, especially on a global scale. As a result, laws are unable to be enforced. Another legal problem for such global marketplaces appears to be determining which applicable legislation and jurisdiction to obey.

Several marketplaces set their rules and laws based on their nation of origin or as specified in their agreements, making them only subject to the laws of that country [14]. In Amazon, for example, users must agree to use the services based on the Federal Arbitration Act, applicable federal law, and the laws of the state of Washington. While on eBay, they must follow the law of the state of Utah or the American Arbitration Association ("AAA") in the case of arbitration.

In the proposed data marketplace, a seller and a buyer negotiate, then state their terms and conditions before submitting them to the smart contract. To solve this issue, the proposed system relies on the DRC, which works as an arbitration system. When a dispute is submitted, buyers can select one or two representatives from the marketplace as well as the sellers, or the system will select them instead. The representatives are assumed experts in the area. Therefor, in the event that the buyer files a claim, the arbitrators will study the claim and provide their decision based on the offer submitted to the smart contract.

8 Conclusion

In this work, a framework for a decentralized data marketplace based on blockchains and smart contracts is proposed. To prevent fraud, the system requires participants to provide a security deposit. In the event of a disagreement, the smart contract will refer the dispute to the DRC for resolution. The paper shows technologies such as blockchains and artificial intelligence being used to overcome challenges and concerns. Also, how the data market has evolved into a worldwide market is explored.

References

1. Alqwadri, A., Azzeh, M., Almasalha, F.: Application of machine learning for online reputation systems. Int. J. Autom. Comput. **18**(3), 492–502 (2021)
2. Bag, S., Azad, M.A., Hao, F.: A privacy-aware decentralized and personalized reputation system. Comput. Secur. **77**, 514–530 (2018)
3. Bar-Isaac, H.: Reputation and survival: learning in a dynamic signalling model. Rev. Econ. Stud. **70**(2), 231–251 (2003)
4. Bughin, J., Seong, J., James, M., Chui, M., Joshi, R.: Modeling the global economic impact of AI—mckinsey (2018). www.mckinsey.com/featured-insights/artificial-intelligence/notes-from-the-AI-frontier-modeling-the-impact-of-ai-on-the-world-economy. Accessed 06 Mar 2022
5. Introduction to smart contracts—ethereum.org (2021). https://ethereum.org/en/developers/docs/smart-contracts/. Accessed 14 Mar 2021
6. Hynes, N., Dao, D., Yan, D., Cheng, R., Song, D.: A demonstration of sterling: a privacy-preserving data marketplace. Proc. VLDB Endow. **11**(12), 2086–2089 (2018). https://doi.org/10.14778/3229863.3236266
7. Jha, V., Ramu, S., Shenoy, P.D., Venugopal, K.: Reputation systems: evaluating reputation among all good sellers. Data-Enabled Discov. Appl. **1**(1), 1–13 (2017)
8. Kim, M.S., Ahn, J.H.: Management of trust in the e-marketplace: the role of the buyer's experience in building trust. J. Inf. Technol. **22**(2), 119–132 (2007)
9. Miao, H., Li, A., Davis, L.S., Deshpande, A.: Towards unified data and lifecycle management for deep learning. In: 2017 IEEE 33rd International Conference on Data Engineering (ICDE), pp. 571–582. IEEE (2017)
10. Minhas, N.N.: Why iota is better and getting better than blockchains?—by noman nasir minhas—nerd for tech—medium. https://medium.com/nerd-for-tech/why-iota-is-better-and-getting-better-than-blockchains-b6eb62bf8b87. Accessed 17 July 2022
11. Pfeiffer, T., Nowak, M.A.: Digital cows grazing on digital grounds. Curr. Biol. **16**(22), R946–R949 (2006)
12. Prova, A.A., Akter, T., Islam, M.R., Uddin, M.R., Hossain, T., Hannan, M., Hossain, M.S.: Analysis of online marketplace data on social networks using LSTM. In: 2019 5th International Conference on Advances in Electrical Engineering (ICAEE), pp. 381–385. IEEE (2019)
13. Disclaimer (2022). https://www.reuters.com/info-pages/disclaimer/
14. Rosenthal, L., Mithal, M., Donohue, M., Sheer, A.: Consumer protection global electronic marketplace looking (2000). https://www.ftc.gov/sites/default/files/documents/reports/consumer-protection-global-electronic-marketplace-looking-ahead/electronicmkpl.pdf
15. Sharma, P., Lawrenz, S., Rausch, A.: Towards trustworthy and independent data marketplaces. In: Proceedings of the 2020 The 2nd International Conference on Blockchain Technology, pp. 39–45 (2020)
16. Soska, K., Kwon, A., Christin, N., Devadas, S.: Beaver: a decentralized anonymous marketplace with secure reputation. Cryptology ePrint Archive (2016)
17. Souza, R., et al.: Provenance data in the machine learning lifecycle in computational science and engineering. In: 2019 IEEE/ACM Workflows in Support of Large-Scale Science (WORKS), pp. 1–10. IEEE (2019)
18. Trabucchi, D., Buganza, T., Pellizzoni, E.: Give away your digital services: leveraging big data to capture value new models that capture the value embedded in the data generated by digital services may make it viable for companies to offer those services for free. Res. Technol. Manag. **60**(2), 43–52 (2017)

19. Travizano, M., Sarraute, C., Ajzenman, G., Minnoni, M.: Wibson: a decentralized data marketplace. arXiv preprint arXiv:1812.09966 (2018)
20. Witkowski, M., Artikis, A., Pitt, J.: Experiments in building experiential trust in a society of objective-trust based agents. In: Falcone, R., Singh, M., Tan, Y.-H. (eds.) Trust in Cyber-societies. LNCS (LNAI), vol. 2246, pp. 111–132. Springer, Heidelberg (2001). https://doi.org/10.1007/3-540-45547-7_7
21. Yoo, H., Ko, N.: Blockchain based data marketplace system. In: 2020 International Conference on Information and Communication Technology Convergence (ICTC), pp. 1255–1257. IEEE (2020)

Formulate Full View Camera Sensor Coverage by Using Group Set Coverage

Hongwei Du[1], Zhao Zhang[2(✉)] ⓘ, Zhenhua Duan[3], Cong Tian[3], and Ding-Zhu Du[4] ⓘ

[1] Department of Computer Science and Technology, Harbin Institute of Technology, Shenzhen Graduate School, Shenzhen, China
hongwei.du@ieee.org
[2] College of Mathematics and Computer Science, Zhejiang Normal University, Jinhua, Zhejiang 321004, China
hxhzz@sina.com
[3] ICTT and ISN Laboratory, Xidian University, Xian 710071, China
{zhhduan,ctian}@mail.xidian.edu.cn
[4] Department of Computer Science, University of Texas at Dallas, Richardson, TX 75080, USA
dzdu@utdallas.edu

Abstract. Full view is an important subject in the study of wireless camera sensor coverage. It involves three issues, camera direction selection, camera location selection, and moving-directional target coverage. In this paper, we study them step by step, from one issue, two issue, to three issues. In each step, we formulate a group set cover- age problem, and study its computational complexity and approximation solutions. Especially, we employ a new type of approximations, the global approximation of local optimality for nonsubmodular optimization.

1 Introduction

Nowadays, the camera sensor plays an important role in our daily life. It has been installed in almost everywhere, such as supermarkets, home, street intersections, cars, etc. The camera sensor is widely used on tracing criminal activities. Currently, it is also used for tracing COVID-19 virus. In study of camera sensors, the coverage is an important issue.

The camera sensor is a type of directional sensor. The covering region of a camera sensor is a sector with center at the camera sensor (Fig. 1). The radius and the angle of the sector are called *sensing radius* and *sensing angle*, respectively. A target point is said to be *covered* by a camera sensor if it lies in the covering region of the camera sensor. The *sensing direction* is represented by the

---

Supported by National Natural Science Foundation of China (61772154, U20A2068), Zhejiang Provincial Natural Science Foundation of China (LD19A010001) and Natural Science Foundation of USA (1907472).

Z. J. Haas et al. (Eds.): WiCON 2022, LNICST 464, pp. 76–90, 2023.
https://doi.org/10.1007/978-3-031-27041-3_6

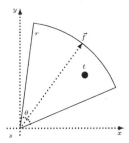

Fig. 1. Camera sensor s with sensing radius r, angle θ, direction f covers a target t.

ray dividing the sensing angle evenly, which is usually adjustable continuously or discretely.

Consider a set of target points and a camera sensor. When the sensing direction is rotated to different positions, the camera sensor would cover different subsets of target points. Therefore, each camera sensor would generate a *group* of subsets of target points. Using a group of subsets to represent a camera sensor, each camera sensor coverage problem may be formulated as a group set cover problem.

Among various coverage requirements, the full view is a tough one. However, it is very important since it enable the sensor system to monitor moving targets.

In this paper, we are going to study the full-view camera sensor coverage problem, which involves three issues:

- Camera sensing direction selection.
- Camera location selection.
- Coverage of moving-directional targets.

We organize our study into three steps based on consideration of one issue, two issues, until all three issues. In each step, we will formulate considered camera coverage problem into a group set coverage problem. Since in all three steps, formulated group set coverage problems are NP-hard, we design and analysis of its approximation solution.

Related Works. The sensor coverage was studied initially on wireless sensors with omni antennas and a set of target points or a target area. For example, Cardei *et al.* [1] studied the maximum lifetime coverage problem on a set of homogeneous wireless sensors with omni antennas and a set of target points and raised a long-standing open problem on the existence of polynomial-time constant-approximation algorithm. Ding *et al.* [2] gave the first positive solution for the open problem by presenting a polynomial-time 4-approximation, and Li and Jin [3] found a PTAS (polynomial-time approximation scheme). Wu *et al.* [4] studied the connected sensor cover problem on homogeneous wireless sensors with omni antennas and a target area, and raised an open problem on the existence of polynomial-time constant-approximation algorithm. Actually, they showed the existence of a polynomial-time $O(r)$-approximation and a polynomial-time $O(\log^2 n \log \log n)$-approximation where r and n are two unrelated parameters, which strongly suggests the existence of a polynomial-time constant-approximation. However, this problem is still open today.

Meanwhile, many efforts [5–10] have been made on extending research work from wireless sensors with omni antennas to directional sensors, i.e., wireless sensors with directional antennas so that the covering region is as shown in Fig. 1. Such extension may meet surprising trouble. For example, for wireless sensors with omni antennas, the minimum sensor cover problem has PTAS [10]. However, for directional sensors covering target points, the corresponding minimum sensor cover problem has not been found to have a polynomial-time constant-approximation so far [5].

The camera sensor is a type of directional sensors. In the study of camera sensors, the popular target object is the directional target, such as the human face [11] which can be identified only from certain range of direction. A directional target u has a facing angle at u and a facing direction which bisects the facing angle evenly (Fig. 2). A directional target u is *covered* by a camera sensor a if u lies in the covering region of s and segment su lies in both the sensing angle of s and the facing angle of u as shown in the middle of Fig. 3. In the study of the camera sensor coverage on directional targets, many efforts [12–14] have been made in the literature. Among them, it may be worth mentioning the work of Wang and Cao [15] who proposed an important concept "full view". A directional target is *full-view* covered by a set of camera sensors if for the target in any facing direction, there exists a camera sensor covering the target. An area is *full view* covered by a set of camera sensors if a directional sensor lying at any point in the area can be full view covered by the set of camera sensors.

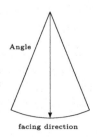

Fig. 2. Directional target.

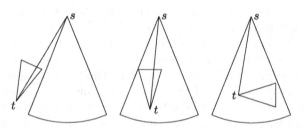

Fig. 3. A directional target t is covered by a camera sensor s (in middle case).

Many issues on full view have been studied in the literature, such as full view barrier cover [16,17], full view area coverage [18,19], lifetime of full view coverage [20], orientation scheduling [21]. However, none of them have touched the maximum coverage problem studied in this paper, especially for full view coverage.

Our Contribution. In this paper, we study full-view coverage in camera sensor networks, in which every camera's direction is adjustable and every target has a moving direction. Our study consists of three steps.

1. In the first step, we study how to select the camera direction and formulate it into the maximum group set coverage problem. This problem is proved to be NP-hard and it has a polynomial-time $(1 - 1/e)$-approximation. In this step, considered targets are target points or fixed-directional targets.
2. In the second step, we transform each moving-directional target into a set of fixed-directional targets, so that the full-view camera coverage problem can be formulated into the maximum group set coverage with composed targets. This is also NP-hard. We will present an approximation which has a global performance ratio $(1 - 1/e)^{\alpha}(1 + \varepsilon)$ for local optimality.
3. In the third step, we give a constraint on the number of cameras and face a camera location selection problem. Our formulation is the maximum group set coverage with size constraint and composed targets. We show that this is an NP-hard problem which also has an approximation with a global performance ratio $(1 - 1/e)^{\alpha}(1 + \varepsilon)$ for local optimality.

The global approximation for local optimality is a new type of approximation algorithms for nonsubmodular optimizations [22]. The study of such a type of approximations is in the background that classic approximation performance measure, the ratio of objective function values between approximation solution and (global) optimal solution does not work well. In this paper, we are going to employ the technique of nonconvex relaxation to obtain the global approximation for local optimality.

2   Problem Formulation

Consider a heterogeneous camera sensor network. We will formula various camera sensor coverage problems into group set cover problems.

Note that each camera can rotate its sensing direction, and at each orientation, it covers a subset of target points or a subset of fixed-directional targets. Therefore, selecting a sensing direction corresponds to selecting one subset from a group. Hence, the sensing direction selection problem for covering the maximum number of target points or fixed-directional targets can be formulated as the following problem.

Problem 1 (Maximum Group Set Coverage). *Given m groups $\mathcal{G}_1$, $\mathcal{G}_2$, ..., $\mathcal{G}_m$ of subsets of a finite set X, select one subset from each group to cover the maximum total number of elements.*

To reduce the maximum full-view coverage problem to a group set coverage problem, we replace each full-view directional target by a finite number of fixed-directional targets as follows.

Lemma 1. *Consider a directional target t with facing angle α. Then t can be replaced by $\lceil 4\pi/\alpha \rceil$ fixed-directional targets with facing angle at most $\alpha/2$ such that if these fixed-directional targets are covered by a set of camera sensors, $\mathcal{S}$, then t is full-view covered by $\mathcal{S}$.*

Proof. Divide angle 2π at t evenly into $\lceil 4\pi/\alpha \rceil (= h)$ angles α_1, ..., α_h each of at most $\alpha/2$. Replace target t by h targets at location of t with fixed facing angles α_1, ..., α_h, respectively (Fig. 4).

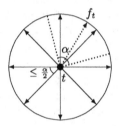

Fig. 4. Proof of Lemma 1.

Then for any orientation of target t, its facing direction must be contained in an angle α_i. This angle α_i must be entirely contained in the facing angle of t in current orientation. Since the target with facing direction α_i is covered by the set of camera sensors, $\mathcal{S}$, we can immediately see that target t in current orientation is covered by $\mathcal{S}$. $\qquad\qquad\square$

Now, the full-view coverage of a directional target is represented by a composition of several fixed-directional targets. Hence, the sensing direction selection problem for full-view directional targets can be formulated as follows.

Problem 2 (Maximum Group Set Coverage with Composed Targets).
Consider m groups $\mathcal{G}_1$, $\mathcal{G}_2$,..., $\mathcal{G}_m$ of subsets of a finite set X. All elements in X are partitioned into subsets X_1, X_2,... X_r, each called a composed target. The problem is to select one subset from each group to cover the maximum total number of composed targets, where a composed target is said to be covered if all elements in the composed target are covered.

Note that each composed target X_t corresponds to a full-view directional target t and all elements in X_t correspond to fixed-directional targets obtained from decomposing the full-view directional target t by Lemma 1. We may assume that for any camera sensor s, the line segment ts does not overlap with any boundary of the decomposition (otherwise the decomposition can be rotated a little to avoid overlap). This property implies the following observation.

Lemma 2. *For every composed target X_t, no subset in any group $\mathcal{G}_i$ covers two elements in X_t.*

Now, consider the camera sensor allocation problem. Since each possible location for camera sensor may also be represented by a group of subsets, selecting k locations for camera sensors corresponds to selectiing k groups. Therefore, the camera sensor allocation problem for full-view directional targets can be formulated as the following problem.

Problem 3 (Maximum Group Set Coverage with Size Constraint).
Consider m groups $\mathcal{G}_1, \mathcal{G}_2,..., \mathcal{G}_m$ of subsets of a finite set X. All elements in X are partitioned into subsets $X_1, X_2,..., X_r$, each called a composed target, *and they satisfy property sated in Lemma 2. Given an integer $k > 0$, the problem is to select k groups and then select one subset from each selected group to cover the maximum total number of composed targets.*

The camera sensor allocation for target points and fixed-directional targets can be formulated into a special case of Problem 3; in such a case, every composed target contains only one element.

3   Maximum Group Set Coverage

3.1   Complexity

A *group set cover* is a collection of subset groups $\mathcal{G}_1, \mathcal{G}_2, ..., \mathcal{G}_m$ such that all elements can be covered by $\cup_{i=1}^{m} S_i$ where S_i is selected from group $\mathcal{G}_i$. The group set cover problem can be seen as an extension of the set cover problem, since the latter can be viewed as a special case of the former in which each group has only one subset.

Problem 4 (Group Set Cover). *Given a collection of subset groups $\mathcal{G}_1, \mathcal{G}_2, ..., \mathcal{G}_m$, does this collection form a group set cover?*

Theorem 1. *The group set cover problem is NP-complete.*

Proof. The problem belongs to NP since we can one subset from each group and check if their union cover all elements in polynomial-time. To show NP-hardness of the group set cover problem, consider a well-known P-hard problem, the minimum set cover problem. Its decision version is as follows: Given a collection $\mathcal{C}$ of subsets of a finite set X, and an integer $k > 0$, find out whether there are at most k subsets in $\mathcal{C}$ such that their union contains X.

To construct a polynomial-time reduction, we set $\mathcal{G}_1 = \mathcal{G}_2 = \cdots = \mathcal{G}_k = \mathcal{C}$. Then $\mathcal{C}$ has a subcollection of at most k subsets (say $\{S_{i_1}, S_{i_2}, ..., S_{i_\ell}\}$ with $\ell \leq k$) covering X if and only if $\{\mathcal{G}_1, \mathcal{G}_2, ..., \mathcal{G}_\ell\}$ and $\{S_{i_1}, S_{i_2}, ..., S_{i_\ell}\}$ form a group set cover, where S_{i_j} is viewed to be a set selected from group $\mathcal{G}_j$.

Corollary 1. *The maximum group set coverage problem is NP-hard.*

3.2   Approximation Solution

The maximum group set coverage problem can be formulated into a 0–1 linear programming as follows: Consider m groups $\mathcal{G}_1, ..., \mathcal{G}_m$ of subsets of a finite set X. Note that an indicator for an event is a 0–1 variable to indicate whether the event occurs or not. Let x_{iS} be the indicator for event that subset S is selected from group $\mathcal{G}_i$. Denote $n = |X|$ and $\mathcal{G} = \mathcal{G}_1 \cup \cdots \cup \mathcal{G}_k$. Let y_j be the indicator for event that element j is covered by some selected subset.

$$\max \ y_1 + y_2 + \cdots + y_n \qquad\qquad (ILP1)$$

$$\text{s.t. } \ y_j \leq \sum_{i=1}^{m} \sum_{S:j \in S \in \mathcal{G}_i} y_{iS} \quad \forall j = 1, ..., n,$$

$$\sum_{S:S \in \mathcal{G}_)} y_{iS} \leq 1 \quad \text{for all } i = 1, ..., m,$$

$$y_j \in \{0, 1\} \quad \text{for all } j = 1, ..., n,$$

$$x_{iS} \in \{0, 1\} \quad \text{for all } S \in \mathcal{G} \text{ and } i = 1, 2, ..., m.$$

By LP-relaxation and randomized rounding technique, we can compute an approximation (x_{iS}, y_j) such that following result holds. The computation time is $O((n + mg)^{3.5})$ where $n = |X|$, m is the number of groups and g is the maximum number of subsets in a group. The detail can be found in [26].

Theorem 2.

$$E\left[\sum_{j=1}^{n} y_j\right] \geq (1 - e^{-1})opt_1$$

where opt_1 is the objective value of an optimal solution for the group set coverage problem (ILP1).

4   Maximum Group Set Coverage with Composed Targets

Note that the maximum group set coverage problem can be considered as a special case of the maximum group set coverage problem with composed targets, in which every composed target contains only one element. Since the former is NP-hard, so is the latter. Therefore, we only focus on algorithm design and analysis in this section.

Consider m groups $\mathcal{G}_1, ..., \mathcal{G}_m$ of subsets of a finite set X which is partitioned into τ composed targets $X_1, X_2, ..., X_\tau$, i.e., $X = X_1 \cup X_2 \cup \cdots X_\tau$ and $X_t \cap X_{t'} = \emptyset$ for $1 \leq t < t' \leq \tau$. Recall the observation made in Lemma 2. Let x_{iS} be the indicator for event that subset S is selected from group $\mathcal{G}_i$. Denote $n = |X|$ and $\mathcal{G} = \mathcal{G}_1 \cup \cdots \cup \mathcal{G}_k$. Let y_j be the indicator for event that element j is covered by some selected subset. The following is a 0–1 multi-linear programming.

$$\max \sum_{t=1}^{\tau} \prod_{j \in X_t} y_j \qquad\qquad (INLP2)$$

$$\text{s.t. } y_j \leq \sum_{i=1}^{m} \sum_{S:j \in S \in \mathcal{G}_i} x_{iS} \quad \text{for all } j = 1, ..., n,$$

$$\sum_{S:S \in \mathcal{G}_i} x_{iS} \leq 1 \quad \text{for all } i = 1, ..., m,$$

$$y_j \in \{0,1\} \quad \text{for all } j = 1, ..., n,$$

$$x_{iS} \in \{0,1\} \quad \text{for all } S \in \mathcal{G}_i \text{ and } i = 1, 2, ..., m.$$

Its relaxation is as follows.

$$\max \sum_{t=1}^{\tau} \prod_{j \in X_t} y_j \qquad\qquad (NLP2)$$

$$\text{s.t. } y_j \leq \sum_{i=1}^{m} \sum_{S:j \in S \in \mathcal{G}_i} x_{iS} \quad \text{for all } j = 1, ..., n,$$

$$\sum_{S:S \in \mathcal{G}_i} x_{iS} \leq 1 \quad \text{for all } i = 1, ..., m,$$

$$0 \leq y_j \leq 1 \quad \text{for all } j = 1, ..., n,$$

$$0 \leq x_{iS} \leq 1 \quad \text{for all } S \in \mathcal{G}_i \text{ and } i = 1, 2, ..., m.$$

Let (y_j^*, x_{iS}^*) be a $(1 - \varepsilon)$-approximate solution for local optimality of the multilinear programming (NLP2). A randomized rounding is executed as follows.

Randomized Rounding: With probability x_{iS}^*, randomly select one subset S from each group $\mathcal{G}_i$ (i.e., set $x_{iS} = 1$ and $x_{iS'} = 0$ for $S' \neq S$). Set

$$y_j = \begin{cases} 1 & \text{if element } j \text{ is covered by a selected subset,} \\ 0 & \text{otherwise.} \end{cases}$$

Let (x_{iS}, y_j) be a solution obtained from this randomized rounding. Similar to the proof of Lemma 3, we have the following properties.

Lemma 3. $E[y_j] \geq (1 - e^{-1}) y_j^*.$

Proof. For each $j = 1, ..., n,$

$$\text{Prob}[y_j = 1] = 1 - \prod_{i=1}^{m} \prod_{S:j \in S \in \mathcal{G}_i} (1 - x_{iS}^*) \geq 1 - \left(\frac{\sum_{i=1}^{m} \sum_{S:j \in S \in \mathcal{G}_i} (1 - x_{iS}^*)}{K_j} \right)^{K_j}$$

$$= 1 - \left(1 - \frac{\sum_{i=1}^{m} \sum_{S:j \in S \in \mathcal{G}_i} x_{iS}^*}{K_j} \right)^{K_j} \geq 1 - \left(1 - \frac{y_j^*}{K_j} \right)^{K_j}.$$

where $K_j = |\{(i, S) \mid j \in S \in \mathcal{G}_i\}|).$

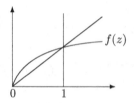

Fig. 5. Function $f(z)$.

Since the function $f(z) = 1 - (1 - \frac{z}{K_j})^{K_j}$ is monotone increasing and concave in $[0, 1]$, the function curve is above the line segment between two points $(0, f(0))$ and $(1, f(1)$ (Fig. 5). Note that $f(0) = 0$ and $f(z) = 1 - (1 - \frac{1}{K_j})^{K_j}$. Therefore,

$$f(z) \geq \left(1 - \left(1 - \frac{1}{K_j}\right)^{K_j}\right) z \geq (1 - e^{-1})z.$$

Thus,

$$\mathrm{Prob}[y_j = 1] \geq (1 - e^{-1})y_j^*.$$

Hence, $E[y_j] = \mathrm{Prob}[y_j = 1] \geq (1 - e^{-1})y_j^*$. □

Lemma 4. $E[\prod_{j \in X_t} y_j] = \prod_{j \in X_t} E[y_j]$.

Proof. By Lemma 2, for a fixed composed target t, events $\{y_j = 1\}_{j \in X_t}$ are independent. Therefore, this lemma holds. □

Theorem 3. *Let (y_j, x_{iS}) be an approximate solution obtained by the above randomized rounding. Then*

$$E\left[\sum_{t=1}^{\tau} \prod_{j \in X_t} y_j\right] \geq (1 - e^{-1})^{\alpha}(1 - \varepsilon)lopt_2$$

where $lopt_2$ is the objective value of a local optimal solution of (NLP2) and $\alpha = \max_{1 \leq t \leq \tau} |X_t|$.

Proof. By Lemmas 3 and 4, we have

$$E\left[\sum_{t=1}^{\tau} \prod_{j \in X_t} y_j\right] = \sum_{t=1}^{\tau} E\left[\prod_{j \in X_t} y_j\right] = \sum_{t=1}^{\tau} \prod_{j \in X_t} E[y_j] \geq (1 - e^{-1})^{\alpha} \sum_{t=1}^{\tau} \prod_{j \in X_t} y_j^*$$
$$= (1 - e^{-1})^{\alpha}(1 - \varepsilon) \cdot lopt_2.$$

The theorem is proved. □

We summarize the above randomized algorithm into Algorithm 2.

Algorithm 1 Approximation for maximum group set coverage with composed targets

---

input m groups $\mathcal{G}_1$, $\mathcal{G}_2$, ..., $\mathcal{G}_m$ of subsets of a finite set X and a partition of X into
  composed targets $X = X_1 \cup X_2 \cup \cdots \cup X_\tau$.

output a collection $\mathcal{S}$ of subsets of X.

0:   $\mathcal{S} \leftarrow \emptyset$;
1:   solve (NLP2) to obtain a $(1 - \varepsilon)$-approximate solution (x_{iS}^*, y_j^*);
2:   **for** $i = 1$ **to** m **do**
3:       select one subset S from $\mathcal{G}_i$ with
         probability x_{iS}^*;
4:       $\mathcal{S} \leftarrow \mathcal{S} \cup \{S\}$
5:   **end-for**
6:   **return** $\mathcal{S}$.

The running time of Algorithm 1 depends on the running time for computing local optimal solutions (Kuhn-Tucker points) of (NLP2), which is a multilinear maximization with linear constraints. By a sequence of linear programs [23,24], a sequence of feasible points can be generated to be globally convergent to those local optimal solutions. However, it is open to analyze the running time to obtain a $(1 - \varepsilon)$-approximation. In fact, those algorithms have linear convergence rate, which means that under certain condition, the number of steps can be bounded by a polynomial with respect to $O(1/\varepsilon)$. However, in general case, such an upper bound is proved only for quadratic objective function [27].

5   Maximum Group Set Coverage with Size Constraint

Note that the element coverage problem can be viewed as a special case of the composed target coverage problem. In such a case, every composed target contains only one element. Therefore, with size constraint, we only study composed targets. Moreover, the problem is NP-hard since unconstrained case is. In the following, we design approximation algorithm for this size constrained case.

Consider m subset groups $\mathcal{G}_1, ..., \mathcal{G}_m$ on finite set X which is partitioned into τ composed targets $X_1, X_2, ..., X_\tau$, i.e., $X = X_1 \cup X_2 \cup \cdots X_\tau$ and $X_t \cap X_{t'} = \emptyset$ for $1 \le t < t' \le \tau$. Note that Lemma 2 is assumed for these composed targets. Let x_{iS} be the indicator for event that subset S is selected from group $\mathcal{G}_i$. Let $|X| = n$ and suppose an integer $k \ge 1$ is given. Let y_j be the event that element j is covered by a selected subset and z_i the indicator for event that a subset is selected from group $\mathcal{G}_i$. The following is a 0–1 multi-linear programming.

$$\max \sum_{t=1}^{\tau} \prod_{j \in X_t} y_j \qquad\qquad (INLP3)$$

$$\text{s.t. } y_j \leq \sum_{i=1}^{m} \sum_{S:j \in S \in \mathcal{G}_i} x_{iS} \quad \text{for all } j = 1, ..., n,$$

$$\sum_{S:S \in \mathcal{G}_i} x_{iS} \leq z_i \quad \text{for all } i = 1, ..., m,$$

$$\sum_{i=1}^{m} z_i \leq k$$

$$y_j \in \{0,1\} \quad \text{for all } j = 1, ..., n,$$

$$z_i \in \{0,1\} \quad \text{for all } i = 1, ..., m,$$

$$x_{iS} \in \{0,1\} \quad \text{for all } S \in \mathcal{G} \text{ and } i = 1, 2, ..., m.$$

Its relaxation is as follows.

$$\max \sum_{t=1}^{\tau} \prod_{j \in X_t} y_j \qquad\qquad (NLP3)$$

$$\text{s.t. } y_j \leq \sum_{i=1}^{m} \sum_{S:j \in S \in \mathcal{G}_i} x_{iS} \quad \text{for all } j = 1, ..., n,$$

$$\sum_{S:S \in \mathcal{G}_i} x_{iS} \leq z_i \quad \text{for all } i = 1, ..., m,$$

$$\sum_{i=1}^{m} z_i \leq k,$$

$$0 \leq y_j \leq 1 \quad \text{for all } j = 1, ..., n,$$

$$0 \leq z_i \leq 1 \quad \text{for all } i = 1, ..., m,$$

$$0 \leq x_{iS} \leq 1 \quad \text{for all } S \in \mathcal{G} \text{ and } i = 1, 2, ..., m.$$

Let (y_j^*, x_{iS}^*, z_i^*) be a $(1-\varepsilon)$-approximate solution for local optimality of nonlinear programming (NLP3). A randomized rounding can be executed as follows.

Randomized Rounding: Consider m collections of k groups as follows:

$$\mathcal{C}_1 = \{\mathcal{G}_1, \mathcal{G}_2, ..., \mathcal{G}_k\}, \ \mathcal{C}_2 = \{\mathcal{G}_2, \mathcal{G}_3, ..., \mathcal{G}_{k+1}\}, \ ... \ \mathcal{C}_m = \{\mathcal{G}_m, \mathcal{G}_1, ..., \mathcal{G}_{k-1}\}.$$

First, select one collection $\mathcal{C}_\ell$ with probability p_ℓ, where $\{p_\ell\}_{\ell=1}^{m}$ is a solution to the following equation system.

$$(a_{i\ell}) \cdot \begin{pmatrix} p_1 \\ \vdots \\ p_m \end{pmatrix} = \begin{pmatrix} z_1^* \\ \vdots \\ z_m^* \end{pmatrix} \qquad\qquad (1)$$

and $(a_{i\ell})$ is an $m \times m$ matrix with

$$a_{i\ell} = \begin{cases} 1 & \text{if } \mathcal{G}_i \in \mathcal{C}_\ell, \\ 0 & \text{otherwise.} \end{cases} \tag{2}$$

Note that $(a_{i\ell})$ is a circulant matrix which is nonsingular. Hence equation system (1) has a unique solution. Since group $\mathcal{G}_i$ belongs to k collections $\mathcal{C}_i, \mathcal{C}_{i-1}, \ldots, \mathcal{C}_{i-k+1}$, equation system (1) can be rewritten as

$$\sum_{\ell=i-k+1}^{i} p_\ell = z_i^* \text{ for } i = 1, \ldots, m, \tag{3}$$

where "+" is in the sense of modular m.

Next, for each group $\mathcal{G}_i$ in the selected collection $\mathcal{C}_\ell$, randomly select one subset S from $\mathcal{G}_i$ with probability x_{iS}^*/z_i^* (and no subset of $\mathcal{G}_i$ is selected with probability $1 - \sum_{S \in \mathcal{G}_i} x_{iS}^*/z_i^*$.)

$$y_j = \begin{cases} 1 & \text{if element } j \text{ is covered by a selected subset,} \\ 0 & \text{otherwise.} \end{cases}$$

Lemma 5. $E[y_j] \geq (1 - e^{-1})y_j^*$.

Proof. For each $j = 1, \ldots, n$, let $I_j = \{(i, S) \mid j \in S \in \mathcal{G}_i\}$. Notice that for each $(i, S) \in I_j$,

$$\text{Prob}[(i, S) \text{ is picked}]$$

$$= \sum_{\ell=1}^{m} \text{Prob}[\mathcal{C}_\ell \text{ is picked}] \times \text{Prob}[(i, S) \text{ is picked} \mid \mathcal{C}_\ell \text{ is picked}]$$

$$= \sum_{\ell=i-k+1}^{i} p_\ell \cdot \frac{x_{iS}^*}{z_i^*} = z_i^* \cdot \frac{x_{iS}^*}{z_i^*} = x_{iS}^*,$$

where the third equality is because of (3). Then

$$\text{Prob}[y_j = 0] = \prod_{(i,S) \in I_j} \text{Prob}[(i,S) \text{ is not picked}] = \prod_{(i,S) \in I_j} (1 - x_{iS}^*)$$

$$\leq \left(\frac{\sum_{(i,S) \in I_j} (1 - x_{iS}^*)}{K_j} \right)^{K_j} = \left(1 - \frac{\sum_{(i,S) \in I_j} x_{iS}^*}{K_j} \right)^{K_j}$$

$$\leq \left(1 - \frac{y_j^*}{K_j} \right)^{K_j},$$

where $K_j = |I_j|$. Hence,

$$E[y_j] = \text{Prob}[y_j = 1] \geq 1 - \left(1 - \frac{y_i^*}{K_j} \right)^{K_j} \geq (1 - e^{-1})y_j^*$$

The lemma is proved. □

Lemma 6. $E[\prod_{j \in X_t} y_j] = \prod_{j \in X_t} E[y_j]$.

Proof. It is the same as the proof of Lemma 4.   □

Theorem 4. *Let* (y_j, x_{iS}) *be the approximate solution obtained by the above randomized rounding. Then*

$$E\left[\sum_{t=1}^{\tau} \prod_{j \in X_t} y_j\right] \geq (1 - e^{-1})^{\alpha}(1 - \varepsilon)lopt_3$$

where $lopt_3$ *is the objective value of a local optimal solution for (NLP3) and* $\alpha = \max_{1 \leq t \leq \tau} |X_t|$.

Proof. It is similar as the proof of Theorem 3.   □

We summarize the above algorithm into Algorithm 3.

Algorithm 2 Approximation for maximum group set coverage with size constraint and composed targets

---
input m groups $\mathcal{G}_1, \mathcal{G}_2, ..., \mathcal{G}_m$ of subsets of a finite set X, a partition of X into
    composed targets $X = X_1 \cup X_2 \cup \cdots \cup X_{\tau}$, and an integer $k > 0$.
output a collection $\mathcal{S}$ of subsets of X.
0:    $\mathcal{S} \leftarrow \emptyset$;
1:    Solve (NLP3) to obtain a $(1 - \varepsilon)$-approximate solution (x_{iS}^*, y_j^*, z_i^*);
2:    Solve equation system (1) to obtain p_{ℓ} for $\ell = 1, 2, ..., m$;
3:    Select one collection $\mathcal{C}_{\ell}$ with probability p_{ℓ};
4:    **for** each $i \in \mathcal{C}_{\ell}$ **do**
5:        select one subset S from $\mathcal{G}_i$ with probability x_{iS}^*/z_i^*;
6:        $\mathcal{S} \leftarrow \mathcal{S} \cup \{S\}$
7:    **end-for**
8:    **return** $\mathcal{S}$.

The running time of Algorithm 2 depends on computing a local optimal solution of (NLP3), which is an open problem in the situation stated at the end of last section.

6   Conclusion

In this paper, the group set coverage problem is proposed as a mathematical formulation for the study of camera sensor coverage problems. Through such a formulation, approximation algorithms are successfully designed for several maximization problems on camera sensor coverage.

A challenge is to study the minimization problem for group set coverage. Given a collection of subset groups on a finite set, find a minimum subcollection which is a group set cover. This may not be a proper research problem since it is NP-complete to determine whether a collection of subset groups is a group set cover, that is, it is NP-hard to determine whether the input has a feasible solution or not. According to Theorem 2, a proper research problem may be stated as follows: Given a collection of subset groups on a finite set, find a minimum subcollection covering at least $1 - 1/e$ percentage of all elements (i.e., for which there is an efficient selection that select one subset from each group such that at least $1 - 1/e$ portion of all elements are covered by selected subsets).

The above mentioned challenge may suggest us to study geometric version of group set coverage. Actually, the camera sensor coverage has some geometric structure which has been lost when it is formulated into the group set coverage problem. How to formulate a geometric version of group set coverage in order to reflect the geometric structure of camera sensor coverage? It may be an interesting problem in our future research.

References

1. Cardei, M., Thai, M., Li, Y., Wu, W.: Energy-efficient tar get coverage in wireless sensor networks. In: IEEE INFOCOM 2005, Miami, USA (2005)
2. Ding, L., Wu, W., Willson, J.K., Wu, L., Lu, Z., Lee, W.: Constantapproximation for target coverage problem in wireless sensor networks. In: Proceedings of The 31st Annual Joint Conference of IEEE Communication and Computer Society (INFOCOM) (2012)
3. Li, J., Jin, Y.: A PTAS for the weighted unit disk cover problem. In: Halldórsson, M.M., Iwama, K., Kobayashi, N., Speckmann, B. (eds.) ICALP 2015. LNCS, vol. 9134, pp. 898–909. Springer, Heidelberg (2015). https://doi.org/10.1007/978-3-662-47672-7_73
4. Lidong, W., Hongwei, D., Weili, W., Li, D., Lv, J., Lee, W.: Approximations for minimum connected sensor cover. In: INFOCOM (2013)
5. Ai, J., Abouzeid, A.A.: Coverage by directional sensors in randomly deployed wireless sensor networks. J. Comb. Optim. 11(1), 1 (2006)
6. Astorino, A., Gaudioso, M., Miglionico, G.: Optimizing sensor cover energy for directional sensors. In: AIP Conference Proceedings, vol. 1776. No. 1. AIP Publishing LLC (2016)
7. Li, D., Liu, H., Lu, X., Chen, W., Du, H.: Target Q-coverage problem with bounded service delay in directional sensor networks. IJDSN 8 (2012)
8. Liu, Z., Jia, W.: GuojunWang: area coverage estimation model for directional sensor networks. IJES 10(1), 13–21 (2018)
9. Lu, Z., WU, W., Li, W.W.: Target coverage maximisation for directional sensor networks. IJSNet 24(4), 253–263 (2017)
10. Sung, T.-W., Yang, C.-S.: Voronoi-based coverage improvement approach for wireless directional sensor networks. J. Netw. Comput. Appl. (JNCA) 39, 202–213 (2014)
11. Yu, Z., Yang, F., Teng, J., Champion, A.C., Xuan, D.: Local face-view barrier coverage in camera sensor networks. In: Proceedings of International Conference on Computer Communications (INFOCOM), 26 AprilC1 May, HongKong (2015)
12. Yang, C., Zhu, W., Liu, J., Chen, L., Chen, D., Cao, J.: Self-orienting the cameras for maximizing the view-coverage ratio in camera sensor networks. Pervasive Mob. Comput. 17, 102–121 (2015)
13. Cheng, B., Cui, L., Jia, W., Zhao, W., Hancke, G.P.: Multiple Region of Interest Coverage in Camera Sensor Networks for Tele- Intensive Care Units. IEEE Trans. Indus. Inform. 12(6), 2331–2341 (2016)

14. Hong, Y., et al.: Projection-Based Coverage Algorithms in 3D Camera Sensor Networks for Indoor Objective Tracking. In: CSoNet, pp. 309–320 (2019)
15. Wang, Y., Cao, G.: On full-viewcoverage in camera sensor networks. In: Proceeding International Conference on Computer Communications. In: (INFOCOM), pp. 10–15 April, 2011, Shanghai, China (2011)
16. Gao, X., Yang, R., Wu, F., Chen, G., Zhou, J.: Optimization of full-View barrier coverage with rotatable camera sensors. In: Proceedings of International Conference on Distributed Computing Systems (ICDCS), 5C8 June, 2017, Atlanta, GA, USA, pp. 870–879 (2017)
17. Ma, H., Yang, M., Li, D., Hong, Y., Chen, W.: Minimum camera barrier coverage in wireless camera sensor networks. In: The Proceedings of International Conference on Computer Communications (INFOCOM), pp. 25–30 March, 2012, Orlando, FL, USA (2012)
18. He, S., Shin, D., Zhang, J., Chen, J., Sun, Y.: Full-view area coverage in camera sensor networks: dimension reduction and near-optimal solutions. IEEE Trans. Veh. Technol. **64**(9), 7448–7461 (2016)
19. Hsiao, Y., Shih, K., Chen, Y.: On full-view area coverage by rotatable cameras in wireless camera sensor networks. In: Proceedings of International Conference on Advanced Information Networking and Applications (AINA), 27–29 March, TaiPei, Taiwan (2017)
20. Li, C., Bourgeois, A.G.: Lifetime and full-view coverage guarantees through distributed algorithms in camera sensor networks. In: Proceedings of International Conference on Parallel and Distributed Systems (ICPDS), Shenzhen, China, pp. 15–17 (2017)
21. Zhang, Q., He, S., Chen, J.: Toward optimal orientation scheduling for full-view coverage in camera sensor networks. In: Proceedings of International Conference on Distributed Computing Systems (GLOBECOM), Nara, Japan, pp. 27–30 (2016)
22. Ding-Zhu, D., Pardalos, P.M., Hu, X., Wu, W.: Introduction to Combinatorial Optimization, Springer (2022). https://doi.org/10.1007/978-3-031-10596-8
23. Charkhgard, H., Savelsbergh, M., Talebian, M.: A linear programming based algorithm to solve a class of optimization problems with a multi-linear objective function and affine constraints. Comput. Oper. Res. **89**, 17–30 (2018)
24. Drenick, R.F.: Multilinear programming: duality theories. J. Optim. Theor. Appl. **72**(3), 459–486 (1992). https://doi.org/10.1007/BF00939837
25. Weili, W., Zhang, Z., Ding-Zu, D.: Set function optimization. J. Oper. Res. Soc. China **7**(2), 183–193 (2019)
26. Du, D.-Z., Pardalos, P.M., Wu, W.: Mathematical Theory of Optimization. Springer (2010). https://doi.org/10.1007/978-1-4757-5795-8
27. Ye, Y.: On the complexity of approximating a KKT point of quadratic programming. Math. Program. **80**, 195–211 (1998)

Delay-Aware Hash Tree for Blockchain on Vehicular Delay Tolerant Networks

Joong-Lyul Lee[1]([✉]) [iD] and Joobum Kim[2] [iD]

[1] Department of Mathematics and Computer Science,
University North Carolina at Pembroke, Pembroke, NC 28372, USA
`joonglyul.lee@uncp.edu`
[2] Department of Information Technology, Middle Georgia State University,
Macon, GA 31206, USA
`joobum.kim@mga.edu`

Abstract. Blockchain (BC) technology is being applied to various applications with a lot of interest in data security. One of these applications is being applied in Vehicular Ad-hoc Networks (VANETs). Due to the high mobility of VANETs, frequent changes of the network topology occur and the network connection can be lost. These cause a high delay and network partitioning. Therefore, a new research paradigm called Vehicular Delay Tolerant Networks (VDTNs) is introduced to study these issues. When BC technology is applied to VANETs, it constructs a data gathering tree or schedules a routing path in the network layer for efficient data collection and handling network disruption. Furthermore, frequent topology updates happen. However, if the BC hash tree is not updated in the application layer, this causes an increase in network delay due to the inconsistency between the data gathering tree and the hash tree. In this paper, we describe this problem and propose new greedy algorithms to construct a hash tree that considers the network connection time on VDTNs. In such a hash tree, the inconsistency between the hash tree and the data gathering tree can be resolved by constructing the data gathering tree in consideration of the network connection time. Additionally we analyze the time complexity of the proposed algorithms.

Keywords: Blockchain · VANETs · VDTN · Hash tree

1 Introduction

Blockchain (BC) technology is receiving a lot of attention along with the popularity of data security and is a very stable, secure technology due to the characteristics of distributed technology. As an example of data security in BC, many mobile devices record online shopping and payment history. These histories can be altered or forged by cyber attackers. If this information is created using BC, it can be protected against data falsification from cyber attackers. The representative application technology using the BC is the cryptocurrency that is currently attracting much attention [1].

© ICST Institute for Computer Sciences, Social Informatics and Telecommunications Engineering 2023
Published by Springer Nature Switzerland AG 2023. All Rights Reserved
Z. J. Haas et al. (Eds.): WiCON 2022, LNICST 464, pp. 91–101, 2023.
https://doi.org/10.1007/978-3-031-27041-3_7

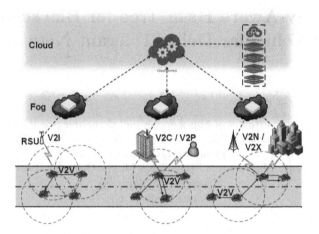

Fig. 1. A Vehicular-Fog-Cloud (VFC) Framework for BC

This BC is being applied to Vehicular Ad-hoc Networks (VANETs) [2,3]. Figure 1 presents a Vehicular-Fog-Cloud (VFC) framework when BC is applied to VANETs. VANETs are connected to five different types of communication devices. These five different types of communication devices are as follows: Vehicle to Infrastructure (V2I), Vehicular to Vehicle (V2V), Vehicle to Cloud (V2C), Vehicle to Pedestrian (V2P), Vehicle to Network (V2N), Vehicle to Everything (V2X) [4,5]. VANETs have high network delay, frequent network disconnection, and partitioning due to high mobility. A new research paradigm called vehicular delay tolerant networks (VDTNs) is introduced to study these issues. Delay-tolerant networking (DTN) continues to provide network connectivity even when heterogeneous network failures occur. VDTNs are similar to the characteristics of DTN in that network partitions or network disconnections occur [6,7].

When BC technology is applied to VANETs, it does not consider highly dynamic network topology [8,9]. VANET nodes construct a network topology for a short period to transmit data to the Cloud data center through Fog nodes as shown in Fig. 1. Due to the movement of VANET nodes over time, the network topology for transmitting data changes, and then the hash tree (eg. Merkle tree [10,11]) in BC does not change. This discrepancy between the data gathering tree and the hash tree in BC causes the network delay to increase. To compensate for this shortcoming, we propose new greedy algorithms to construct a hash tree for BC based on a data scheduling graph.

Contribution of this paper: The main contributions of this paper can be summarized as follows:

1. When the BC is applied to VANETs, the network topology changes frequently due to the high mobility of the VANET. We notice that the discrepancy between the changed network topology and the hash tree in the BC causes a problem of increasing network delay, and define this problem in this paper.

2. We propose new greedy algorithms that construct a hash tree for BC based on the data collection schedule for VANETs with high mobility and describe the time complexity of the proposed algorithms.

To the best of our knowledge, this is the first research work about network delay caused by the discrepancy between the hash tree and data gathering tree (routing path) in BC technology of VANETs, where the network topology changes most frequently over time.

The rest of this paper is structured as follows. Section 2 describes the network model, problem formulation, the proposed algorithm, and the analyzed result. Finally, Sect. 3 concludes this paper.

2   System Model and Design

In this section, we describe the core components in the system, notation, problem statement, and the proposed delay-aware hash tree construction algorithms.

2.1   Core Components in the System

Vehicle Node (VN). A vehicle with a wireless onboard unit (OBU) is connected to an Internet through a Road Side Unit (RSU) which is connected to the backbone network around the road. Each VANET node transmits necessary safety-related information for driving such as road surface condition information, traffic information, weather information, etc. to the Cloud center through the Fog node by communicating with other nodes or RSU.

Cluster Head Node (CHN). The VANET node constructs a topology to collect safety-related information or provide network connectivity to each node. This node that constructs and controls the topology is the cluster head node (CHN).

Road Side Unit (RSU). The Road Side Unit (RSU) connected to the Backbone network is installed on the roadside and provides network connectivity to passing cars, thereby providing Internet connectivity.

Fog Node (FN). The information collected by the VANET nodes is sent to the Cloud center, and the information from numerous VANET nodes is concentrated in on the data center, creating a network bottleneck. To overcome these shortcomings, nearby servers (Fog nodes) provide connectivity and accessibility. These Fog nodes (FN) process the information collected from the VANET nodes and send them to the Cloud center.

Cloud Data Center (CDC). The information collected from the Fog nodes is stored in the Cloud data center (CDC), and the stored information is analyzed. The analyzed useful information is provided to each client.

2.2 Notation and Problem Statement

Definition 1 (Graph by vehicular node v). *Given a graph $G = (V, E)$ by each VANET node v_n and each edge $E = (v_i, v_j)$ existing within the transmission range of VANET node v_i and v_j.*

Definition 2 (Communication range of vehicular node v). *The communication range c_{v_i} of a node is defined as the communication range of each VANET node v_i.*

Definition 3 (Network connection of vehicular node v_i and v_j). *The network connection $N(v_i, v_j)$ of VANET nodes v_i, v_j is defined as the minimum communication range of VANET nodes v_i, v_j, i.e. $N(v_i, v_j) = min\,(c_{v_i}, c_{v_j}) : v_i, v_j \in V\}$.*

Definition 4 (Graph by time space). *Given a graph $G = (V_{(n,t)}, E_{(i,j,t)})$ by time spaces and each VANET node has location $V_{(n,t)} = (x_t, y_t)$ and each edge $E_{(i,j,t)} = (V_{(i,t)}, V_{(j,t)})$ in the time space.*

Definition 5 *Network Connection* metric space). *Consider the Network Connection metrics space $(V_{(i,j)}, \delta_{(i,j)})$, where v_i and v_j are in the set of VANET nodes. For each pair of VANET nodes $v_i, v_j \in V$, $\delta_{(i,j)}(StartTime\_stamp(st), End\,Time\_stamp(et))$ is an estimated network connection time duration.*

1. $\delta_{(i,j)}(st, et) >= 0$
2. $\delta_{(i,j)}(st, et) = \delta_{(j,i)}(st, et)$ if $v_i \neq v_j$
3. $\delta_{(i,j)}(st, et) = 0$ if $v_i = v_j$

Problem 1. *Given a set of the vehicular set $V = \{v_1, v_2, v_3, \cdots, v_n\}$ and time constant $t \geq t_{max}$, we want to construct a hash tree with no additional network delay based on a data gathering tree to collect data efficiently on predictable VDTNs which provide continuous network connectivity despite frequent network failures.*

As shown in Fig. 2-(a), VANET nodes construct a data transmission tree to send and receive data efficiently. However, this data transmission tree is changed continually as time goes by due to the mobility of VANETs. If the BC Hash tree and VANET data transmission tree are the same as in Fig. 2-(a), there will be no delay beyond the expected network delay. If the VANET data transmission tree is updated, there may be a case of inconsistency with the BC Hash tree.

As shown in Fig. 2-(b), when the data transmission tree is updated within the same tree, the data is transmitted inefficiently. For example, when the cluster head (Black node) changes to the terminal node due to the VANET node's

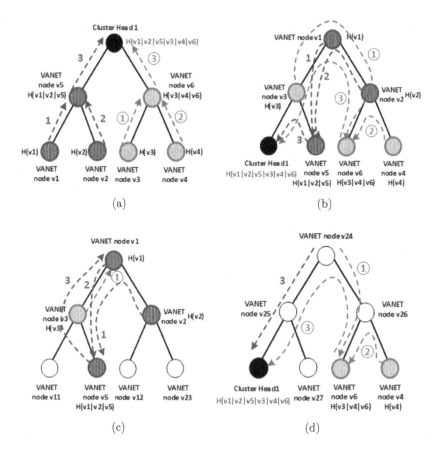

Fig. 2. Discrepancy between data gathering tree and hash tree on VDTN: (a) A case where the data gathering tree and hash tree are identical, and (b) A case where the data gathering tree and hash tree are not the same, (c), and (d) A case where the nodes of the hash tree are split into two data gathering trees.

mobility, VANET node 1 and VANET node 2 are forwarded to VANET node 3 after hashing the data with the previous terminal nodes(Red arrows 1, 2, and 3). After calculating the Hash value added with its data value, VANET node 3 is transmitted to the current end node, which is the head of the previous network transmission tree. VANET node 3 and VANET node 4 transmit their data hash values to VANET node 6. Then, after calculating the hash value of the received data and the hash value of its data, the VANET node 6 transmits the hash data to the cluster head which is changed to the current terminal node(Green arrows 1, 2, and 3).

Figures 2-(c) and (d) show the case in which the nodes in Fig. 2-(a) are mixed with other nodes to form two new data gathering trees due to the mobility of VANET nodes. As the cluster head (Black node) exists in the tree in Fig. 2-(d), VANET node 1 and VANET node 2 in Fig. 2-(c) transmit the hash value to VANET node 3. Then, this hash value is again transmitted to the cluster head (Black node) in the terminal node in 2-(d) (Red arrows 1, 2, and 3). VANET node 3 in Fig. 2-(c) and VANET node 4 in Fig. 2-(d) transmit the hash value to VANET node 6, and VANET node 6 transmits the hash value to the cluster head (Green arrows 1, 2, and 3). As shown in this example, the data collection tree is frequently updated based on the network layer. However, a Merkle tree is used to calculate the data hash value in the BC, and this tree does not update when the data gathering tree is changed.

In a DTN, many existing algorithms consider scheduling to transfer data, but there is no algorithm considers both scheduling and delay. As seen in the example in Fig. 2, delay as well as scheduling for data delivery are important parts that cannot be ignored.

Therefore, we propose new algorithms considering scheduling and delay for BC on VDTNs.

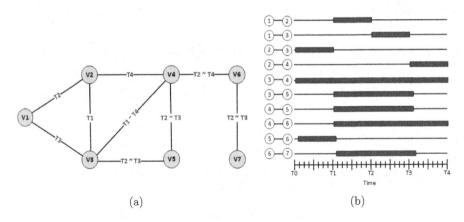

(a)   (b)

Fig. 3. A complete graph of the time-evolving network

As shown in Fig. 3-(a), it creates a complete graph based on a network connection and time-evolving network. In a time-evolving network, each VANET node has a network connection and network duration with the neighbor node in different time slots as in Fig. 3-(b).

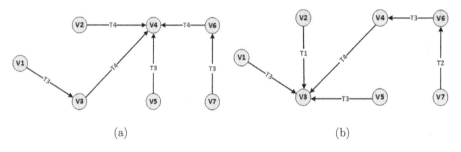

Fig. 4. Scheduling graphs for data collection based on Fig. 3

2.3 Delay-aware Hash Tree on Predictable VDTNs

Phase I: VANET Set-Up. As the movement of the VANET nodes is predictable, it creates a complete graph based on network connected time. This research method has been studied in many papers [12,13]. Furthermore, it has a connected schedule between nodes during a specific time as in Fig. 3-(b). It selects a root node set choosing the highest time-stamp with the longest network connection time. In Fig. 3-(b), the time-stamp with the longest connection time is the connection link of nodes 3 and 4. Therefore, nodes 3 and 4 are included in the root node candidate sets.

Phase II: Scheduling Data Collection. Node 3 and node 4 are the root node candidates. When node 4 is selected as the root node, node 4 selects the highest timeslot in the connecting link with the neighboring nodes as shown in Fig. 4-(a). Node 4 selects nodes 2, 3, 5, and 6 as neighboring nodes, and selects the highest timestamp that can also select timestamps. If there is a node that has not been selected in this round, the node with the highest time-stamp among the neighboring nodes connects with the neighboring node. However, the selected neighbor nodes choose a timestamp that is lower than the timestamp selected by the root node but is selectable higher. In Fig. 4-(a), node 3 selects node 1 with timestamp 3, and node 6 selects node 7 with timestamp 3 in the next round. In Fig. 4-(b), node 3 is selected as the root node. Neighbors 1, 2, 4, and 5 are selected by selecting the highest timestamp that node 3 can select among the neighboring nodes. Since there is a node that was not selected in this round, node 4 among the child nodes selects node 6 in the next round. As there are still unselected nodes, node 6 checks circularity and selects child node 7 in the next round.

Algorithm 1. Data Scheduling algorithm based on VDTN

Input: a set of vehicle V^*, a set of time stamps and duration T^*;
Output: a cluster set C^*;
1:
2: $S \leftarrow$ a set of all visiting nodes;
3: $V \leftarrow$ a set of all vehicle nodes;
4: $T^*_{List} = Sort\{\delta_{(i,j)}(st_1, et_1), \delta_{(k,l)}(st_2, et_2)...\}$ by endTimeSlot;
5: $R^* =$ select the root node candidate group among the nodes with the longest and highest timestamp (et) from T^*_{List};
6:
7: **while** $V \neq \{\emptyset\}$ **do**
8:      Pick a node v_i from R^* and remove node v_i from V;
9:      Add a node v_i to S and C^*;
10:     Select the neighbor node of node v_i and add neighbor node v_j to S;
11:     Select the highest time slot of node v_j;
12:     **if** *timestamp of* $v_j \leq$ *timestamp of the root* **then**
13:         Add child node list C^*;
14:         remove node v_j from V;
15:     **end if**
16: **end while**
17:
18: Return cluster set C^*;

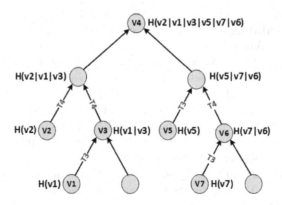

Fig. 5. A Dealy-aware Hash Tree based on Fig. 4-(a)

Algorithm 2. DHT construction algorithm

Input: a set of cluster C^*;
Output: hash tree H;

1:
2: Pick a root node v_i from C^* and remove the node from C^*;
3: $H\_root = v_i$;
4: **for** i to n **do**
5:     $child\_node = child\_node$ of v_i;
6:     **if** $child\_node.size > 0$ **then**
7:         ADDCHILDNODE($child\_node$);
8:     **end if**
9:     $i++$;
10:     $H_{level}++$;
11: **end for**
12:
13: **function** ADDCHILDNODE($child\_node$)
14:     **if** $child\_node.size == 1$ **then**
15:         Add $H.left\_child \leftarrow child\_node$;
16:         Add $H.right\_child \leftarrow dummy\_node$;
17:         $child\_node.size = child\_node.size - 1$;
18:     **else if** $child\_node.size == 2$ **then**
19:         Add $H.left\_child \leftarrow child\_node$;
20:         Add $H.right\_child \leftarrow child\_node$;
21:         $child\_node.size = child\_node.size - 2$;
22:     **else if** $child\_node.size > 2$ **then**
23:         Add $H.left\_child \leftarrow dummy\_node$;
24:         Add $H.right\_child \leftarrow dummy\_node$;
25:         $left\_child\_node.size = \lceil child\_node.size/2 \rceil$;
26:         $right\_child\_node.size = \lfloor child\_node.size/2 \rfloor$;
27:         ADDCHILDNODE($left\_child\_node$);
28:         ADDCHILDNODE($right\_child\_node$);
29:     **end if**
30: **end function**
31:
32: Return hash tree H;

Phase III: Delay-aware Hash Tree (DHT). The root hash value of the hash tree stored in BC. This hash tree is a binary tree structure. The data gathering schedule trees in Fig. 4-(a) and (b) are not binary trees. Therefore, after constructing a tree considering scheduling for data gathering, this tree is converted into a binary tree as in Fig. 5. It pops up the root node from the cluster set that is the output from Algorithm 1. As shown in Fig. 5, when there are two or more child nodes, the level of the tree is increased and a dummy node is added. The algorithm terminates when there are no more child nodes.

A hash value $h_{(j,k)} = H(v_i)$ is computed with $1 \leq k \leq 2^n$. The leaf node of the hash tree has level $j = 0$ and the root node has level $j = n$. The number of nodes in a level is from left to right. Therefore, $h_{(0,0)} = H(v_1)$, $h_{(1,0)} = H(v_1|v_2)$ and $h_{(2,0)} = H(v_1|v_2|v_3)$.

Theorem 1. *The time complexity of the proposed Algorithm 1 on VDTN is O(E).*

Proof. Initially, an algorithm selects a root node in a cluster. It executes as many as the number of VANET edges. Therefore, the time complexity of the proposed algorithm is $O(E)$.

Theorem 2. *The time complexity of the proposed Algorithm 2 is O(log$_2$V).*

Proof. This algorithm is to convert from a tree set for efficient data collection to a binary tree. And it repeats as many as the level of the binary tree. Therefore, the time complexity of the proposed algorithm is $O(log_2V)$.

3   Conclusion

A data gathering tree constructs for efficient data collection in VANETs. It frequently changes due to high mobility. However, the hash tree in BC is not updated like the data gathering tree when BC is applied to VANETs. If the data collection tree and hash tree are not identical, then there is a problem in which network delay increase. In this paper, we describe this problem and propose algorithms for constructing a tree that collects data at a specific time based on the mobility expected as a solution and construct a hash tree based on this data gathering tree on VDTNs. We showed the time complexity of the proposed algorithms. In future work, we have a plan to simulate these algorithms and perform performance comparisons with the other algorithms.

References

1. Nakamoto, S..: Bitcoin: A peer-to-peer electronic cash system
2. Li, H., Pei, L., Liao, D., Sun, G., Xu, D.: Blockchain meets VANET: an architecture for identity and location privacy protection in VANET. Peer-to-Peer Netw. Appl. **12**(5), 1178–1193 (2019)
3. Deng, X., Gao, T.: Electronic payment schemes based on blockchain in VANETs. IEEE Access **8**, 38296–38303 (2020)
4. Lee, M., Atkison, T.: VANET applications: past, present, and future. Veh. Commun. **28**, 100310 (2021)
5. Cunha, F., et al.: Data communication in VANETs: protocols, applications and challenges. Ad Hoc Netw. **44**, 90–103 (2016)
6. Kang, H., Ahmed, S.H., Kim, D., Chung, Y.-S.: Routing protocols for vehicular delay tolerant networks: a survey. Int. J. Distrib. Sens. Netw. **11**(3), 325027 (2015)
7. Cheng, P.-C., Lee, K.C., Gerla, M., Härri, J.: GeoDTN+ Nav: geographic DTN routing with navigator prediction for urban vehicular environments. Mob. Netw. Appl. **15**(1), 61–82 (2010)
8. Kim, S.: Impacts of mobility on performance of blockchain in VANET. IEEE Access **7**, 68646–68655 (2019)

9. Xie, L., Ding, Y., Yang, H., Wang, X.: Blockchain-based secure and trustworthy internet of things in SDN-enabled 5G-VANETs. IEEE Access **7**, 56656–56666 (2019)
10. Merkle, R.C.: Secrecy, Authentication, and Public Key systems. Stanford university (1979)
11. Becker, G.: Merkle signature schemes, merkle trees and their cryptanalysis. Ruhr-University Bochum. Technical report (2008)
12. Lee, J.-L., Hwang, J., Park, H.-S., Kim, D..: On latency-aware tree topology construction for emergency responding VANET applications. In: IEEE INFOCOM 2018-IEEE Conference on Computer Communications Workshops (INFOCOM WKSHPS), pp. 57–63 IEEE (2018)
13. Lee, J.-L., Hwang, J., Park, H., Kim, D.: Ad hoc communication topology construction for delay-sensitive internet of vehicle applications. Wirel. Commun. Mob. Comput. 2022 (2022)

Learning the Propagation of Worms in Wireless Sensor Networks

Yifan Wang(✉) , Siqi Wang , and Guangmo Tong

University of Delaware, Newark, DE 19711, USA
{yifanw,wsqbit,amotong}@udel.edu

Abstract. Wireless sensor networks (WSNs) are composed of spatially distributed sensors and are considered vulnerable to attacks by worms and their variants. Due to the distinct strategies of worms propagation, the dynamic behavior varies depending on the different features of the sensors. Modeling the spread of worms can help us understand the worm attack behaviors and analyze the propagation procedure. In this paper, we design a communication model under various worms. We aim to learn our proposed model to analytically derive the dynamics of competitive worms propagation. We develop a new searching space combined with complex neural network models. Furthermore, the experiment results verified our analysis and demonstrated the performance of our proposed learning algorithms.

Keywords: Wireless sensor network · Multi-worm propagation · Complex neural network

1 Introduction

Due to the recent advances in wireless and micro-mechanical sensor technologies, wireless sensor networks (WSNs) have been widely used in various real-time applications, for example, target tracking, biological detection, health care monitoring, environmental sensing and etc. [9,16,17,22,26,29]. WSNs are composed of the spatially distributed sensors that are low-cost, small-sized, low-energy, and multi-functional [10,16,35]. Each sensor is designed to sense and collect environmental information. It has the ability to carry out a local computation to obtain the required data and will transfer the required data to a higher-level host [3,35]. Besides, the communication paradigm of WSNs is based on the broadcasting such that each sensor can communicate with its neighbors directly [3,32].

The computer worms are the programs that can be disseminated across the network by self-replicating to exploit the security or policy flaws [28,36]. Although many advantages of the sensors are proposed, WSNs are vulnerable to attacks by worms and variants. One reason is that sensor network protocols primarily concentrate on power conservation, and each sensor is usually assigned to a limited resource. Therefore it generally has a weak defense mechanism [19,30]. Besides, since the spread of worms usually relies on the information involved in the infected

© ICST Institute for Computer Sciences, Social Informatics and Telecommunications Engineering 2023
Published by Springer Nature Switzerland AG 2023. All Rights Reserved
Z. J. Haas et al. (Eds.): WiCON 2022, LNICST 464, pp. 102–115, 2023.
https://doi.org/10.1007/978-3-031-27041-3_8

sensors and WSNs often embed an efficient propagation mechanism, the worms can achieve a rapid propagation speed [2, 4, 16]. Furthermore, some worms will upgrade and be more complicated in order to propagate successfully, which will result in a widespread destruction [35]. Therefore, worms and variants become one of the main threats to network security.

In order to control the spreading of worms, people seek to understand the dynamic behaviors of worms. In practice, worms utilize different propagation strategies. For example, scan-based techniques will identify the vulnerable sensors based on the IP address [34, 39]. Topology-based techniques allow worms to spread through the topology neighbors [35]. Many studies have modeled these propagation procedures mathematically. Most researchers proposed propagation models based on the classic epidemic models, for example, SIR and SEIR models [12, 15]. In recent works, extensions to the epidemic models have been proposed: Some studies considered the hybrid dynamic of worms and antivirus propagation [1, 6, 11]. Some works investigated the virus behavior containing the stability analysis of WSNs [14, 27, 38].

Considering a WSN composed of a number of sensors, the transmission rates for different worms vary based on the distinct mechanism embedded in the sensors. That means that for different worms and sensors, the dynamic behavior will vary [7, 37]. Meanwhile, both scan-based and topology-based propagation strategies select the targets based on the features related to the sensors [25, 35]. Since there is a basic similarity between worm propagation through wireless devices and the information diffusion process over the regular network, from this standpoint, we propose a discrete communication model based on the competitive diffusion models under multiple worms. We seek to learn our proposed model to derive the dynamics of competitive worms propagation analytically. Our contributions can be summarized as follows.

- **Propagation Model Design.** We design a communication model that simulates the propagation of the competitive worm. Our model includes the special case with the hybrid dynamics with virus and patch, which provides a new aspect to the antivirus protection design.
- **Searching Space Analysis.** We develop a new searching space combined with the complex-valued neural network. To our best knowledge, this provides a starting point for analyzing the worms propagation model.
- **Empirical Studies.** We provide experimental validation of our model compared with some baseline methods.

The paper is organized as follows. In the next section, we introduce some related works of the different propagation models. Section 3 illustrates the structure of the communication model and formulates the learning problem. Section 4 describes the learning framework, including the searching space design and the learning algorithm. Experiments are given in Sect. 5.

2   Related Work

A large number of models have been proposed to analyze the dynamics of worm propagation in WSNs based on epidemic models. Kephart et al. first proposed the idea of formulating the worm's propagation based on simple epidemic models. They assumed each sensor or host stays in one of two states: susceptible or infectious. And the infected sensor will not change its infectious state [15]. In recent works, Abdel et al. proposed an extension SIR model by considering antivirus dynamics that add the antidotal state to each sensor [1]. And the authors present a unified study of the epidemic-antivirus nonlinear dynamical system. The work in [2] designed a fractional-order compartmental epidemic model by accounting for the global stability analysis. Several studies added the quarantined constraints for each sensor to the epidemic models [16,20,21].

For multiple worms propagation, authors in [32] proposed a model that supports the sleep and work interleaving schedule policy for the sensor nodes. They assigned different infect probabilities to each worm when the infected nodes attempted to infect other nodes. However, they did not specify the relationship among these worms, and it is hard to track the dynamic of different worms. [24] developed a SEjIjR-V Epidemic Model with differential exposure, infectivity, and communication Range. Besides, they generate the epidemic thresholds for each sensor corresponding to different worms. In our work, we formulate a worms propagation model based on the works in [23,33]. And inspired by them, we develop an explicitly complex-valued neural network to exactly simulate the worms' propagation process.

3   Preliminaries

In this section, we present the communication model and problem settings.

3.1   Communication Model

We consider the wireless network as a directed graph $G = (V, E)$, where V and E denote the sensors and the communication links, respectively. Let $|V| = N$ and $|E| = M$. For each node v, its in-neighbors is denoted by $N_v \subseteq V$. It is assumed that K different worms are spread over the network, and each worm $k \in [K]$ propagates from a set of sensors $S^k \in V$. For each node $v \in V$, there is a set of threshold $\Theta_v = \{\theta_v^1, ..., \theta_v^K\}$ that represents its vulnerabilities to different worms, where $\theta \in [0, \infty)$. For each edge $(u, v) \in E$, there is a set of weights $W_{(u,v)} = \{w_{(u,v)}^1, ..., w_{(u,v)}^K\}$ indicates its levels of transmission with different worms, where $w \in [0, \infty)$. We assume that a node can only be infected by one worm and suppose that the spread of worms continuous step by step based on the following rules.

- Initialization. For nodes $v \in S^k$, they are k-infected; Otherwise, the nodes stay innocent.

- Step t. There are two stages during each step. Let $S_{t-1}^k \subseteq V$ be the k-infected nodes at the end of step $t - 1$.
  - Stage 1. For each innocent node v, it can be possibly infected by the worms in set $P_v^t \subseteq [K]$, where

$$P_v^t = \left\{ k \Big| \sum_{u \in N_v \cap S_{t-1}^k} w_{(u,v)}^k \geq \theta_v^k \right\}. \tag{1}$$

  - Stage 2. Node v will finally be infected by worm k^* such that

$$k^* = \underset{k \in P_v^t}{\arg\max} \sum_{u \in N_v \cap S_{t-1}^k} w_{(u,v)}^k \tag{2}$$

   Once a node is infected, its status will not change during the propagation. For tie breaking, each node is more vulnerable with the worm with a large index.
- Termination. The propagation process ends when no nodes can be infected. We can observe that $t \leq N$.

3.2   Problem Settings

We begin by presenting some notations that are used in the rest of the paper.

Notations. For a complex number $a+ib$, a is the real part and b is the imaginary part, where $a, b \in \mathbb{R}$. For convenience, we use (a, b) to simplify the notation. During the propagation process, for a step $t \in [N]$, we denoted the status of each node $v \in V$ by a complex-valued vector $I_t(v) \in \mathbb{C}^K$: If v is k-infection, then the k_{th} element in $I_t(v)$ is $1 + i0$ and the rest elements are $0 + i0$; If v is a innocent node, then all the elements in $I_t(v)$ are $0 + i0$. The status over all nodes, named all-infection status, is then formulated as a matrix $\mathcal{I}_t \in \mathbb{C}^{K \times N}$ by concatenating I_t for each node, where $\mathcal{I}_{t,v} = I_t(v)$. Furthermore, to simplify, we assume that $K = 2^P$ where $p \in \mathbb{Z}^+$.

We are interested in learning propagation functions given the collected propagation data.

Definition 1. *Given a network graph and a communication model, the propagation function $F : \mathbb{C}^{K \times N} \rightarrow \mathbb{C}^{K \times N}$ maps from initial all-infection status $\mathcal{I}_0$ to the final status $\mathcal{I}_N$.*

Definition 2. *The propagation data set D is a set of initial-final status pairs with size $Q \in \mathbb{Z}^+$, where*

$$D = \{(\mathcal{I}_0, \mathcal{I}_N)^i\}_{i=1}^Q. \tag{3}$$

Given a new initial-final status pair $(\mathcal{I}_0, \mathcal{I}_N)$, let $\hat{\mathcal{I}}_N$ be the predicted final all-infection status, we use l to measuring the loss.

$$l(\hat{\mathcal{I}}_N, \mathcal{I}_N) = \frac{1}{N} |\{v : \hat{\mathcal{I}}_{N,v} \neq \mathcal{I}_{N,v}, v \in V\}| \tag{4}$$

The problem can be formally defined as follows.

Problem 1. Given the graph structure G and a set of propagation data D draw from some distribution $\mathcal{D}$, we wish to find a propagation function $F : \mathbb{C}^{K \times N} \rightarrow \mathbb{C}^{K \times N}$, that minimizes the generalization error L, where

$$L(F) = \mathbb{E}_{(\mathcal{I}_0, \mathcal{I}_N) \sim \mathcal{D}} l(F(\mathcal{I}_0), \mathcal{I}_N) \tag{5}$$

4   A Learning Framework

In this section, for the communication model, we first design a searching space that composed by the complex neural network. Then the learning algorithm is proposed given such searching space.

4.1   Hypothesis Space Design

In this section, we construct the hypothesis space for Problem 1 by simulating the propagation process as a finite complex-valued Neural Network (CVNNs) from local to global. Assume that for the complex-valued neuron n at layer $l+1$, it is linked with m numbers of neurons in the previous layer, then the output of neuron n is described as follows:

$$H_n^{l+1} = \sigma_n^{l+1} \left(\sum_{i=1}^{m} W_{in}^l H_n^l + T_n^l \right) \tag{6}$$

Here W_{in}^l denotes the weight connecting the neuron n and the neuron i from the previous layer, σ_n^{l+1} denotes the activation function on neuron n, T_n^l is the bias term.

Local Propagation. For the local propagation, it simulates the diffusion process during every step t. It starts by receiving the all-infection status $\mathcal{I}_t \in \mathbb{C}^{K \times N}$ at the end of step t. Figure 1 illustrates an example of local propagation process.

Stage 1. We aim to find out all the possible worms that can infect the each innocent nodes. During this stage, each worm diffuses separately and follows a linear threshold process. Therefore, we wish the links between the layers represents the topology in the WSNs and the activation function can be simply defined as the threshold functions. In addition, the communication model indicates that once a node is affected, it will never change the status. Therefore, for each node, we add one link towards it self at the next layer with a relatively large value. The propagation can be simulated by

$$\mathbf{H}^2 = \sigma^1(\mathbf{W}^1 \mathbf{H}^1 + \mathbf{T}^1), \tag{7}$$

where for $i, j \in [N]$ and $k, l \in [K]$, we have

$$\mathbf{W}_{i \cdot K + k, j \cdot K + l}^1 := \begin{cases} (w_{(i,j)}^k, 0) & \text{if } (i, j) \in E \text{ and } k = l \\ 1000 & \text{if } i = j \text{ and } k = l \\ (0, 0) & \text{otherwise} \end{cases}$$

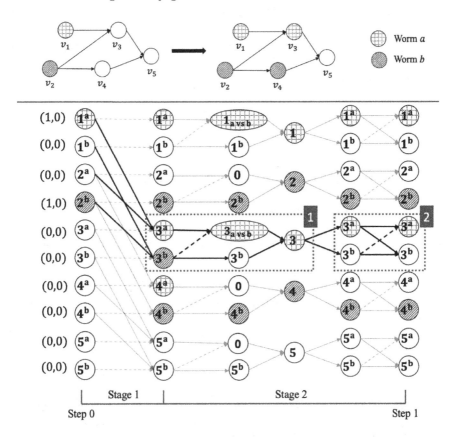

Fig. 1. Local propagation structure. Suppose that two competitive worms are disseminated in the network. The top part of the figure shows the propagation process during one step across a small WSN. The neural network below shows the corresponding designed neural network during one step and each stages are simulated by several layers. We focus on the activation flow on node 3 using highlight lines. Specially, the idea of the structure in the boxes labeled with 1 and 2 are discussed in Fig. 2 and 3.

$$\sigma^1_{j \cdot K+l}(x) := \begin{cases} x & \text{if } \mathrm{Re}(x) \geq \theta^l_j \\ (0,0) & \text{Otherwise} \end{cases} . \tag{8}$$

$$T^1_{j \cdot K+l}(x) := (0, l) \tag{9}$$

Stage 2. With the input $\mathbf{H}^2$ from phase 1, this stage determines the final infect status of each node. That is for a node $i \in V$, we want to find out the largest value among the sub-array

$$\left[\mathrm{Re}(\mathbf{H}^2_{i+1}), \mathrm{Re}(\mathbf{H}^2_{i+2}), ..., \mathrm{Re}(\mathbf{H}^2_{i+K}) \right]. \tag{10}$$

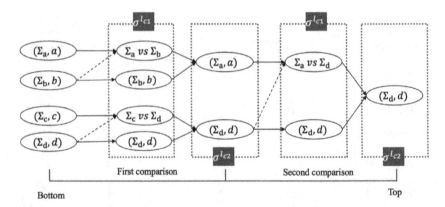

Fig. 2. Hierarchy structure of pairwise comparisons. This figure shows the structure of box 1 in Fig. 1. To better illustration, suppose that there are four different
worms: a, b, c and d and thereby with two pairwise comparison. The nodes in the bottom layer represent the sub-array 10. All the weights on the solid links are $1 + i0$
and the weights on the dash links are $-1 + i0$. During each comparison process, the
first layer implements the activation function in Eq. 11 such that: if the prior one has
the larger value of real part, the node returns the difference; Otherwise, it will return
$(0, 0)$. Therefore, by combining the second layer l^{c2}, the output is exactly the larger
value between two nodes.

Intuitively, finding the largest value among Eq. 10 can be implemented through
a hierarchy structure of pairwise comparisons. Starting from the sub-array, each
hierarchy compares every two neighboring elements and passing the larger value
to the next level, which leads to a P hierarchy levels structure.

From bottom to top, for node $v \in [N]$, in each hierarchy level $p \in [P]$, the
size of input elements $I_p = \frac{K}{2^{p-1}}$ and the size of output elements $O_p = \frac{K}{2^p}$. Each
level can be decoded by two layers: l^{c1} and l^{c2}.

In l^{c1}, for $i, j \in [I_p]$,

$$
\mathbf{W}_{i,j}^{c1} := \begin{cases} (1, 0) & \text{if } i = j \\ (0, -1) & \text{if } j = i - 1 \text{ for } j = 2n + 1 \text{ where } n \in \{0, 1, 2, ..., I_p - 1\} \\ (0, 0) & \text{otherwise} \end{cases}
$$

$\sigma^{l_{c1}}$ is defined as follows:

$$
\sigma^{l_{c1}}(x) := \begin{cases} (\text{Im}(x), \text{Re}(x)) & \text{if } \text{Im}(x) \geq 0 \\ (0, 0) & \text{otherwise} \end{cases} \tag{11}
$$

In l^{c2}, for $i \in [I_p]$ and $j \in [O_p]$,

$$
\mathbf{W}_{i,j}^{l_{c2}} := \begin{cases} (1, 0) & \text{if } i = 2 \cdot j \text{ or } i = 2 \cdot j - 1 \\ (0, 0) & \text{otherwise} \end{cases}
$$

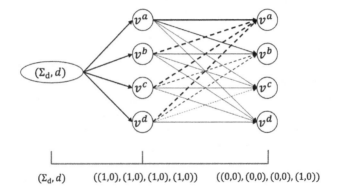

Fig. 3. Structure of the format adjustment. This figure shows the structure of box 2 in Fig. 1. Suppose that there are four different worms: a, b, c and d. For a node $v \in V$, at the end of one step, we assume it is d-active. All the weights on the solid links are $1 + i0$ and the weights on the dash links are $-1 + i0$. In addition, the threshold on each node v^k of each layer is k, where $k \in \{a, b, c, d\}$. The bottom vectors in the figure below shows the format of each layer.

$\sigma^{l_{c2}}$ is defined as follows.

$$\sigma^{l_{c2}}(x) := x$$

By repeatedly using these two layers P times, the output of stage 2 is $\mathbf{H}^{2P+2} \in \mathbb{C}^N$. For $i \in [N]$ and $k \in [K]$, each node in $\mathbf{H}^{2P+2}$ holds the value as follows,

$$\mathbf{H}_i^{2P+2} = \left(\max_{k \in K}\{\mathrm{Re}(\mathbf{H}_{i+k}^2)\}, \arg\max_{k \in K}\{\mathrm{Re}(\mathbf{H}_{i+k}^2)\} \right), \qquad (12)$$

where the real part for each node i indicates the largest incoming weights among all the worms, and the imaginary part is the corresponding worm index.

Format Adjustment. In order to simulate the global worm propagation process, we need to make the format of the output at the end of local propagation be same as the input, that is $\mathbf{H}^{2Z+3} = \mathcal{I}_{t+1} \in \mathbb{C}^{K \times N}$. Two layers are added. Figure 3 shows an example of the structure of the format adjustment. The two layers can be formulated as follows.

$$\mathbf{H}^{2P+2+i} = \sigma^{2Z+2+i}(\mathbf{W}^{2Z+2+(i-1)}\mathbf{H}^{2Z+2+(i-1)}), \qquad (13)$$

where $i = \{1, 2\}$. The first layer can be seen as a transition layer. The number of the output nodes will be recovered as the input, and the real number of each node are set to 0. For the imaginary part, its value will be equal to 1 if the node's corresponding worm's index is no large than the real part in Eq. 12. Therefore, it is formulated as follows. For each $i, j \in [N]$, $k \in [K]$, we have

$$\mathbf{W}^{2P+3}_{i \cdot K, j \cdot K + k} := \begin{cases} (1,0) & \text{if } i = j \\ (0,0) & \text{otherwise} \end{cases}$$

and

$$\sigma^{2P+3}_{j \cdot K + k}(x) := \begin{cases} (1,0) & \text{if Im}(x) \text{ and Im}(x) \geq k \\ (0,0) & \text{Otherwise} \end{cases}. \tag{14}$$

The last layer are designed to extract the all-infection status at the end of local propagation, and that is $\mathbf{H}^{2P+4} = \mathcal{I}_t$
where for each $i, j \in [N]$, $k, l \in [K]$, we have

$$\mathbf{W}^{2P+4}_{i \cdot K + k, j \cdot K + l} := \begin{cases} (1,0) & \text{if } i = j \text{ and } l \geq k \\ (-1,0) & \text{if } i = j \text{ and } l < k \\ (0,0) & \text{otherwise} \end{cases}$$

and

$$\sigma^{2P+4}_{j \cdot K + l}(x) := \begin{cases} (1,0) & \text{if Re}(x) > l \\ (0,0) & \text{Otherwise} \end{cases}. \tag{15}$$

We can then obtain the following lemma.

Lemma 1. *The local propagation under transmission model can be simulated by a complex neural network with $2P + 4$ layers.*

From Local to Global. The output of local propagation complex neural network can be viewed as the input for the next time step. We can repeatedly using the local network to exactly simulated the whole propagation process. We denoted such global complex neural network by M_C. Therefore, we can obtain our hypothesis space of Problem 1.

Definition 3. *Taking the weights $W_{(u,v)}$ for $(u, v) \in E$ and thresholds Θ_v for $v \in V$ as the parameters, the hypothesis space $\mathcal{F}$ is the set of all possible M_C.*

4.2   Learning Algorithm

Given the hypothesis space $\mathcal{F}$, the propagation function F based on the propagation model is now implemented as a complex neural network model. Instead of directly learning the F, we seek to learn a complex neural network model from $\mathcal{F}$ that can minimize the generalization error in Eq. 5. Same as the neural network, learning in complex neural networks refers to the process of modifying the parameters involved in the network such that the learning objectives can be achieved. And it is natural to use a gradient-based approach to reach our learning goals. [13] shows that it is unnecessary to limit using the activation functions that are complex differentiable, or holomorphic, and they state that those functions that are differentiable with respect to the real part and the imaginary part of each parameter are also compatible with backpropagation. Following this idea,

Table 1. Main results. Each simulation is implemented with 600 training samples, 400 testing samples and 4 worms.

		F1 score	Precision	Recall	Accuracy
ER graph	Proposed method	$0.469_{(6.E-03)}$	$0.419_{(6.E-03)}$	$0.629_{(6.E-03)}$	$0.727_{(3.E-03)}$
	RegularNN	$0.408_{(4.E-03)}$	$0.329_{(4.E-03)}$	$0.590_{(6.E-03)}$	$0.695_{(3.E-03)}$
	SVM	$0.184_{(0)}$	$0.192_{(0)}$	$0.201_{(0)}$	$0.498_{(1.E-03)}$
	Random	$0.182_{(2.E-03)}$	$0.200_{(2.E-03)}$	$0.200_{(2.E-03)}$	$0.200_{(2.E-03)}$
Sensors network	Proposed method	$0.408_{(1.E-02)}$	$0.372_{(1.E-02)}$	$0.575_{(1.E-02)}$	$0.684_{(6.E-03)}$
	RegularNN	$0.208_{(1.E-02)}$	$0.302_{(6.E-02)}$	$0.450_{(3.E-02)}$	$0.597_{(3.E-03)}$
	SVM	$0.146_{(8.E-04)}$	$0.117_{(3.E-03)}$	$0.205_{(3.E-04)}$	$0.537_{(3.E-03)}$
	Random	$0.176_{(7.E-03)}$	$0.200_{(4.E-03)}$	$0.200_{(8.E-03)}$	$0.199_{(7.E-03)}$

we initialized two groups of parameters corresponding to the real and imaginary parts and trained them separately. And we utilize the complexPytorch package, a high-level API of PyTorch, to implement layers and functions [5,18,31]. Note that, in the activation function 8, 14 and 15, they are not differentiable everywhere. We use a tanh function to approximately return the gradients during the training.

5 Experiments

In this section, we evaluated our proposed method by experiments. We compare our method with several baseline algorithm on synthetic and real worlds networks.

5.1 Settings

WSN Data. We adopt two types of graph structures to evaluate our proposed method: one synthetic graph and a real-world WSN. One synthetic graph is a randomly generated Erdős-Rényi (ER) graph with 200 nodes and 0.2 edge probability [8]. The real-world WSN is collected from 54 sensors deployed in the Intel Berkeley Research lab[1].

Communication Model and Sample Generating. The number of worms are select from 2, 4, 8. For each node v, the threshold value of worm k, θ_v^k, is generated uniformly random from $[0,1]$. The weight on each edge (u,v) of worm k is set as $w_{(u,v)}^k = \frac{1}{|N_v|+k}$. For each graph, we generate a sample pool $D = \{(\mathcal{I}_0, \mathcal{I}_N)^i\}_i^{1000}$ with $N/2$ seeds and each seed is selected uniformly at random. Each selected seed node is assigned to worm uniformly at random. Given $\mathcal{I}_0$, $\mathcal{I}_N$ is generated follow the communication model (Table 3).

---

[1] http://db.csail.mit.edu/labdata/labdata.html.

Table 2. Impact of the different number of worms. Each simulation is implemented with 600 training samples, 400 testing samples, and 100 seeds.

Number of worms	F1	Precision	Recall	Accuracy
2	$0.717_{(3.E-02)}$	$0.657_{(1.E-02)}$	$0.948_{(3.E-02)}$	$0.803_{(2.E-02)}$
4	$0.469_{(6.E-03)}$	$0.419_{(6.E-03)}$	$0.629_{(6.E-03)}$	$0.727_{(3.E-03)}$
8	$0.277_{(4.E-03)}$	$0.206_{(5.E-03)}$	$0.313_{(5.E-03)}$	$0.656_{(3.E-03)}$

Table 3. Impace of the different number of seeds. Each simulation is implemented with 600 training samples, 400 testing samples, and 4 worms.

Number of seeds	F1 score	Precision	Recall	Accuracy
50	$0.332_{(4.E-03)}$	$0.277_{(4.E-03)}$	$0.579_{(7.E-03)}$	$0.676_{(4.E-03)}$
100	$0.469_{(6.E-03)}$	$0.419_{(6.E-03)}$	$0.629_{(6.E-03)}$	$0.727_{(3.E-03)}$
150	$0.549_{(5.E-03)}$	$0.524_{(4.E-03)}$	$0.626_{(4.E-03)}$	$0.733_{(3.E-03)}$

Baseline Method. We consider two baseline algorithms: RegularNN and Support Vector Machine (SVM). RegularNN is a real-valued deep neural network model with $4 \cdot N$ layers. The activation functions are set as a combination of linear, ReLU, and sigmoid. We aim to compare ComplexNN, which explicitly simulates the diffusion process, with the regular designed neural network. Since the proposed problem is a binary classification task, we implement the SVM algorithm. Besides, the random method with a random prediction is also considered.

Implementation. The size of the training set is selected from $\{200, 400, 600\}$ and the testing size is 400. During each simulation, the train and test samples are randomly selected from the sample pool. For each method, we use F1 score, precision, recall, and accuracy to evaluate the performance. Besides, the number of simulations for each setting is set to 5, and we report the average performance together with the standard deviation.

5.2   Observations

Table 1 shows the main results. Each cell includes the average value and its corresponding standard deviation. We can observe that our method outperforms other methods. Compared to the RegularNN, the proposed method are able to improve the prediction errors. And this shows the advantage of using an explicit model. Besides, it shows that the performance of each algorithm is increased given a larger graph.

Impact of Number of Worms. Table 2 gives the simulation results for our proposed method under the different numbers of worms. We can observe that with a lower number of worms, the performance is improved. One plausible reason is that the number of worms determines the size of the number of input and output features for our model. And it meets the nature of neural network training properties.

Imbalanced Class Distribution. The simulation results for our proposed method under the different number of seeds are given in Table 2. We see that the performance is increased when more seeds are provided. Since our model is a binary classifier, a small number of seeds leads to an imbalance class distribution. It is an inherent issue in predicting the node status in that the majority of the nodes tend to be inactive.

6 Conclusion

In this paper, we formulate a propagation model for multiple worms and propose a complex-valued neural network model. In particular, our designed complex-valued neural network model simulates the propagation process exactly. Overall our method outperforms classic supervised learning methods. However, it is not sufficiently stable for different data within the different numbers of worms and seeds. And it is possible that there exists an advanced representation strategy for the neural network design that can achieve a better performance, which is one direction for our future work. In addition, encouraged by the possibility of using a complex-valued neural network to simulate the worms' propagation models, we believe it would be interesting to apply our method to the traditional epidemic model.

References

1. Abdel-Gawad, H.I., Baleanu, D., Abdel-Gawad, A.H.: Unification of the different fractional time derivatives: an application to the epidemic-antivirus dynamical system in computer networks. Chaos, Solitons Fractals **142**, 110416 (2021)
2. Achar, S.J., Baishya, C., Kaabar, M.K.: Dynamics of the worm transmission in wireless sensor network in the framework of fractional derivatives. Math. Methods Appl. Sci. **45**(8), 4278–4294 (2022)
3. Akyildiz, I.F., Su, W., Sankarasubramaniam, Y., Cayirci, E.: Wireless sensor networks: a survey. Comput. Netw. **38**(4), 393–422 (2002)
4. Awasthi, S., Kumar, N., Srivastava, P.K.: A study of epidemic approach for worm propagation in wireless sensor network. In: Solanki, V.K., Hoang, M.K., Lu, Z.J., Pattnaik, P.K. (eds.) Intelligent Computing in Engineering. AISC, vol. 1125, pp. 315–326. Springer, Singapore (2020). https://doi.org/10.1007/978-981-15-2780-7_36
5. Bassey, J., Qian, L., Li, X.: A survey of complex-valued neural networks. arXiv preprint arXiv:2101.12249 (2021)
6. Behal, K.S., Gakkhar, S., Srivastava, T.: Dynamics of virus-patch model with latent effect. Int. J. Comput. Math. **99**, 1–16 (2022)
7. Chakrabarti, D., Leskovec, J., Faloutsos, C., Madden, S., Guestrin, C., Faloutsos, M.: Information survival threshold in sensor and p2p networks. In: IEEE INFOCOM 2007–26th IEEE International Conference on Computer Communications, pp. 1316–1324. IEEE (2007)

8. Erdös, P.: Graph theory and probability. Can. J. Math. **11**, 34–38 (1959)
9. Galluccio, L., Morabito, G.: Impact of worm propagation on vehicular sensor networks exploiting v2v communications. In: 2019 International Conference on Wireless and Mobile Computing, Networking and Communications (WiMob), pp. 1–6. IEEE (2019)
10. Gulati, K., Boddu, R.S.K., Kapila, D., Bangare, S.L., Chandnani, N., Saravanan, G.: A review paper on wireless sensor network techniques in internet of things (IoT). Mater. Today Proc. **51**, 161–165 (2021)
11. Haghighi, M.S., Wen, S., Xiang, Y., Quinn, B., Zhou, W.: On the race of worms and patches: modeling the spread of information in wireless sensor networks. IEEE Trans. Inf. Forensics Secur. **11**(12), 2854–2865 (2016)
12. Han, X., Tan, Q.: Dynamical behavior of computer virus on internet. Appl. Math. Comput. **217**(6), 2520–2526 (2010)
13. Hirose, A., Yoshida, S.: Generalization characteristics of complex-valued feedforward neural networks in relation to signal coherence. IEEE Trans. Neural Netw. Learn. Syst. **23**(4), 541–551 (2012)
14. Hu, Z., Wang, H., Liao, F., Ma, W.: Stability analysis of a computer virus model in latent period. Chaos, Solitons Fractals **75**, 20–28 (2015)
15. Kephart, J.O., White, S.R., Chess, D.M.: IEEE spectrum. Comput. Epidemiol. **30**(5), 20–26 (1993)
16. Khanh, N.H.: Dynamics of a worm propagation model with quarantine in wireless sensor networks. Appl. Math. Inf. Sci **10**(5), 1739–1746 (2016)
17. Krishnamachari, B.: Networking Wireless Sensors. Cambridge University Press, Cambridge (2005)
18. Matthès, M.W., Bromberg, Y., de Rosny, J., Popoff, S.M.: Learning and avoiding disorder in multimode fibers. Phys. Rev. X **11**(2), 021060 (2021)
19. Mishra, B.K., Keshri, N.: Mathematical model on the transmission of worms in wireless sensor network. Appl. Math. Model. **37**(6), 4103–4111 (2013)
20. Mishra, B.K., Tyagi, I.: Defending against malicious threats in wireless sensor network: a mathematical model. Int. J. Inf. Technol. Comput. Sci. **6**(3), 12–19 (2014)
21. Mishra, B.K., Srivastava, S.K., Mishra, B.K.: A quarantine model on the spreading behavior of worms in wireless sensor network. Trans. IoT Cloud Comput. **2**(1), 1–12 (2014)
22. Nain, M., Goyal, N.: Localization techniques in underwater wireless sensor network. In: 2021 International Conference on Advance Computing and Innovative Technologies in Engineering (ICACITE), pp. 747–751. IEEE (2021)
23. Narasimhan, H., Parkes, D.C., Singer, Y.: Learnability of influence in networks. In: Advances in Neural Information Processing Systems, vol. 28 (2015)
24. Nwokoye, C., Umeugoji, C., Umeh, I.: Evaluating degrees of differential infections on sensor networks' features using the sejijr-v epidemic model. Egypt. Comput. Sci. J. **44**(3) (2020)
25. Nwokoye, C.N.H., Madhusudanan, V.: Epidemic models of malicious-code propagation and control in wireless sensor networks: an indepth review. Wirel. Per. Commun. **125**, 1–30 (2022). https://doi.org/10.1007/s11277-022-09636-8
26. Ojha, R.P., Srivastava, P.K., Sanyal, G., Gupta, N.: Improved model for the stability analysis of wireless sensor network against malware attacks. Wirel. Pers. Commun. **116**(3), 2525–2548 (2021)
27. Qin, P.: Analysis of a model for computer virus transmission. Math. Prob. Eng. 2015 (2015)

28. Rajesh, B., Reddy, Y.J., Reddy, B.D.K.: A survey paper on malicious computer worms. Int. J. Adv. Res. Comput. Sci. Technol. **3**(2), 161–167 (2015)
29. Regin, R., Rajest, S.S., Singh, B.: Fault detection in wireless sensor network based on deep learning algorithms. EAI Trans. Scalable Inf. Syst. **8**, e8 (2021)
30. Srivastava, A.P., Awasthi, S., Ojha, R.P., Srivastava, P.K., Katiyar, S.: Stability analysis of SIDR model for worm propagation in wireless sensor network. Indian J. Sci. Technol. **9**(31), 1–5 (2016)
31. Trabelsi, C., et al.: Deep complex networks. In: International Conference on Learning Representations (2018). https://openreview.net/forum?id=H1T2hmZAb
32. Wang, X., Li, Q., Li, Y.: EiSiRS: a formal model to analyze the dynamics of worm propagation in wireless sensor networks. J. Comb. Optim. **20**(1), 47–62 (2010)
33. Wang, Y., Tong, G.: Learnability of competitive threshold models. In: Raedt, L.D. (ed.) Proceedings of the Thirty-First International Joint Conference on Artificial Intelligence, IJCAI-22, pp. 3985–3991. International Joint Conferences on Artificial Intelligence Organization (2022). https://doi.org/10.24963/ijcai.2022/553. main Track
34. Wang, Y., Wen, S., Cesare, S., Zhou, W., Xiang, Y.: The microcosmic model of worm propagation. Comput. J. **54**(10), 1700–1720 (2011)
35. Wang, Y., Wen, S., Xiang, Y., Zhou, W.: Modeling the propagation of worms in networks: a survey. IEEE Commun. Surv. Tutorials **16**(2), 942–960 (2013)
36. Weaver, N., Paxson, V., Staniford, S., Cunningham, R.: A taxonomy of computer worms. In: Proceedings of the 2003 ACM workshop on Rapid Malcode, pp. 11–18 (2003)
37. Yao, Y., Sheng, C., Fu, Q., Liu, H., Wang, D.: A propagation model with defensive measures for PLC-PC worms in industrial networks. Appl. Math. Model. **69**, 696–713 (2019)
38. Zarin, R., Khaliq, H., Khan, A., Khan, D., Akgül, A., Humphries, U.W.: Deterministic and fractional modeling of a computer virus propagation. Results Phys. **33**, 105130 (2022)
39. Zou, C.C., Towsley, D., Gong, W., Cai, S.: Routing worm: A fast, selective attack worm based on IP address information. In: Workshop on Principles of Advanced and Distributed Simulation (PADS'05), pp. 199–206. IEEE (2005)

Resource Management, Routing, and Internet Computing

5G Channel Forecasting and Power Allocation Based on LSTM Network and Cooperative Communication

Zhangliang Chen and Qilian Liang[(✉)]

The University of Texas at Arlington, Arlington 76010, USA
zhangliang.chen@mavs.uta.edu, liang@uta.edu

Abstract. In this paper, a forecasted channel system on the basis of Long-Short Term Memory (LSTM) neural network is devised to deal with the problem of gradient disappearance in the Recurrent Neural Network (RNN) specialized in dealing with time series problems. Then, the designed arithmetic is performed and the performances are compared with the real channel, and small Root Mean Square Error (RMSE) is obtained, which shows the high accuracy of the prediction. After that, based on the channel forecasted by using the LSTM network, the power allocation based on cooperative communication is derived, and compare the power results without cooperative communication. For the single-relay cooperative scenarios, a power allocation schema under the end goal to maximize the information transmission rate (ITR) at the destination node is proposed. The realization process of this scheme is constructing the information transmission rate function of the destination node under the condition of setting the total power transmitted is a fixed value by the node. When the ITR of the destination node is the maximum, the source node and relay node achieved the optimal transmission power values. Therefore, system performance is improved by optimizing power allocation method of the transmitting nodes. By comparing with other schemes, it is verified that the power allocation scheme proposed in this paper has better performance and saves system resources.

Keywords: LSTM · 5G · Channel forecasting · Cooperative communication · Power allocation

1 Introduction

In recent years, with the rapid development of global wireless broadband communication technology, the number of mobile user groups has increased rapidly, and there are more and more requirements for the service quality of communication networks and high-speed multimedia applications [1].

Channel forecasting and power allocation are key techniques for wireless communication [2]. If the state of the channel can be predicted, the power in the channel will be allocated reasonably, more power will be distributed on the sub-channel with good

This work was supported by U.S. National Science Foundation (NSF) under Grant CCF-2219753.

Z. J. Haas et al. (Eds.): WiCON 2022, LNICST 464, pp. 119–133, 2023.
https://doi.org/10.1007/978-3-031-27041-3_9

state, and less power will be distributed on the sub-channel with bad state [3], so as to realize the high efficiency of power allocation [4].

Wireless signal can be considered as a time series, and Recurrent Neural Network (RNN) is one of the most potential tools for time series modeling. The neural network model of RNN adds the features of time series. The hidden layer of the RNN model has feedback edges [5]. The input of each hidden layer includes both the current sample features and the information brought by the previous time series. It can achieve high-accuracy predictions performance [6].

However, RNNs also have some drawbacks. For standard RNN networks, the time span of information that can be used in practice is very limited. When we use information from a relatively recent time point to solve the task of the current moment, RNN can effectively learn the information of the historical moment. However, when we need to use historical information that differs from the current moment information for a long time, the ability of RNN to learn information will be weakened, which is the problem of RNN's gradient disappearance. Long Short Term Memory (LSTM) can be considered as a special form of RNN network, which is superimposed a long term memory function on the RNN, the persistence of the RNN network can be maintained, which allows the long-term dependence of the model on the neural network to be realized [7]. The biggest advantage here is that the LSTM network itself can do the function of remembering information for a long time, which is independent of what it learns through data training. As explained in the previous paragraph, the vanishing gradient phenomenon is ubiquitous in traditional RNN networks [8]. The LSTM network was born to solve this shortcoming. A long-term memory function that keeps information from decaying is superimposed on the traditional RNN network.

In this paper, a 5G channel forecasting system based on the LSTM neural network is proposed, In addition, the cooperative communication is derived to achieve high efficient power allocation based on the forecasted 5G channel by using the LSTM network. The forecasting accuracy of LSTM network and comparison of the performance of power allocation based on cooperative communication with equal power distribution method is presented in Sect. 4.

2   Channel Forecasting Based on LSTM Network

2.1   Introduction and Structure of LSTM Network Model

Long short-term memory network is a variant of recurrent neural network [9], which is mainly used to solve long-term time-dependent problems. For example, in image description, speech recognition, and natural language processing, the LSTM model has performed well and is widely used in academic and industry fields.

Figure 1 shows the structure of a neuron in an LSTM network. The LSTM network is essentially a unidirectional chain structure, and the internal structure of each neuron on the chain is the same, which is the same as the structure of RNN. But the difference of LSTM is that three new structures and special memory units are added to solve the gradient vanishing. The three gate structures are input gate, forget gate and output gate [10]. The gate structure contains the Sigmoid function layer, which can compress the value between 0–1, which helps to remember useful information for a long time or forget redundant information. When the previous data is needed, the activation function will be multiplied by 0 to get 0 output, and this part of the information will not be passed to the next neuron as input [11]. Similarly, when encountering information data that needs to be memorized, it will be multiplied by 1 and still save itself, and then passed to the next neuron as input information. It is through this selective memory or forgetting of information that the LSTM network can save a part of useful information for a long time, and the basis for this phenomenon is the newly added three gate structures and memory units, and the problem of gradient vanishing can be solved [12].

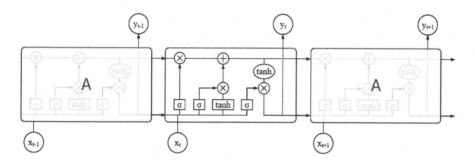

Fig. 1. Structure diagram of LSTM

In Fig. 1, x_t indicates the input at time t, or we can call it the CSI at time t. σ is the Sigmoid function, it is an activation function. $\otimes$ represents the calculation of element multiplication, and the forget gate, input gate and output gate is established by the combination of σ and $\otimes$ together, which are respectively shown from left to right [13]. The information passing through the forget gate will be decided whether it needs to be forgotten, the signal passing through the input gate will be retained and added to the memory unit as a component, and the output of the next hidden state will be determined by the output gate.

2.2   The Training Principle of LSTM

The training method of the LSTM model covers the calculation process of forward calculation and back propagation. The specific calculation process is as follows:

1. Forward calculation process:
   (a) Forget gate: The input vector at time t and the output vector of the output layer at time $t - 1$ jointly determine the output state of the forgetting gate at time t. The calculation method is shown in Eq. (1).

$$f_t = \sigma \left(W_f \cdot (y_{t-1}, x_t) + b_f \right) \tag{1}$$

where: f_t is the output vector at time t, σ is the activation function, W_f is the weight matrix, concated by matrix W_{fy} and matrix W_{fx}, y_{t-1}, x_t are the output vector of the output layer at time $t - 1$ and the input vector of the input layer at time t, respectively. b_f is the bias term.

Among them, W_f can be presented as:

$$(W_f) \begin{pmatrix} y_{t-1} \\ x_t \end{pmatrix} = (W_{fy} W_{fx}) \begin{pmatrix} y_{t-1} \\ x_t \end{pmatrix}$$

$$= W_{fy} y_{t-1} + W_{fx} x_t \tag{2}$$

(b) Input gate: The input gate can be represented by the Eq. (3), and the meanings represented by the symbols in the formula are similar to those of the forget gate, which will not be repeated here.

$$i_t = \sigma \left(W_i \cdot (y_{t-1}, x_t) + b_i \right) \tag{3}$$

(c) Memory unit: The state of the memory unit at the current moment can be calculated in two steps. First, the output at time $t - 1$ and the input at time t are used to calculate the state $\hat{c}_t$ of the current input unit. Its calculation expression can be expressed as:

$$\hat{c}_t = tanh \left(W_c \cdot (y_{t-1}, x_t) + b_c \right) \tag{4}$$

Then calculate the memory cell state c_t at the current moment:

$$c_t = f * c_{t-1} + i_t * \hat{c}_t \tag{5}$$

The $*$ symbol in the formula is the multiplication operation between each element. The unit state $\hat{c}_t$ input by the LSTM at the current moment and the long-term memory c_{t-1} are combined through the memory unit.

(d) Output gate:

$$o_t = \sigma \left(W_o \cdot (y_{t-1}, x_t) + b_o \right) \tag{6}$$

$$y_t = o_t * tanh(c_t) \tag{7}$$

y_t represents the final output of the LSTM model at the current time, that is, the spectral prediction value at time t. It can be seen from Eq. (7) that the output of the output gate and the state of the memory unit at the current moment jointly determine the value of y_t.

2. Back propagation process of error:

Similar to the RNN model, the calculation of the error back propagation of the LSTM model also uses the value of the error term σ, and according to the calculated error term, the gradient descent method is used to update the weights. In the training process of the LSTM model, there are 4 groups of weights that the model needs to learn, and the specific learning parameters are shown in Table 1:

The weight matrix plays a different role in the derivation process of backpropagation, so it is divided as follows:

$$W_o = [W_{oy}, W_{ox}]$$
$$W_f = [W_{fy}, W_{fx}]$$
$$W_i = [W_{iy}, W_{ix}]$$
$$W_c = [W_{cy}, W_{cx}] \tag{8}$$

Table 1. Learning parameters

Module	Weight matrix	Bias item
Output gate	W_o	b_o
Forget gate	W_f	b_f
Input gate	W_i	b_i
Memory unit	W_c	b_c

Assuming that the error (loss function) is E, and the output at time t is y_t, then the error term δ_t of the output layer at time t is:

$$\delta_t = \frac{\partial E}{\partial y_t} \qquad (9)$$

For the above four weight matrices, there are four weighted inputs, which correspond to f_t, i_t, c_t and o_t at time t, respectively. Let their corresponding error terms be δ_{ft}, δ_{it}, δ_{ct} and δ_{ot}, respectively, then:

$$\delta_{o_t}^T = \frac{\partial E}{\partial(W_o \cdot (y_{t-1}, x_t) + b_o)}$$
$$= \frac{\partial E}{\partial y_t} \cdot \frac{\partial y_t}{\partial o_t} \cdot \frac{\partial o_t}{\partial(W_o \cdot (y_{t-1}, x_t) + b_o)}$$
$$= \delta_t^T * tanh(c_t) * o_t * (1 - o_t) \qquad (10)$$

In the same way, the error term of forget gate, input gate and memory cell can be known from the chain rule.

The error propagation along the time direction is to calculate the error term δ_{t-1} at time t_1, and the expression of δ_{t-1} is:

$$\delta_{t-1} = \delta_{o_t}^T W_{oy} + \delta_{f_t}^T W_{fy} + \delta_{i_t}^T W_{iy} + \delta_{\hat{c}_t}^T W_{cy} \qquad (11)$$

The calculation formula for the propagation of the error term to the upper layer can be expressed as:

$$\delta_{t-1}^l = \frac{\partial E}{\partial(W \cdot (y_t, x_t) + b)}$$
$$= (\delta_{o_t}^T W_{ox} + \delta_{f_t}^T W_{fx} + \delta_{i_t}^T W_{ix} + \delta_{\hat{c}_t}^T W_{cx}) * f'(W \cdot (y_t, x_t) + b) \qquad (12)$$

where $W \cdot (y_t, x_t) + b)$ represents the weighted input of layer $l - 1$, and f is the activation function of layer $l - 1$.

Taking the output gate as an example, the calculated error term is used to calculate the gradient of each weighting matrix and the gradient of the bias term at time t. The calculation can be expressed as:

$$\frac{\partial E}{\partial W_{oy,t}} = \frac{\partial E}{\partial(W_o \cdot (y_{t-1}, x_t) + b_o)} \cdot \frac{\partial(W_o \cdot (y_{t-1}, x_t) + b_o)}{\partial W_{oy,t}} = \delta_{o_t} y_{t-1}^T \qquad (13)$$

$$\frac{\partial E}{\partial W_{ox,t}} = \frac{\partial E}{\partial (W_o \cdot (y_{t-1}, x_t) + b_o)} \cdot \frac{\partial (W_o \cdot (y_{t-1}, x_t) + b_o)}{\partial W_{ox,t}} = \delta_{o_t} x_{t-1}^T \quad (14)$$

$$\frac{\partial E}{\partial b_{o,t}} = \frac{\partial E}{\partial (W_o \cdot (y_{t-1}, x_t) + b_o)} \cdot \frac{\partial (W_o \cdot (y_{t-1}, x_t) + b_o)}{\partial b_{o,t}} = \delta_{o_t} \quad (15)$$

The final gradient is the sum of the gradients at each time:

$$\frac{\partial E}{\partial W_{oy}} = \sum_{j=1}^{t} \delta_{o_j} y_{j-1}^T; \quad (16)$$

$$\frac{\partial E}{\partial W_{ox}} = \sum_{j=1}^{t} \delta_{o_j} x_j^T \quad (17)$$

$$\frac{\partial E}{\partial b_o} = \sum_{j=1}^{t} \delta_{oj} \quad (18)$$

In the same way, the weight matrix and the gradient of the bias term of the forget gate, input gate and memory unit can be obtained.

3 Power Allocation Based on Cooperative Communication

In cooperative communication, nodes cooperate with each other, which can not only expand the communication range [14], but also improve the information transmission rate of the system. The research on resource allocation in cooperative communication mainly focuses on power allocation. By rationally allocating the power of nodes, the system performance can be improved while the power consumption can be reduced [15].

When a relay node cooperates with other nodes to transmit information, it should not only consider improving the system performance, but also consider when to cooperate, with whom and how to cooperate [16]. Compared with the straight forward communication link, cooperative communication has better transmission quality and channel capacity, but the structure of cooperative communication is complex and the amount of calculation is large [17]. The direct transmission link has a simple structure and low complexity. Due to the limited wireless communication resources, the main goal of cooperative communication is to improve the performance of the communication network and allocate power reasonably under the premise that the total power of the wireless communication system is constrained [18].

3.1 Cooperative Communication System Model

As shown in Fig. 2, the system model includes three nodes, which is source node S, relay node R and destination node D. There are two transmission links in the communication

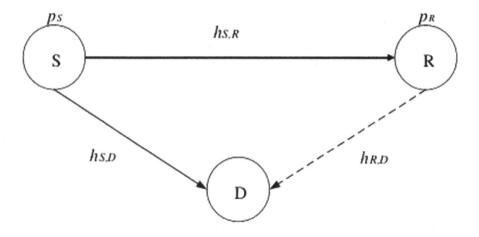

Fig. 2. Cooperative communication system model

with different transmission time: the first link at time one, node S sends signals to the node R and the node D directly; at the second link at time two, the node R transmits the signal to the node D through DF transmission [19]. The node D cooperates and decodes the signals received from the node S and node R to obtain diversity gain.

In the system model, the channel coefficients of the three links are $h_{S,D}$, $h_{S,R}$, and $H_{r,d}$, respectively. The noises of the three links are independent of each other and are Gaussian white noise with 0 mean and variance σ^2. p_R is the transmission power from node R. In the first time slot, the information transmission rates $R_{S,D}$ and $R_{R,D}$ obtained by the node R and node D are expressed as:

$$R_{S,D} = \frac{1}{2}log_2(1 + \gamma_{S,D})$$
$$R_{S,R} = \frac{1}{2}log_2(1 + \gamma_{S,R}) \tag{19}$$

Among them, $\frac{1}{2}$ in the equation is because the whole transmission process includes two transmission time slots. The S-D link has a SNR of $\gamma_{S,D} = \frac{p_S H_{S,D}}{\sigma^2}$, and the S-R link has a SNR of $\gamma_{S,R} = \frac{p_S H_{S,R}}{\sigma^2}$.

In the second time slot, the information transmission rate $R_{R,D}$ obtained by the destination node is expressed as:

$$R_{R,D} = \frac{1}{2}log_2(1 + \gamma_{R,D}) \tag{20}$$

where the SNR of R-D link is $\gamma_{R,D} = \frac{p_R H_{R,D}}{\sigma^2}$.

3.2 Power Allocation

Introduction to Power Allocation. Power allocation is to calculate the optimal power allocation factor with the goal of maximizing the QoS performance at the destination node under the condition of constraining the total power of the node [20]. In the problem of power allocation, this paper takes the information transmission rate as the optimization goal to reduce power consumption when the system performance is optimal.

1. Define Variables
   The node power allocation vector is expressed as:

$$P = [p_S, p_R] \tag{21}$$

   Compare the information transmission rate of the relay node and the destination node, and express the minimum value $f(p_S, p_R)$ as

$$f(p_S, p_R) = \min(R_{S,D} + R_{R,D}, R_{S,D}) \tag{22}$$

2. Target Optimization
   In the system model, the proposed power allocation scheme should not only ensure the maximum information transmission rate of the destination node, but also minimize the power consumption of the entire transmission process and reduce the power consumption overhead. The optimization objective function is represented by the following equation:

$$\max_{p_S, p_R} f(p_S, p_R) \tag{23}$$

The constraints are expressed as:

$$p_S + p_R \leq p_{tot} \tag{24}$$

$$log^2(1 + p_S H_{S,D}) + log^2(1 + p_R H_{R,D}) \geq log^2(1 + p_S H_{S,R}) \tag{25}$$

$$p_S \geq 0, p_R \geq 0 \tag{26}$$

Among them, $\sigma^2 = 1$, Eq. (23) is the optimization objective function, Eq. (24) is the constraint condition of the transmission power from node S and node R, Eq. (25) is the maximum value reached by the destination node rate, Eq. (26) is the transmission power values of node S and node R are greater than 0.

On the foundation of above three constraints, the optimization state is described as, under the premise of ensuring that the power of the node is positive and constraining the total transmit power of the node, the goal is to maximize the information transmission rate of the destination node, so as to obtain the optimal relationship between the node S and node R.

3.3   The Power Allocation Algorithm for Cooperative Communication

In order to decline the squander of resources and improve the system performance, a power allocation scheme is proposed in the single-relay cooperative communication model. The power allocation scheme is to establish a convex optimization function of the maximum information transmission rate of the destination node under the constraint of ensuring the total transmit power [21], and use the Lagrangian function to optimize the transmission power of node S and node R.

The steps of the algorithm are as follows:

Step1: The Lagrange equations for optimizing objective Eqs. (22) to (24) are expressed as:

$$L(p_S, p_R) = f(p_S, p_R) + \lambda[log_2(1 + p_S H_{S,D}) + log_2((1 + p_R H_{R,D}) \\ - log_2(1 + p_S H_{S,R})] + \mu(p_S + p_R - p_{tot}) \tag{27}$$

where $\lambda \geq 0$ is the Lagrange multiplier under power constraints.

Step2: According to the Karush-Kuhn-Tucker condition, set the partial derivatives of $L(p_S, p_R)$ to p_S and p_R to 0 respectively. The optimal solutions p_S^* and p_R^* should satisfy the following equations:

$$\frac{\partial L}{\partial p_S^*} = \frac{1}{2ln2}\left[\frac{H_{S,D} + 2\lambda H_{S,D}}{(1 + p_S H_{S,D})} - \frac{2\lambda H_{S,R}}{(1 + p_S H_{S,R})})\right] + \mu \tag{28}$$

$$\frac{\partial L}{\partial p_R^*} = \frac{H_{R,D}(1 + 2\lambda)}{2ln2(1 + p_R H_{R,D})} + \mu \tag{29}$$

Step3: In the optimization Eq. (30), under the condition that the total power of the node is constrained, when the information transmission rate of the destination node reaches the maximum, the optimal power p_S^* and p_R^* of the source node and the relay node are respectively:

$$p_S^* = min\left(\frac{1 + 2\lambda}{2\mu ln2} - \frac{1}{H_{R,D}}, p_{tot}\right) \tag{30}$$

$$p_R^* = max\left(\frac{H_{R,D}(1 + 2\lambda)}{2ln2(1 + p_R H_{r,d})} + \mu\right)^+ \tag{31}$$

where, $(\cdot)^+ = max(\cdot, 0)$

Equations (28) to (31) are the optimal solutions of the optimization problem (23).

4   Simulations and Performance Analysis

4.1   5G Channel Forecasting Based on LSTM Network

In this section, the simulation of 5G channel forecasting based on LSTM is derived.

The parameters of simulated channels are shown in Table 2. We selected 10000 channels, and performed average value of 10000 times forecasting. During the forecasting, first 90% of observations is used to train the model, and last 10% data is used

Table 2. Simulation parameters

Frequency (GHz)	28.0	Bandwidth (MHz)	800
TXPower (dBm)	30.0	Environment	NLOS
Scenario	UMi	Pressure (mBar)	1013.25
Humidity	50	Temperature (Celsius)	20.0
Rain Rate (mm/hr)	0.0	Polarization	Co-Pol
Foliage	No	DistFol (m)	0.0
Foliage Attenuation (dB)	0	TX Array Type	URA
RXArray Type	URA	Num of TX Elements	64
Num of RX Elements	64	TXAziHPBW	10
TXElvHPBW	10	RXAziHPBW	10
RXElvHPBW	10		

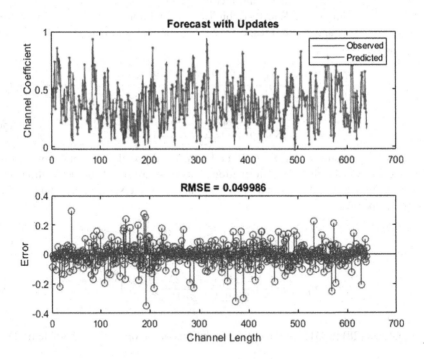

Fig. 3. Comparison and RMSE of forecasting by using actual observation

to test. Through experiments, we selected the optimal LSTM network parameters, used a two-layer neural network with 330 hidden units, and performed 2000 iterations of training.

Then, we forecasted values for multiple time steps, and updated the network with each forecasting. After each step of forecasting, use the previous forecasted value as the input to the function. Because the CSI has been obtained, the actual value of the time step between each forecasting is used to replace the forecasted value to update the network state. The comparison of forecasting accuracy and RMSE is performed in Fig. 3. The RMSE is about 0.05. We can conclude that our optimized model parameters for LSTM network can achieve a relatively high forecasting accuracy.

4.2 Power Allocation Based on Cooperative Communication

Information Transmission Rate of Destination Node vs Power of Source Node. The initial value of the power of the source node is set to 10 dBm, which is linearly increased to 20 dBm according to the step size of about 1 dBm. The influence of the transmit power of the source node on the information rate of the destination node under different power schemes is analyzed as shown in Fig. 4.

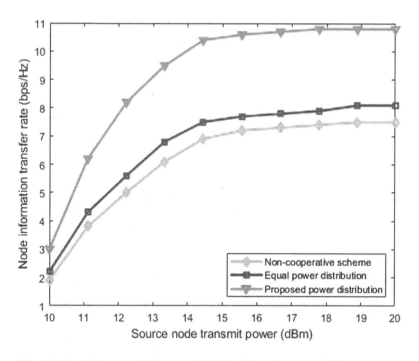

Fig. 4. Information transmission rate of destination node vs power of source node

Figure 4 describes the change of the information rate of the destination node when the power of the source node changes. The scheme in this paper can maximize the information rate of the destination node under the premise of constraining the total transmit power of the node, and effectively reduce the transmit power of the source node. Compared with the other two schemes, this scheme can improve the information transmission rate of the destination node, especially when the transmit power is small.

Information Transmission Rate of Destination Node vs Power of Relay Node. The initial value of the relay node power is set to 10 dBm, and it is linearly increased to 20 dBm in steps of about 1 dBm. Compare the power allocation scheme proposed in this paper with the equal power distribution, and study the influence of the relay node power on the information rate of the destination node as shown in the Fig. 5 shown.

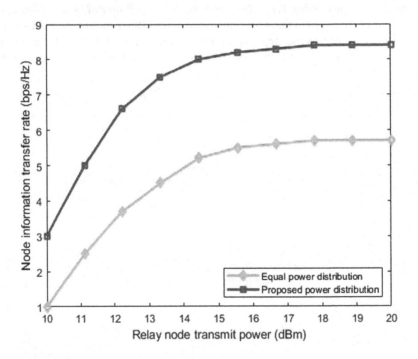

Fig. 5. Information transmission rate of destination node vs power of relay node

Figure 5 describes the change of the information rate of the destination node when the power of the relay node changes. First of all, the figure shows that in the process of linear increase of relay node transmit power, the change of destination node information rate shows an upward trend, which is because with the increase of relay node transmit power, the power used for information transmission becomes larger, Therefore, the information transmission rate at the destination node is improved. Secondly, compared with the equal power scheme, the proposed scheme obtains better information rate of the destination node. The proposed scheme not only improves the information transmission rate of the destination node, but also reduces the power consumption of the relay node, due to cooperative diversity helps to improve the information transmission rate at the destination node. In addition, Fig. 5 presents that when the relay node power is low, both power allocation schemes improve the information transmission rate of the destination node. However, the scheme proposed in this paper has a higher information transmission rate of the destination node when the transmit power of the relay node changes, reflecting the constraints on the total power of the node. The power allocation scheme proposed in this paper can maximize the information rate of the destination node.

Information Transmission Rate of Destination Node vs Distance of Relay Node. The initial value of the relay node position is set to 20 m, and linearly increases to 110 m in steps of 10 m. Comparing the power allocation scheme proposed in this paper with the equal power allocation scheme, the difference between the information transmission rate of the destination node and the position of the relay node The relationship is shown in Fig. 6.

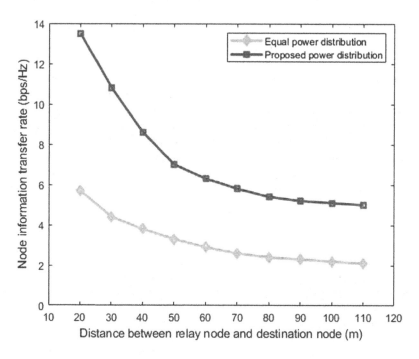

Fig. 6. Information transmission rate of destination node vs distance of relay node

Figure 6 presents the change in the information rate of the destination node when the position of the relay node changes. Compared with the equal power allocation scheme, when the relay node is located closer, the information rate of the destination node decreases rapidly with its increase. When the position of the successor node is very large, the existence of interference limitation makes the information transmission rate of the destination node tend to a stable value. The proposed scheme is better than the equal power allocation scheme in response to the change of the information rate of the destination node.

5   Conclusion and Future Work

In this paper, the simulated 5G channel is forecasted by using LSTM network. Based on that, cooperative communication is proposed to improve the performance of wireless communication. The optimal LSTM model parameters are obtained to achieve the RMSE about 0.05 of testing data set. In addition, a power allocation algorithm based on cooperative communication is proposed and the comparisons of proposed scheme with non-cooperative system and equal power allocation scheme discussed.

The LSTM model in the recurrent neural network as the main analysis tool is implemented in the paper. However, the LSTM neural network has a complex structure, which requires a lot of experiments and theoretical analysis to select the type of activation function for the network level, which optimization algorithm to use, and even to design several layers of neural network structure. The selection of hyperparameters in wireless communication channel forecasting using LSTM network is also an important follow-up research work in this paper. In addition, the work of this paper is mainly based on the relay selection strategy. Research in other directions, such as power control and coding cooperation, is also the focus of cooperative communication. In addition to the capacity-maximizing power allocation strategy mentioned in this paper, we can also study the power consumption of different forwarding methods, the probability of interruption, and the power allocation strategy when the channel quality meets a certain standard, and explore the power allocation from the perspective of various combinations of improvement.

References

1. Capar, F., Martoyo, I., Weiss, T., Jondral, F.: Analysis of coexistence strategies for cellular and wireless local area networks. In: 2003 IEEE 58th Vehicular Technology Conference. VTC 2003-Fall (IEEE Cat. No. 03CH37484), vol. 3, pp. 1812–1816. IEEE (2003)
2. Nosratinia, A., Hunter, T.E., Hedayat, A.: Cooperative communication in wireless networks. IEEE Commun. Mag. **42**(10), 74–80 (2004)
3. Jayaweera, S.K.: Virtual mimo-based cooperative communication for energy-constrained wireless sensor networks. IEEE Trans. Wireless Commun. **5**(5), 984–989 (2006)
4. Senon, M., et al.: Channel capacity of indoor MIMO systems in the presence of spatial diversity. In: Sulaiman, H.A., Othman, M.A., Othman, M.F.I., Rahim, Y.A., Pee, N.C. (eds.) Advanced Computer and Communication Engineering Technology. LNEE, vol. 315, pp. 53–61. Springer, Cham (2015). https://doi.org/10.1007/978-3-319-07674-4_6

5. Kolodzy, P., Avoidance, I.: Spectrum policy task force. Fed. Commun. Comm. Wash. DC Rep. ET Docket **40**(4), 147–158 (2002)

6. Su, W., Sadek, A.K., Liu, K.R.: Cooperative communication protocols in wireless networks: performance analysis and optimum power allocation. Wirel. Pers. Commun. **44**(2), 181–217 (2008). https://doi.org/10.1007/s11277-007-9359-z

7. Feng, D., Jiang, C., Lim, G., Cimini, L.J., Feng, G., Li, G.Y.: A survey of energy-efficient wireless communications. IEEE Commun. Surv. Tutorials **15**(1), 167–178 (2012)

8. Sutton, R.S., McAllester, D., Singh, S., Mansour, Y.: Policy gradient methods for reinforcement learning with function approximation. In: Advances in Neural Information Processing Systems, vol. 12 (1999)

9. Tumuluru, V.K., Wang, P., Niyato, D.: A neural network based spectrum prediction scheme for cognitive radio. In: 2010 IEEE International Conference on Communications, pp. 1–5. IEEE (2010)

10. Yan, Z., et al.: DeHiB: deep hidden backdoor attack on semi-supervised learning via adversarial perturbation. In: Proceedings of the AAAI Conference on Artificial Intelligence, vol. 35, no. 12, pp. 10585–10593 (2021)

11. Zhao, Y., Luo, S., Yuan, Z., Lin, R.: A new spectrum prediction method for UAV communications. In: 2019 IEEE 5th International Conference on Computer and Communications (ICCC), pp. 826–830. IEEE (2019)

12. He, Y., Yu, F.R., Zhao, N., Leung, V.C., Yin, H.: Software-defined networks with mobile edge computing and caching for smart cities: a big data deep reinforcement learning approach. IEEE Commun. Mag. **55**(12), 31–37 (2017)

13. Wang, T., Wen, C.-K., Wang, H., Gao, F., Jiang, T., Jin, S.: Deep learning for wireless physical layer: opportunities and challenges. China Commun. **14**(11), 92–111 (2017)

14. Gerasimenko, M., et al.: Cooperative radio resource management in heterogeneous cloud radio access networks. IEEE Access **3**, 397–406 (2015)

15. Zhao, Y., Li, S., Jin, F.: Identification of influential nodes in social networks with community structure based on label propagation. Neurocomputing **210**, 34–44 (2016)

16. Cover, T., Gamal, A.E.: Capacity theorems for the relay channel. IEEE Trans. Inf. Theor. **25**(5), 572–584 (1979)

17. Koohestani, M., Hussain, A., Moreira, A.A., Skrivervik, A.K.: Diversity gain influenced by polarization and spatial diversity techniques in ultrawideband. IEEE Access **3**, 281–286 (2015)

18. Zou, Y., Zheng, B., Zhu, X.: A new cooperative diversity scheme for next generation wireless network. In: 2008 5th IEEE Consumer Communications and Networking Conference, pp. 938–942. IEEE (2008)

19. Di, C., Li, F., Li, S.: Sensor deployment for wireless sensor networks: a conjugate learning automata-based energy-efficient approach. IEEE Wirel. Commun. **27**(5), 80–87 (2020)

20. Chang, C.-W., et al.: Adaptive resource allocation for OFDM-based single-relay cooperative communication systems over Rayleigh fading channels. In: 2013 Second International Conference on Robot, Vision and Signal Processing, pp. 214–219. IEEE (2013)

21. Zhou, F., Du, M.: A wavelet coding scheme used in multi-source relay-based cooperative communication. In: 2013 22nd Wireless and Optical Communication Conference, pp. 45–49. IEEE (2013)

Fog Resource Sharing to Enable Pay-Per-Use Model

Zahid Khan[1]([✉]), Hasan Ali Khattak[1], Assad Abbas[2], and Samee U. Khan[3]

[1] National University of Sciences and Technology (NUST), Islamabad, Pakistan
{zkhan.msit19seecs,hasan.alikhattak}@seecs.edu.pk
[2] Department of Computer Science, COMSATS University Islamabad,
Islamabad, Pakistan
assadabbas@comsats.edu.pk
[3] Electrical and Computer Engineering, Mississippi State University, Starkville, USA
skhan@ece.msstate.edu

Abstract. Advancements in the Internet of Things and Information Communication and Technologies have increased the demand for real-time services. Thus computing resources are migrated from the cloud to fog networks to give the users near real-time experiences. Fog computing resources containing storage and networks that are shifted from core to edge to minimize the latency while using the applications-application implementation nearest to fog nodes that reduce the latency however burden leans on the density of users. The fog network performance degrades because of the over-subscription of fog nodes. In this work, we have proposed a method that depends on alliance establishment for resource management while using the model that will charge according to the usage of network resources. We assume that the cluster contains one prime node with several fog nodes. Firstly, the customer needs information regarding the application requirement for the clusters then the prime node evaluates the capacity of the fog node, which fulfills desired demands of the end user. According to end-user requirements, the prime node among the cluster selects the specific symmetry batch nodes. Additionally, in this work, we have suggested an extension of resource handling regarding fog networks, combining end-user demands for the service and allocating individual nodes against the batch application.

Keywords: Fog computing · Pay-per-use model · Coalition formation · Game theoretic approaches

1 Introduction

The Internet of Things (IoT) has completely replaced the regular communication between the physical and digital frameworks that define the different IoT devices. IoT devices are contributing more than 11 zettabytes of total data worldwide. The fog/edge computing moderates the demand for the utilization of cloud data centers for IoT instances. The perception of the fog/edge computing domain consists

© ICST Institute for Computer Sciences, Social Informatics and Telecommunications Engineering 2023
Published by Springer Nature Switzerland AG 2023. All Rights Reserved
Z. J. Haas et al. (Eds.): WiCON 2022, LNICST 464, pp. 134–143, 2023.
https://doi.org/10.1007/978-3-031-27041-3_10

of computing resources like servers, the processor in terms of cores, data centers, and network devices like routers, switches, bridges, hubs, etc. In fog networks, nodes are highly distributed as compared to cloud setups. On the other perspective, cloud architecture is extended to the edge by fog networks while the fog networks use the properties that are being employed in the cloud architecture [13].

The pay-per-use model allocates the network's resources against end-user requests to avail of the service. Existing literature did not consider fog networks regarding business models. The fog networks have offered a platform to cope with the end-user application requirements. For optimization of resources as it was used earlier in the presence of a single cluster where researchers have offered the model to turn down the latency of service provisioning.

Existing literature considers distinct fog network parameters like fog node capacity, reliability, and delay. However, the work-related business perspective does not exist in fog networks [3]. We suggested the model which charges the price according to the use of network resources. The fog network provides support for designing and managing resources, which is essential for the fog network. In general, fog and cloud are different networks because one is distributed while the second is centralized, so both networks cannot use common schemes.

In this paper, we presented a pay-per-use model which depends on alliance establishment for resource management in fog networks. There is a partnership between fog nodes in the same cluster but non-cooperative behavior between individual groups. The customer desires to get a trade-off between delay and price against the services. This paper assumes that the collection contains one master node with multiple fog nodes. Firstly, the customer needs information regarding the requirement of the application then the master node evaluates the fog node that fulfills the end-user resource requirement [12].

The master node selects the local balance subset of fog nodes according to end-user requirements. After that, to reduce the price to be paid and service delay, the applicant selects the specific symmetry batch nodes of the fog network. Additionally, we suggested a resource-handling extension in fog networks. At the same time, the pay-per-use model is used to allocate the network's resources against end-user requests to avail of the application services [11].

The rest of the document is organized as follows: Sect. 2 presents a review of the literature, whereas Sect. 3 gives a system model for the pay-per-use model along with the problem statement. Section 4 explains the pay-per-use model. Next, Sect. 5 presents the experimental results, and finally, Sect. 6 concludes this paper following the direction of future work.

2   Literature Review

The existing literature focuses on reducing the latency in fog networks. However, the authors suggest a scheme that allocates the resources by using a fog network, so this is the combined problem for setup. The authors Nguyen, Bao-le, and Bhargava suggest a scheme to allocate the resources that is a purchaser-retailer game in which the services behave like purchasers while resources of fog network behave like distinct products [10].

The researchers assess the symmetry of each service while formulating curvilinear problems. Management of resource of fog network Abedin, Aslam, and Hong focusing the quality of service needs ultrareliable low latency communication with increment in broadband services [2]. The authors designed a combined customer alliance and scheme for resource deployment by using bilateral parallel games that verify a strong coalition between the infrastructure of fog networks and IoT devices.

In previous work, researchers discussed related resources deployment depends on pay-per-use for diversified services of fog network. Farooq and Zhu presented a scheme that relies on the price for deployment of implicit storage in which researchers focused on diversified services [6].

In the sensor cloud paper, Misra and Chakraborty suggested a technique comprising a pricing model related to the distribution of resources that focuses on service reliability. In another research, Misra and Chakraborty proposed a game theoretic resource allocation scheme for sensor cloud [9]. Researchers observed system deploys resources to the customers depending on the price that is finalized by a centralized system, also known as the cloud. The authors proposed an alternate scheme for sensor records. In another paper authors, Aazam proposed a resource deployment technique based on user requirements that depend on factual documentation [1]. Therefore, all these schemes have used a centralized approach for resource allocation that is not applicable in distributed fog networks.

In Fog prime paper, Misra and Mondal suggested a technique for deploying resources that depend on the dynamic cost to explore the bargain between the service delay and related price [8]. The authors used a game that is an active corporation - generation to finalize the deployment of resources technique regionally inside the cluster.

Hence, there is a need for a scheme regarding the deployment of resources in the fog network that uses the model that is pricing based to provide service of the fog network. In this work, we have presented an extension for the resource handling-related fog networks which combines end-user demands for the service and allocates individual nodes against the batch application. In this research, we used dynamic corporation-generation to finalize the deployment of resources technique regionally inside the local cluster. Another point is that in the proposed solution, authors have operated a profitability game that finalizes nodes and focuses on the tradeoff.

In the existing literature, the authors mainly covered unlike features of fog networks. The researchers discussed issues related to mobility and implications regarding mobility in terms of fog networks. Therefore, the authors did not discuss connected fog networks that are based on the price to be paid against the usage of network resources. We have suggested that policies related to pricing play a vital role in fog networks for resource allocation as in cloud networks. Additionally, a centralized approach is used as a resource allocation scheme in a cloud environment. So the centralized approach is not applicable in distributed fog networks. Finally, there is a need of a system that deploys the fog network resources that depend on price according to the usage of resources to provide service. Every cluster contains one coordinator node, which is known as a prime node.

3   System Architecture

This proposed solution suggests a system that depends on a fog network that contains several nodes with several customers. The nodes of the fog network are distributed over the terrestrial area and formulate clusters. One node in each cluster performs as an administrator who is known as the Prime node, as shown in Fig 1. Constraints like computation capacity and residual energy must be fulfilled by a node to become a leading or prime node. When the selection of the prime node is completed, every fog node joins the cluster based on the nearest leading or prime node. The node remains in the ownership of the service provider, but end users just utilize the services according to their requirements by using a pay-per-use model.

Table 1. Resource allocation features of fog networks

Resource allocation on the bases of pricing	Features of fog networks				
	Decentralized	Heterogeneous	Dynamic configuration	Fog	Cloud
Chakraborty [4]	No	No	Yes	No	Yes
Farooq [6]	No	No	Yes	Yes	No
Abedin [2]	Yes	Yes	Yes	Yes	No
Nguyen [10]	No	Yes	No	No	Yes
Chanra [5]	Yes	Yes	Yes	Yes	No
Halima [7]	No	No	Yes	No	Yes
Zhang [14]	Yes	No	No	Yes	No
Aazam [1]	No	No	No	No	Yes

3.1   Problem Statement

This model contains three layers one is the cloud, the second is fog, and the third is the end user. The fog layer is the middle that consists of hardware and software resources and provides communication between the end user and the cloud. The fog layer consists of fog nodes, and the node is basically a device or system that contains a processor, memory, and storage. There are multiple clusters in the middle layer. Each set includes one prime node and multiple fog nodes. The prime node of every group is responsible for allocating the resources to the end user according to the customer's request.

Before allocating resources, there will be an agreement between the end user and the owner of the fog network regarding the service being offered and its charges as well as the duration of the service. The ultimate consumer will be levied according to the consumption of fog network resources. In this paper, we focus on the middle (fog) layer to improve the network's performance by using the pay-per-user model. We present an extension of resource management in fog networks while combining the end-user demands for the service and allocating individual nodes against batch applications, as this problem is not discussed in previous literature.

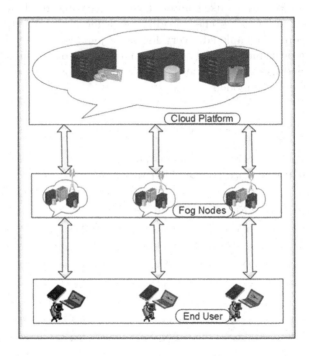

Fig. 1. Schematic Diagram of Fog Resource Sharing to enable pay-per-use Model architecture.

3.2   Selection of Prime Node and Creation of Cluster

The method which was suggested in previous studies was described in a set of equations. In this paper, some of the equations of earlier studies have been used according to the needs of this paper. We applied the Master Node Selection, and Cluster formation Method [8] that is abridged below. We assume that the prime node is elected based on the satisfaction of the Following condition as shown in Eq. 1.

$$C_f \geq C_{th} \quad \text{also} \quad E_f \geq E_{th} \tag{1}$$

Here C_f denotes the computation while E_f is the remaining energy of fog node f, sequentially. In another way, Cth and Eth are the threshold values of C_f and E_f and the selection of prime node based on Cth and Eth as given in Eq. 2.

$$I_{mi,mj} = \sqrt{(\frac{C_{mi} - C_{mj}}{C_{th}})^2 + (\frac{E_{mi} - E_{mj}}{E_{th}})^2} \tag{2}$$

C denotes the number of prime nodes or clusters, and C is selected by the prime node by using the p-dispersion technique. Two prime nodes, mi and mj have the dispersion index that shows Euclidean distance in the two-dimensional x-axis and y-axis. Prime node optimize the fn(C) and $fn(C) = minI_{mi,mj} : 0 < i < j < |F|$. When the group of a prime node is confirmed, then every fog node joins the cluster that contains the geographically closest prime node. After receiving the confirmation from the end-user prime node deploy the applications.

In this work, we assume that t is used to denote the time instant and end-user denoted by n that belongs to N, which is the group of end users. $A_n(t)$ Denote request to offer the group application from the prime node of the cluster. Based on the end-user request prime node finalize the suitable fog node f and then confirm to the end user n. End users accept the offer from the prime node according to its requirement and price of services. After finalization of the fog node, the end user confirms to the cluster's respective prime node. When the applications are deployed, then the end user will be charged an amount $p_{max}^{a_n}$ against the application that is being served to the end user $a_n \in A_n(t)$. So the following equation must be fulfilled as represented in Eq. 3.

$$p_a^n(t) \leq p_{max}^{a_n} \tag{3}$$

Where $p_a^n(t)$ denotes the price that is paid against the deployed application by the end user. The cluster's prime node is responsible for avoiding the over-subscription of the fog node by using Eq. 4s.

$$\sum_{a \in A_n(t),} x_{a,f} m_a \leq M_f and \sum_{a \in A_n(t),} x_{a,f} c_a \leq C_f \tag{4}$$

Where $x_{a,f}$ is the binary variable that shows the relation between fog node f and application a. The variable $m_a and c_a$ shows the application's memory and central processing unit resources.

$$X_{a,f} = \begin{cases} 1, & \text{if application deployed to fog node f after confirmation from the end user} \\ 0, & \text{otherwise} \end{cases} \tag{5}$$

This works on the first come, first serve model (FIFO) to process the applications, but it can be well managed by redistribution of applications that are being done.

4   Pay-Per-Use Model for Resource Administration

This model communicates between the prime node and fog nodes that reside in the same cluster. In this proposed solution, there is the urge for scheme-related pricing comprised of resource allocation in fog networks which use models to provide service regarding fog networks. In this paper, we present an extension that resource management and, on the other hand, integrate the service request from the ultimate consumers, equipping a single fog node for each subgroup of application. Dynamic alliance game is being used in research which further streamlines resource allocation plans in local clusters. Furthermore, we employ a utility game for selecting fog nodes and also focus on tradeoffs.

Dynamic coalition gameplay a vital role in the social group of players to communicate between them. This also applies to different environments, and fog nodes handle every application for a limited time. We assume that there will be random changes regarding active applications and the requirement for resources. That is why a dynamic coalition game is an appropriate option.

In this paper, the prime nodes work as team leaders that confirm the cluster performance of the fog network regarding contentment of the fog nodes, detain, and under or over the employment of resources. Similarly, in this work, when service is availed by the end-user, it will confirm its contentment regarding an application that is offered by the fog network. Two parameters are used to evaluate the contentment by end users on the acceptable delay, and the second is the price paid against the service.

5   Experimental Results

In this section, we will discuss the proposed solution's initial experiments that contain the results regarding the network, node load, and latency on fog devices compared to the cloud. Table 2 shows the variables related to the proposed solution that consists of a prime node, fog node, and cloud setup.

The following table shows the experimental results. When the subscriber devices have increased that causing to expand the network traffic, then obviously, performance will affect the proposed solution.

Table 3 shows that as the devices are increased, the network usage and latency will increase in both layers middle and top layers. The middle layer consists of fog devices, and the top layer consists of cloud devices. The main thing is that there is a notable difference in latency and network usage of both the middle and top layers. This shows that a fog network is more efficient as compared to a cloud network. As proposed solution focuses on the middle layer to improve the efficiency of the fog network based on the pay-per-use model. The graphical representation of the results is below.

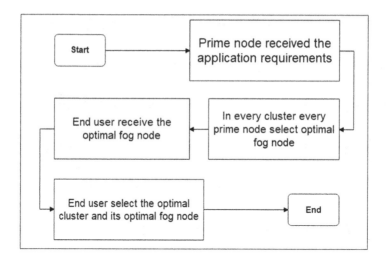

Fig. 2. Flowchart of our proposed pay-per-use model

Table 2. Simulation configuration

Parameters	Cloud	Prime fog node	Fog node
CPU Length (MIPS)	44,800	2,800	2,800
RAM(MB)	40,000	4,000	4,000
UP Link Bandwidth(MB)	100	10,000	10,000
Down Link Bandwidth (MB)	10,000	10,000	10,000
Level	0	1	2
Rate Per MIPS	0.01	0	0
Busy Power (Watt)	1,648	107.339	107.339
Idle power(Watt)	1,332	83.43	83.43

Table 3. Experimental results

Devices	16	20	24	28
Fog Latency (ms)	7.87	8.23	8.59	8.95
Cloud Latency (ms)	8.4	9.5	10.73	12.13
Fog Network Usage (kb)	3198.4	3998	4797	5597
Cloud Network Usage (kb)	27632.16	36099.48	45206	54951

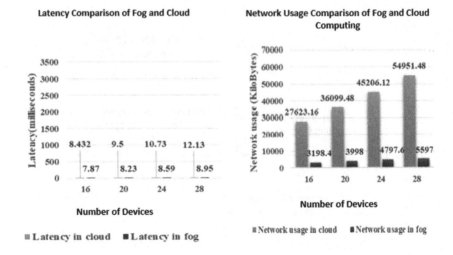

Fig. 3. Comparison of latency and network usage fog and cloud computing

6   Conclusion

In this work, we have compared the latency and network usage of fog computing and cloud computing. The results show that fog computing is more efficient in terms of low latency and less usage of network resources. Furthermore, our target is to achieve more efficiency through resource management in fog networks while combining the end-user demands for the service, and allocating individual nodes against the batch application. The purpose of the proposed solution is to avoid underutilization of the fog network resources.

In the proposed architecture, there are several clusters and several end users as well. In every cluster, there is one prime node and several fog nodes. At starting the end-user request the service to the cluster and the prime node checks by using a dynamic coalition game in which the node is capable of the services that are requested by the end-user and then offers resources against the request. The end user decides on the fog node based on service delay and the price paid against the requested service. In the future, we can extend this work to migrate the fog network services towards the cloud and testify migrated services that turn out to be distributed.

References

1. Aazam, M., Huh, E.-N., St-Hilaire, M., Lung, C.-H., Lambadaris, I.: Cloud customer's historical record based resource pricing. IEEE Trans. Parallel Distrib. Syst. **27**(7), 1929–1940 (2015)
2. Abedin, S.F., Alam, Md.G.R., Kazmi, S.M.A.hsan., Tran, N.H., Niyato, D., Hong, C.S.: Resource allocation for ultra-reliable and enhanced mobile broadband IoT applications in fog network. IEEE Trans. Commun. **67**(1), 489–502, (2018)

3. Awaisi, K.S., et al.: Towards a fog enabled efficient car parking architecture. IEEE Access. **7** , 159100–159111 (2019)
4. Chakraborty, A., Mondal, A., Misra, S.: Cache-enabled sensor-cloud: the economic facet. In: 2018 IEEE Wireless Communications and Networking Conference (WCNC), pp. 1–6. IEEE (2018)
5. Chakraborty, A., Mondal, A., Roy, A., Misra, S.: Dynamic trust enforcing pricing scheme for sensors-as-a-service in sensor-cloud infrastructure. IEEE Trans. Serv. Comput. **14**(5), 1345–1356 (2018)
6. Farooq, M.J., Zhu, Q.: QoE based revenue maximizing dynamic resource allocation and pricing for fog-enabled mission-critical IoT applications. IEEE Trans. Mob. Comput. **20**(12), 3395–3408 (2020)
7. Halima, R.B., Kallel, S., Gaaloul, W., Maamar, Z., Jmaiel, M.: Toward a correct and optimal time-aware cloud resource allocation to business processes. Future Gener. Comput. Syst. **112** ,pp. 751–766 (2020)
8. Subhas Chandra Misra and Ayan Mondal: FOGPRIME: dynamic pricing-based strategic resource management in fog networks. IEEE Trans. Veh. Technol. **70**(8), 8227–8236 (2021)
9. Misra, S., Schober, R., Chakraborty, A.: Race: QoI-aware strategic resource allocation for provisioning Se-aaS. IEEE Trans. Serv. Comput. (2020)
10. Nguyen, D.T., Le, L.B., Bhargava, V.K.: A market-based framework for multi-resource allocation in fog computing. IEEE/ACM Trans. Networking. **27**(3), 1151–1164 (2019)
11. Raja, F.Z., Khattak, H.A., Aloqaily, M., Hussain, R.: Carpooling in connected and autonomous vehicles Current solutions and future directions. ACM Comput. Surv. **1**(1), 1–35 (2021)
12. Yang, Y., Huang, J., Zhang, T., Weinman, J.: Challenges and practices of fog computing, communication, networking, strategy, and economics, Fog and fogonomics (2020)
13. Zafar, F., Khattak, H.A., Aloqaily, M., Hussain, H.: Carpooling in connected and autonomous vehicles current solutions and future directions. ACM Computing Surveys (CSUR), **54**(10s), 1–36 (2022)
14. Zhao, Z., et al.: On the design of computation offloading in fog radio access networks. IEEE Trans. Veh. Techno.**68**(7), pp. 7136–7149 (2019)

An Emergency Information Broadcast Routing in VANET

Liya Xu, Mingzhu Ge$^{(\boxtimes)}$ ⓘ, Anyuan Deng, Jiaoli Shi, and Shimao Yao

Jiujiang University, Jiujiang 332000, China
mingzhug@whu.edu.cn

Abstract. Aiming at the problem that the low efficiency of information transmission caused by the high speed of vehicle and the unstable network topology in the vehicle ad hoc network (VANET), an emergency information broadcast (EIBR) routing in VANET was proposed in this paper. The routing scheme decreases the number of nodes to broadcast packets. A connected dominating set (CDS) is created for the certain road section. Then the CDS is optimized with the approximation method to obtain the minimum connected dominating set (MCDS). The next hop relay node will be selected from the MCDS. In addition, these nodes broadcast the packets by a dynamic probabilistic broadcast strategy. It can enormously lessen the number of broadcast nodes and the transmission collisions, it also can reduce the end-to-end delay consequently. Simulation results have shown the effectiveness of our broadcast routing as compared to the two traditional broadcast protocols NCPR and DMB in the two aspects of the average transmission delay and packet delivery ratio.

Keywords: VANET · Emergency information · MCDS · Probabilistic broadcast · Routing

1 Introduction

In the process of incubating intelligent transportation system (ITS) into reality, vehicular ad hoc network play an indispensable role, moreover, the intelligent networked vehicles, which combine the technologies of VANET and autonomous driving, are the core elements of ITS. The vehicles sever as the nodes collecting traffic information around themselves and broadcasting safety, road conditions and other information by communicating with other vehicles in VANET. It can effectively improve traffic conditions and enhance road safety to reduce the impact of traffic on the environment [1]. VANET is known as a kind of MANET, in which vehicles are not only the nodes receiving information meant for it but also relaying information intended for others in the network, thus information can be transmitted to distant vehicles in a multi-hop method through the relay nodes. Vehicles can establish or join other established VANETs at any time with their movement and without the restriction of fixed facilities. In VANET, vehicles can communicate not only with other vehicles but also with road side units (RSU). It

Z. J. Haas et al. (Eds.): WiCON 2022, LNICST 464, pp. 144–155, 2023.
https://doi.org/10.1007/978-3-031-27041-3_11

accesses the backbone network through roadside units to provide richer services for members in the vehicle.

However, the transmission of information in this network has numerous challenges. The network topology changes extremely quickly owing to the nodes at a high velocity, which results in shorter link duration between nodes. Besides, the mobility of nodes is constrained by the road, which makes the uneven distribution of nodes in the network, it accordingly causes serious network segmentation in VANET. In hot road areas such as intersections, the density of nodes is incredibly high. If all nodes are allowed to broadcast information freely without restriction, it will lead to fierce competition for channel resources and even paralyze wireless transmission in the region. These factors lead to the unreliable transmission of information in VANET. Therefore, it is a considerable significance to search for an efficient broadcast transmission path in VANET.

The main contributions of this work are summarized as follows.

(1) This paper described the importance of routing in VANET and illustrated the challenges of data transmission in the network.
(2) In order to reduce the data broadcast conflict, we design a minimum connected dominant sets construction algorithm and the nodes in the minimum connected dominating set broadcast the packets. Furthermore, these nodes broadcast the packets by a dynamic probabilistic broadcast strategy.
(3) In terms of the average transmission end-to-end delay and packet delivery rate, we evaluate the proposed protocol and compared the results with other schemes.

The remainder of this paper is organized as follows. A brief overview of related work is provided in Section II. The minimum connected dominant sets construction algorithm and the dynamic probabilistic broadcast strategy are presented in Section III. The performance evaluation is given in Section IV. The last Section is conclusion.

2   Related Work

Broadcasting is a basic method of wireless communication in networks. The process is that the node transmits the information packet to the whole network. It acts a significant role in network maintenance and management. In the design of the broadcasting protocol, it possesses many issues remained to solve, such as intense transmission conflict, broadcast storm and hidden terminal.

In [2], vehicles located in a specific road segment employed the slot map broadcast to perform distributed access. All nodes broadcast Hello messages periodically to establish local topology. Each vehicle node utilizes a marker variable to determine whether a packet is redundant or not. However, due to the rapid vehicle nodes and the network topology comparison, the redundancy of data packets is extremely large. It consequently reduces the delivery rate of packets and produces large broadcast latency. Singh et al. proposed a masqueraded probabilistic flooding routing [3]. In the mapping process from node ID to packet, the authors introduced a confusion that is capable of masquerade packets sent by a node to any other nodes as its own packets. In [4], the authors proposed a new probability-based multi-hop broadcast routing to guarantee reliability and low latency. The probability of a node forwarding a packet depends on the distance between the current node and the relay one. But in sparse VANET, there may be insufficient vehicles near the source node to transmit information, which can lead to a sharp drop in the delivery rate of packets.

An adaptive emergency broadcast strategy for VANETs (AVED) is proposed by Chou et al. in [5]. When a traffic accident happens, the current node transmits the emergency messages to all nodes in a certain range. While in AVED, vehicle nodes maintain a routing table through periodical cooperative awareness message, which increases the redundancy of packets. Presented in [6], a recursive broadcast routing is based on the cluster to transmit emergency information in VANET. The algorithm selects a vehicle node as cluster head to broadcast packets. But if some cluster members cannot receive the packet, the cluster head will broadcast the packet repeatedly. It is not suitable for sparse VANET consequently. Virdaus et al. analyzed the influence of broadcast storming for emergency delivery in VANETs [7]. Some scholars proposed many schemes to solve the broadcast storm problems [8, 9, 10, 11]. Yet there are still some unresolved problems in these patterns, such as the redundancy of packets, transmission collision, and transmission delay.

The strategies in [12, 13] and [14], utilize a distance-based broadcast algorithm frequently to appoint the nodes farther away from broadcast ones as the relay node. It lessens the transmission delay of broadcasting data packets through decreasing the value of the hops in the data broadcast transmission process. Moreover, it can further control the amount of redundant broadcast information in the network and improve the utilization efficiency of network resources. While if the reliability of data transmission is not guaranteed, some nodes may not receive data packets. The authors of [15] presented a novel sender-based broadcast protocol in VANET. They designed a control structure based on an index to define control messages. The size of the control messages is determined by a segment-based partition algorithm to adapt the distribution of the relay node. On the other hand, this fashion will add additional overhead in transmission, which affects the transmission efficiency.

To solve the problem of packet collisions and medium contentions along with broadcast storm in VANETs, and inspired by the above-mentioned schemes, we propose an emergency information broadcast routing in this paper, which is based on the idea of reducing the number of nodes to broadcast packets. In our proposed method, a connected dominating set (CDS) is created for the current node, and then optimized to approximate the MCDS. The scheme as presented in our paper greatly lessen the number of broadcast nodes and the transmission collisions, moreover, it also can reduce the end-to-end delay.

3 Routing

3.1 Problem Description

When transmitting emergency data packets, it is demanded that the end-to-end delay of information be severely within a certain given threshold. For example, when congestion occurs in road, the road section near the congestion point will be a local hotspot area, which results in a high local traffic density. If the packets are transmitted according to flooding broadcasting, the problem of broadcast storm mentioned above will arise, which will increase the transmission delay and packet loss rate. This paper researches the routing that can reduce the number of packets transmitted by nodes.

The traditional data transmission is broadcast in VANET. There is no definite destination node for this transmission. The relay node broadcasts the received data to all neighbor nodes, which easily leads to channel congestion, high packet loss rate and so on. The results in [16] show that when data is transmitted by broadcast, the network delivery rate is less than 20%. In order to improve the data transmission efficiency in VANET, this paper divides the highway into cells from the physical level.

In urban environment, roads are generally long rectangular with a length of several kilometers and a width of tens of meters. R represents the maximum distance between two nodes that can transmit packets. The roads are divided into short rectangular cells with 2R, and each cell is assigned an ID. Mark the location of the cell with two points on the diagonal of the short rectangle, as shown in Fig. 1.

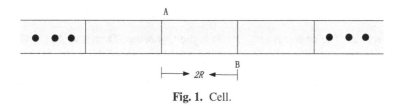

Fig. 1. Cell.

When a road is divided into short rectangles as shown in the above figure, the communication network between vehicle nodes in the road can be designed into a structure composed of physical layer and logical layer, as shown in Fig. 2. The real vehicle nodes are nodes in the physical layer, and each short rectangle is regarded as a virtual node. At the logical level, the broadcast of packets in VANET can build a broadcast tree, and the nodes in the tree are virtual nodes referred to above. Therefore, packets transmission on the road can be regarded as point-to-point transmission.

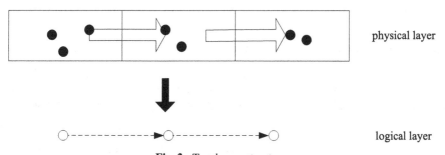

Fig. 2. Two layers structure.

To reduce the number of nodes transmitting packets, a MCDS is constructed for the network composed of physical nodes in above cells. Only the nodes exist in the MCDS can broadcast packets. The construction algorithm of connected dominating set is shown in Sect. 3.4.

3.2 Relevant Definitions

The wireless transmission mode discussed in this paper adopts the omnidirectional transmission mode. In the omnidirectional transmission mode, the wireless coverage area is disc-shaped. In this paper, the transmission range of nodes is represented by the unit disk graph (UDG)[17], that is, all nodes within the disk can communicate with the center node. Let G = (V, E), the V represents the nodes in the graph and the E represents the edges in the graph.

Definition 3–1: Assume that all nodes have the same transmission distance. The nodes relaying packets is considered as the center of the disk and the maximum transmission distance R is considered as the radius. Supposing the distance between two nodes is less than R, they can communicate with each other accordingly.

In VANET, each vehicle has a unique identification. V represents the node of VANET. |V| represents the number of vehicles in VANET. While E represents a connected edge in G, and formula $(v_i, v_j) \in E(G)$ denotes that node v_i and v_j are adjacent.

Definition 3–2: The node set $D \subseteq V(G)$ is the Connected Dominant Set in G, and it indicates for any v, if either $v \in D$ or v is the neighbor node of the nodes existed in D.

Definition 3–3: V represents a node in G. let $Neighbor(v)$ be the neighbor node set of v.

Definition 3–4: $d(v_1, v_2)$ Denotes the distance between v_1 and v_2. Let R be the maximum transmission distance of nodes, thus v_1 and v_2 are connected, provided $d(v_1, v_2) < R$.

3.3 Broadcast Routing Description

This broadcast routing consists of two steps: the first step is that Connected Dominating Set (CDS) is constructed for vehicle nodes of a hot area in VANET; the second one is that the nodes in CDS are selected as the relay nodes to transmit the packets.

3.4 Connected Dominant Sets Construction

The construction of Minimum Connected Dominating Set (MCDS) is an NP-hard problem [18], and that signifies no solution in polynomial time. Hence this paper researches the approximate solution of this problem, and proposes an approximate algorithm to construct MCDS.

Algorithm Description. Initial Connected Graph G with the center of the current node S is constructed. In this paper, an initial connected dominant set is constructed according to the minimum spanning tree method as presented in [19]. Obviously, the greater the degree of a node means the more neighbor nodes of the node, so the connected dominating set construction algorithm should give priority to choose this node. Therefore, the degree of the node can be used as an important parameter to determine the relay node in CDS. Consequently the nodes with greater degrees have higher weights.

Algorithm Implementation. Table 1 describes the algorithm of constructing initial connected graph. Table 2 describes the algorithm of constructing a MCDS. A MCDS is constructed in a cell.

Table 1. Algorithm of constructing initial connected graph

Input: Initial Vertex u_0, The length d Output: $G(V, E)$
1. Initialize set $V = \Phi, E = \Phi$
2. U is the vehicle set that exist in the road section within length a certain d (e.g. 2R), For any $u \in U$, the $d(u, u_0)$ is computed according to their coordinates
3. If $d(u, u_0) < d/2$, then add u to V
4. Delete u from U 5. If U is not empty, go to step 2. Else go to step 6 6. Traverse each node in set V from vertex u and calculate the distance $d(u, u_x)$ between u and u_x in V 7. If $d(u, u_x) < R$, then add (u, u_x) to E. Until all nodes have been traversed 8. Determine that (u, u_x) or (u_x, u) are the same edge. Traverse set E and delete duplicate edges
9. Return $G(V, E)$

Table 2. MCDS Constructing Algorithm

Input: $G(V, E)$ Output: $MCDS$
1. $U = \{u_0\}$, u_0 is the source node
2. $MCDS = \{\Phi\}, CDS_{initial} = \{\Phi\}$
3. Weight each edge in the graph based on the degree of nodes on both sides of the edge
4. Choose one edge (u, v) existed in E and have current maximum weight. Add u or v that is not in U to U 5. Repeat, until $U = V$ 6. U is the $CDS_{initial}$, and $u \in U$ and D(u) > 1 7. For $\forall u_1, u_2, u_1 \in CDS_{initial}, u_2 \in CDS_{initial}$, If $Neighbor(u_2) \subseteq Neighbor(u_1)$, then $MCDS = CDS_{initial} - u_2$. Else $MCDS = CDS_{initial}$ 8. (u, u_x) and (u_x, u) are judged to be the same. Delete duplicate edges in E
9. Return $MCDS$

Algorithm Analysis. We analyze the time complexity of the above two algorithms. Table 1 are c the classic construction graph algorithm, the time complexity is $O(n^3)$. Let's analyze another.

The algorithm in Table 2 mainly consists of four linear steps.

(1) The first step that weights to the edges of graph G. The time complexity of is $O(n)$.
(2) The time complexity of the Prim algorithm is $O(n^2)$.
(3) The time complexity of selecting non-leaf node steps is $O(n)$.
(4) Step to delete redundant nodes. It requires pairs comparing the neighbor nodes number of nodes classified to the initial CDS. For a set with n nodes, the number of this comparison is $O(n^2)$. Let m_1 and m_2 represent the number of neighbor nodes for two nodes. $Max\{m_1, m_2\}$ represents the number of steps to determine whether the neighborhood set of two nodes has a inclusion relationship. The opinion proposed in [20], is that a network is fully connected if each node possesses more than $5.1774 \log n$ neighbors in the network. As a result, m_1 and m_2 are less than $5.1774 \log n$. Therefore, the time complexity of this step is $O(n^2 \log n)$.

Since the above four steps are linear, the time complexity of constructing a MCDS is $O(n^2 \log n)$.

3.5   The Probabilistic Broadcast Strategy

The MCDS is constructed for the network composed of vehicle nodes in the cell. When a packet is transmitted to the cell, only the nodes in CDS can broadcast the packet. In order to further reduce the data transmission conflict, the nodes in the MCDS adopt a Dynamic Probabilistic broadcast strategy to broadcast the packet. The probability of the packet being broadcast by the node is determined by two parameters. One is the average density of the node in VANET. Another is the neighbor coverage set (NCS) of a node for certain packet.

Computing for Average Number of Neighbors of Nodes. In VANET, nodes maintain and update their neighbor sets by periodically sending hello packet. When node x receives the hello packet of node y, it queries whether node y exists in its neighbor table. If it does, it updates the information of node y in its neighbor table. Otherwise, it stores node y in its neighbor table. This paper sets a threshold for the time interval between two nodes sending hello packet. If two nodes do not receive hello packet sent to each other within the given time threshold, they will delete this node in the neighbor table.

Let $\bar{n}$ represent the average number of neighbors for all nodes. The total number of nodes in VANET is represented by N, and the neighbor number of node i is U_i, so $\bar{n}$ can be computed by the following formula.

$$\bar{n} = \frac{1}{N} \sum_{i=1}^{N} U_i \tag{1}$$

The NCS of a Node for Certain Packet. Each node for certain packet has its NCS. It is the set of nodes that coincide in the neighbor table of two nodes. As shown in Fig. 3, vehicle S transmits a packet to A, B, C, H. Both C and H are in the neighbor table of D, and they have received this packet. Therefore, for this packet, the neighbor coverage set of D is C and H.

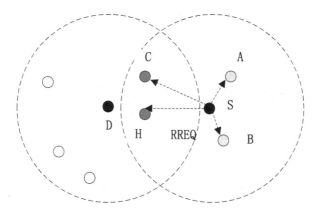

Fig. 3. Packet neighbor coverage set of node.

The Probability Formulation for Broadcasting Packet of Node. The probability of a packet being broadcast by a node is determined by the average density of nodes and the neighbor coverage set of the packet to the node. When a node receives a packet, it first determines the neighbor coverage set of the packet for the node. Obviously, the larger the set of covered neighbor nodes is, the smaller the probability of the packet being broadcast is. Because the larger the node set is, the more number of neighbor nodes that the packet has been transmitted to the node. Therefore, for this node, broadcasting this packet is a repeated broadcast, which will reduce the transmission efficiency.

When the minimum connected dominating set is constructed, this section sets the broadcast probability function formula for the packet P_c in the current node based on the results of above. The average number $\bar{n}$ of neighbors of nodes, is computed in formula (1). The node neighbor coverage set of packet P_c is the number $\tilde{n}$ of nodes that P_c existed in the neighbor table for the current node. The neighbor node number is n for the current node.

The probability Pr that the current node u broadcast a packet is calculated as follows [21].

$$
P_r = \begin{cases} \dfrac{n - \tilde{n}}{\bar{n}}; n \leq \bar{n} \\ \dfrac{n - \tilde{n}}{n}; n > \bar{n} \end{cases} \tag{2}
$$

4   Simulation and Analysis

In the section, this paper computes the end-to-end delay and delivery rate of packets. The experimental parameters are set in Table 3.

Table 3. Parameters.

Parameters	Value
Simulation Size	40 m*10000 m
Number of vehicles	From 5 to 30
Max transmission Distance	250 m
Bandwidth	10Mbps
Type	CBR
Minimum speed	10 m/s
Maximum speed	30 m/s
Packet generation rate	10 per second

This paper compare the emergency information broadcast routing (EIBR) with RBM as presented in [22] and SB adopted by [23] in terms of packet delivery ratio and transmission delay. In SB, the network is divided into adjacent cells. Each cell is assigned a special waiting time. Thus the waiting time of a vehicle that belongs to different cells is not the same. The minimum waiting time allocated to the cell is farthest from the current node, the farthest node consequently can be selected as the relay node first. It guarantees that the distance of each hop about transmitting information is the longest. In the RBM method, the predefined equations are used to allocate the waiting time of each vehicle, and similarly, minimum waiting time allocated to the cell is farthest from the current node for fast transmission.

When the node of VANET is scarce, the packet delivery ratios are close to 100% for all schemes as shown in Fig. 4. While the delivery ratio of packets in RBM decreases significantly with the traffic density increasing, the SB algorithm performs better than the RBM algorithm. Nevertheless, the delivery rate of the proposed broadcast algorithm is still close to 1. In the sparse network, the average transmission delay of SB and RBM algorithm is less than that of the broadcast method proposed in this paper as shown in Fig. 5. The average transmission delay of SB broadcasting increases significantly with vehicle density increasing, while the RBM algorithm and the method proposed in this paper have better performance. Since there will be no transmission conflict to broadcast packets in the sparse network. By comparison, the proposed broadcast algorithm needs to construct CDS, which will cause some delay, meanwhile, the relative distance between nodes decreases with the vehicle density increasing. The SB algorithm promises that the farthest node relays the message first. Sometimes the selected relay node may be not the appropriate next hop, which leads to an increase in the number of repeat broadcasts. The relative distance between nodes decreases with the vehicle density increasing. The number of packets in RMB increases and the number of conflicts increases correspondingly, which cause a rise in the number of repeat broadcasts due to lack of a solution to the collision problem. The proposed broadcast method in this paper broadcasts packets via the nodes in the connected dominant set. The probability of broadcasting collision is extremely reduced. Therefore, the average end-to-end delay is low.

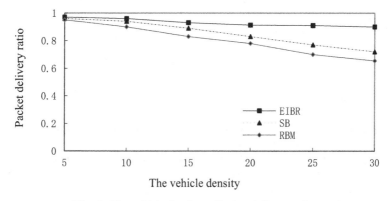

Fig. 4. The vehicle density vs Packet delivery ratios.

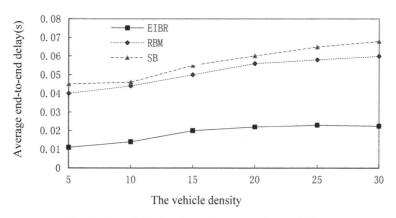

Fig. 5. The vehicle density vs Average end-to-end delay.

5 Conclusion

With the intense Channel competition between a large scale of communication nodes in VANET, it increases the network packet loss rate and decreases the communication efficiency. In case of emergency, the information must be transmitted to relevant vehicles with extremely low delay. This paper designs a broadcasting routing scheme based on a decrease in the number of nodes to broadcast packets. In this paper, an MCDS is constructed for the nodes in the current node communication range, and then the nodes in the MCDS are utilized to broadcast packets. Furthermore, these nodes broadcast the packets by a dynamic probabilistic broadcast strategy. Simulation results show that the proposed method can effectively reduce the transmission delay and improve the packet delivery rate.

Acknowledgement. This work was supported by the NSF(No.1907472), National Science Foundation of China(No.62062045), Science and technology project of Jiangxi Provin-cial Department of Education (No. GJJ211842), Jiangxi Natural Science Foundation (No.

20202BAB202023,20192ACBL20031), Project of Teaching Reform in Jiujiang University(No. XJJGYB-19–47).

References

1. Kaur, R., Singh, T.P., Khajuria, V.: Security issues in vehicular ad-hoc network (VANET). In: 2018 2nd International Conference on Trends in Electronics and Informatics (ICOEI), Tirunelveli, India, pp. 884–889. IEEE (2018)
2. Zhou, M., Wu, M., Ding, Z., Liu, Z., Zhao, F.: performance evaluation of hybrid distributed-centralized TDMA in high-density vehicular networks. IEEE Commun. Lett. **26**(4), 952–956 (2022)
3. Singh, P.K., Agarwal, A., Nakum, G., Rawat, D.B., Nandi, S.: MPFSLP: masqueraded probabilistic flooding for source-location privacy in VANETs. IEEE Trans. Veh. Technol. **69**(10), 11383–11393 (2020)
4. Zeng, X., Yu, M., Wang, D.: A new probabilistic multi-hop broadcast protocol for vehicular networks. IEEE Trans. Veh. Technol. **67**(12), 12165–12176 (2018)
5. Chou, Y., Chu, T.-H., Kuo, S.-Yu., Chen, C.-Y.: An adaptive emergency broadcast strategy for vehicular ad hoc networks. IEEE Sens. J. **18**(12), 4814–4821 (2018)
6. Dong, W., Lin, F., Zhang, H., Yin, Y.: A cluster-based recursive broadcast routing algorithm to propagate emergency messages in city VANETs. In: IEEE 9th International Conference on Communication Software and Networks (ICCSN), Guangzhou, China, pp. 187–190. IEEE (2017)
7. Virdaus, I.K., Kang, M., Shin, S., Kwon, G.-R.: A simulation study: is the broadcast storming really harmful for emergency delivery in VANETs?. In: Proceedings of International Conference on Advanced Technologies for Communication (ATC), Ho Chi Minh City, Vietnam, pp. 666–670. IEEE (2015)
8. Li, P., Zeng, Y., Li, C., Chen, L., Wang, H., Chen, C.: A probabilistic broadcasting scheme for emergent message dissemination in Urban internet of vehicles. IEEE Access **9**, 113187–113198 (2021)
9. Wu, J., Luo, C., Luo Y., Li, K.: Distributed UAV swarm formation and collision avoidance strategies over fixed and switching topologies. IEEE Trans. Cybern. 1–11 (2021)
10. Han, R., Shi, J., Guan, Q., Banoori, F., Shen, W.: Speed and position aware dynamic routing for emergency message dissemination in VANETs. IEEE Access **10**, 1376–1385 (2022)
11. Liu, Z., et al.: PPTM: a privacy-preserving trust management scheme for emergency message dissemination in space–air–ground-integrated vehicular networks. IEEE Internet Things J. **9**(8), 5943–5956 (2022)
12. Fayyad, O.B., Mangoud, M.A.: Multi-hop broadcast protocol based on smart fuzzy inference for vehicular ad-hoc network. In: 3rd Smart Cities Symposium (SCS 2020), IET, online (2020)
13. Luo, Y., Su, X., Yu, Y., Cao, Q., Ni, Z.: Real-time successful broadcasting ratio and distance based broadcast for vehicular ad hoc networks. In: 2020 International Conference on Wireless Communications and Signal Processing (WCSP), Nanjing, China, pp. 1046–1051. IEEE (2020)
14. Arsalan, A., Rehman, R.A.: Distance-based scheme for broadcast storm mitigation in named software defined vehicular networks (NSDVN). In: 2019 16th IEEE Annual Consumer Communications and Networking Conference (CCNC). Las Vegas, NV, USA, pp. 1–4. IEEE (2019)
15. Zhang, H., Zhang, X.: An adaptive control structure based fast broadcast protocol for vehicular ad hoc networks. IEEE Commun. Lett. **21**(8), 1835–1838 (2017)

16. Borgonovo, F., Capone, A., Cesana, M., Fratta, L.: ADHOC MAC: a new, flexible and reliable MAC architecture for ad-hoc networks. In: Proceedings of the IEEE Wireless Communications and Networking. New York, USA, pp. 965–970. IEEE (2003)
17. Marathe, M.V., Breu, H., Hunt, H.B., Ravi, S.S., Rosenkrantz, D.J.: Simple heuristics for unit disk graphs. J. Netw. **25**(2), 59–68 (1995)
18. Garey, M.R., Johnson, D.S.: Computers and intractability-a guide to the theory of NP-completeness. SIAM Rev. **24**(1), 90–91 (1979)
19. Gao W.: Novel connected dominating set algorithm based on minimum spanning tree. J. Comput. Appl. **29**(6), 1489–1493 (2009)
20. Xue, F., Kumar, P.R.: The number of neighbors needed for connectivity of wireless networks. wireless networks. **10**(2), 169–181 (2004)
21. Abdulai, J.D., Ould-Khaoua, M., Mackenzie, L.M., Mohammed, A.: Neighbour coverage: a dynamic probabilistic route discovery for mobile ad hoc networks. In: 2008 International Symposium on Performance Evaluation of Computer and Telecommunication Systems (SPECTS). Edinburgh, UK, pp. 165–172. IEEE (2008)
22. Briesemeister, L., Hommel, G.: Role-based multicast in highly mobile but sparsely connected ad hoc networks. In: 2000 First Annual Workshop on Mobile and Ad Hoc Networking and Computing, Boston, MA, USA, pp. 45–50. IEEE (2000)
23. Fasolo, E., Zanella, A., Zorzi, M.: An effective broadcast scheme for alert message propagation in vehicular ad hoc networks. In: 2006 IEEE International Conference on Communications, Istanbul, Turkey, pp. 3960–3965. IEEE (2006)

IP Lookup Technology for Internet Computing

Yen-Heng Lin and Sun-Yuan Hsieh$^{(\boxtimes)}$

Department of Computer Science and Information Engineering,
National Cheng Kung University, Tainan, Taiwan
`hsiehsy@ncku.edu.tw`

Abstract. Internet protocol (IP) lookup is a key technology that affects
network performance. Numerous studies have inves- tigated IP lookup
and provided solutions for improving lookup algorithms. Herein, we utilized various state-of-the-art algorithms for improving IP lookup performance and explore trie-based algorithms to understand how these algorithms affect memory access or usage and the resulting reductions in IP
lookup times. Moreover, we utizsed parallel data processing for increasing IP lookup throughput. These algorithms are applicable to all tries.
Nevertheless, we conducted experiments by using only binary tries for
simplicity. IP lookup algorithms were tested through simulations using
real IPv4 router tables with 855,997 or 876,489 active prefixes. Finally,
a synthetic architecture combining all of the discussed algorithms was
proposed and evaluated.

Keywords: Internet computing · Router table design · IPv4 ·
Trie-based algorithms · Direct lookup tables · Next-hop tables · Data
communication

1 Introduction

With the rapid development of the Internet, services such as social media,
streaming media, and cloud computing [1] have gradually become a part of
daily life. High-speed Internet is necessary for handling large numbers of internet protocol (IP) packets; however, Internet speed is affected by IP lookup, a key
technology. To send an IP packet to a destination address, it must be transmitted
through multiple routers; nevertheless, connections between routers are not one-
to-one links but are many-to-many links. If a router is to transmit an IP packet
to another router, it uses an IP lookup algorithm to determine an appropriate
next hop to the next router on its own routing table. This IP lookup process is
the bottleneck in Internet communication. Moreover, if the transmitted IP packets are all of minimal size (40 bytes) and if the aggregated link bandwidth is
40 gigabits per second (Gbps), then IP lookup should be performed 125 million
times per second (125 million lookups per second, Mlps) to meet the required
throughput of 8 ns per lookup in this worst-case scenario.

© ICST Institute for Computer Sciences, Social Informatics and Telecommunications Engineering 2023
Published by Springer Nature Switzerland AG 2023. All Rights Reserved
Z. J. Haas et al. (Eds.): WiCON 2022, LNICST 464, pp. 156–175, 2023.
https://doi.org/10.1007/978-3-031-27041-3_12

Classless Inter-Domain Routing (CIDR) [2] was introduced in 1993 as a replacement for the previous classful network addressing architecture on the Internet. Routing table prefixes no longer have fixed lengths of 8, 16, or 24 bits for 32-bit IPv4 [3] addresses; instead, their lengths may vary. In CIDR, a prefix is formatted as a pair of an address and prefix length, as presented in Fig. 1(a); in this figure, the leftmost prefix length address bits indicate the prefix, and the remaining bits can be ignored. For example, the two-bit entry (10*/2 C) indicates that the prefix is 10_2 and the corresponding next hop is router C. When a router receives a incoming packet, it extracts the destination address of the packet and compares it with each prefix entry in the routing table, starting from the leftmost significant bit of the destination address. If numerous prefixes match the address, the router chooses the prefix with the longest length as the best matching prefix (BMP) and forwards the IP packet to the corresponding next-hop router with the longest prefix match (LPM). This is the IP lookup process. For example, in Fig. 1, router A receives an IP packet with a 5-bit destination IP address "10100" that matches the prefixes 1 and 10; therefore, the router chooses 10 with prefix length 2 as the BMP and forwards the packet to the corresponding next-hop router C.

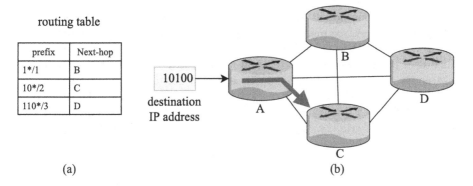

routing table

prefix	Next-hop
1*/1	B
10*/2	C
110*/3	D

(a)   (b)

Fig. 1. (a) Routing table of router A. (b) Forwarding of an incoming IP packet with a 5-bit IP address

Over the past few decades, numerous studies have investigated implementations of IP lookup methods. These methods can be classified into two major categories: hardware-based and software-based methods. In hardware-based methods, parallel data processing can be used to increase lookup speed. Ternary content addressable memory is a prominent hardware-based method [4] and supports highly parallel lookups for entire entries; because it returns the BMP within a single memory access time, its lookup rate can exceed 250 Mlps. However, this method has high power consumption and requires substantial physical space, reducing its practical applicability. In addition, owing to the development of Network Function Virtualization (NFV) technology [5], software-based methods are more suitable than hardware-based methods for applications that require portability. Software-based methods can be further divided into range-based, hash-based, and trie-based methods.

For range-based methods, Zec et al. proposed DXR [6] as an attempt to transform large routing tables into compact lookup structures (range tables) that easily fit into the cache hierarchies of modern CPUs. They further included an additional direct lookup table to divide the range table into 2^k chunks; in the IP lookup process, the first k bits of the destination address are used to reach a certain chunk and identify the LPM more quickly in a smaller range table.

Hash-based IP lookup methods have also been successful. For example, [7] revealed that hashing is an efficient method of achieving an exact match but not LPM. Because the prefixes in the hash table have arbitrary length, the number of leftmost significant bits that must be extracted from the destination address to perform a hash table lookup is unknown. To improve on hash-based methods, Dharmapurikar et al. [8] proposed a method that uses parallel Bloom filters to assess whether a prefix matches an address of a specific length, followed by quickly deleting addresses whose length is inconsistent with the prefix and may otherwise be extracted to the hash table for lookup. Fan et al. proposed another replacement method [9] in which the Bloom filter is replaced with a cuckoo filter to reduce false positives and improve the lookup performance.

Finally, trie-based methods use trie structures to implement IP lookup. The basic trie-based method is the binary trie [10]; however, a drawback of this method is that the tree must be traversed from the root to a leaf to determine the LPM. To alleviate this disadvantage, the priority trie [11] was developed, which uses priority marks to determine whether any longer prefix exists in the child nodes to avoid wasting lookup time. In the fixed-stride multibit trie [12], 2^k children of a node are used to seek k bits at a time, reducing the time complexity from $O(W)$ (binary trie, W = the length of the IP address) to $O(W/k)$. Moreover, the LC-trie [13], patricia trie [14], poptrie [15], and CP-trie [16] have been proposed to increase lookup rate by reducing the trie height and memory consumption.

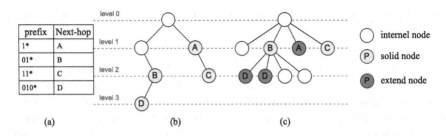

Fig. 2. (a) Routing table. (b) Corresponding binary trie. (c) Corresponding 2-bit stride multibit trie.

In this paper, we focus on trie-based methods with a simple, tiny data structure. Several relevant studies have proposed improvements to the performance of trie-based lookups. Accordingly, we attempt to unify commonly used technologies to help readers understand how this technology improves IP lookup performance. To clearly explain each technology, we include examples with the basic binary trie and the corresponding algorithms for each technology to facilitate the understanding and implementation of these technologies. Moreover, five metrics were used to measure the performance of each technology in our experiment: average Mlps, memory consumption, trie height, average memory accesses, and average update time. These metrics were compared to understand whether the various technologies perform as described.

The remainder of this paper is organized as follows: Sect. 2 describes the binary trie scheme and the k-bit multibit trie scheme and explains how data are stored and searched in trie-based methods. Section 3 describes a direct lookup table algorithm that reduces memory access in the trie. Section 4 describes methods of branching the search of the direct lookup table and trie. Section 5 describes a next-hop table algorithm that reduces the memory consumption of the trie. Section 6 proposes a novel method of synthesizing previous technologies in a trie-based method. Section 7 describes a parallel data processing method that uses multiple threads to increase IP lookup throughput. Section 8 presents the experimental results for a comparison of each algorithm on real IPv4 tables with 855,997 and 876,489 active prefixes and presents the performance of the synthetic method. Finally, Sect. 9 provides our conclusion.

2   Trie-based Scheme

A binary trie is the basic trie-based method. Each node has at most two children, and prefixes can be organized on a digital basis. The search begins from the root, and the bits of the prefix are used to direct the branching. For a bit value of 0, the search moves to the left branch; for a bit value of 1, it moves to the right branch. The search continues until all bits of the prefix are evaluated, and the corresponding next hop is stored in the final branch node. The node storing the next hop is called a solid node; other nodes are called internal nodes. That is, the path from the root to the solid node is equivalent to the prefix, and the value in the solid node is the next hop corresponding to that prefix. Figure 2 presents a routing table stored in a binary trie. For example, the router (010*/3, C) is stored beginning at the root; the first bit is 1, meaning that the search proceeds to the right branch, and the second bit is 1, meaning that the search proceeds to the right branch. Finally, the next hop C is stored in the node.

Searching for the LPM of the destination address on a binary trie is a top-down process from the root. One bit of the destination address is examined at a time. If the bit value is 0, the search proceeds to a left child; otherwise, it proceeds to a right child until it finally proceeds to a null child. When the search reaches a solid node, all branches passed are recorded as the current LPM, and the value stored in the solid node is the corresponding next hop. When the search has been completed, the next hop corresponding to the current LPM is returned. For example, to look up the 5-bit destination address 11011 in Fig. 2, the search begins at the root. The first bit is 1; thus, the search proceeds to right child. This child is a solid node; thus, the next hop A corresponding to LPM 1 is stored. The second bit is also 1; thus, the search again proceeds to the right child, which is also a solid node. We thus store the next hop C corresponding to LPM 11. Finally, the third bit is 0, and the left child is null; therefore, the search stops, and the next hop C corresponding to LPM 11 is returned. Figure 3 presents these search processes.

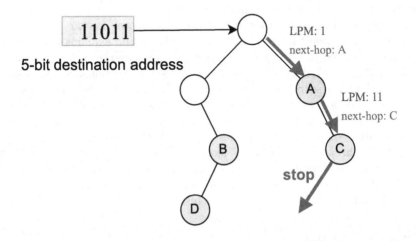

Fig. 3. Search steps for 5-bit destination address in binary trie

In contrast to the binary trie, in the k-bit stride multibit trie, each node has at most 2^k children, and prefixes are stored by using k bits of the prefix at a time to direct the branching. For the example in Fig. 2, to store a router $(1^*/1,$ A) in a 2-bit stride multibit trie, 2 bits are extracted from prefix 1. The length of the prefix is less than 2; thus, we must expand the prefix to obtain a set $\{10,11\}$. On the basis of this set, the next hop A is stored in both the third child and the fourth child from the left. To store another router $(01^*/2,$ B), the store operation directly proceeds to the second child and stores the next hop B in it. However, when the store operation attempts to store a third router $(11^*/2$ C), the store proceeds to third child and determines that the next hop A is already stored in the node. The operation must determine whether the original stored value can be modified. The exact prefix length corresponding to this solid node is unknown because it may have been expanded from a prefix of insufficient length. Thus, more information must be stored in the multibit trie: the prefix length must be stored in the solid node as well. With the prefix length, a decision can be made on whether to save the next hop C because the original next hop A has a prefix length of 1. After a comparison based on prefix length, the next hop A can be changed to C.

The search process for the LPM in a multibit trie is similar to that in a binary trie; however, k bits can be examined simultaneously. Therefore, the multibit trie may be up to k times faster than the original binary trie. In practical applications, the multibit trie does not achieve this performance because the k-bit stride multibit trie requires additional memory consumption due to prefix expansion, thus resulting in more cache misses. Figure 4 presents a search for the 5-bit destination address 11011 in the 2-bit stride multibit trie in Fig. 2. Regarding the binary trie, the next hop C corresponding to LPM 11 is returned.

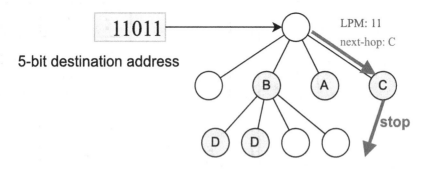

Fig. 4. Search steps for 5-bit destination address in 2-bit stride multibit trie.

3   Direct Lookup Table

Among IP lookup algorithms, trie-based algorithms tend to have lower memory requirements but require a longer search time for the LPM because internal nodes must be traversed to reach the leaf node, resulting in multiple expensive memory accesses. Previous studies [6,15,17] have used an additional array as a lookup table that can examine δ bits of the destination address in O(1) time to direct branching. In this strategy, instead of by traversing internal nodes in the trie, the corresponding next hop can be determined for most destination addresses by using this lookup table only; this can thus reduce the average number of memory accesses. Herein, this strategy is termed a direct lookup table.

The original concept of the direct lookup table was DIR-24-8 [17]; the strategy has two data structures: TBL24 (a direct lookup table) and TBLlong. TBL24 has 2^{24} elements, and each element has a size of 16 bits; one bit is used to determine whether the remaining 15 bits are the next hop or an index to TBLlong. To search in DIR-24-8, the most significant $\delta = 24$ bits of the destination address are first extracted as the index for TBL24, and the value of the element is evaluated. If the first bit of this value is 0, the remaining 15 bits are returned as the next hop; otherwise, the remaining 15 bits multiplied by 256 and then added to the remaining 8 bits of the destination address are used as the index for

TBLlong index. The value of the element in TBLlong is the next hop. Figure 5 presents the search process for a 32-bit destination address. For the incoming destination address (1.0.0.0), the search is directly indexed to 1.0.0 in TBL24, the first bit of which is 0; thus, the next hop A is returned. For the incoming destination address (1.0.1.1), the search is directly indexed to 1.0.1 in TBL24. In this case, the value of the first bit is 1; therefore, a lookup in TBLlong at the index 2×256+1 is performed, and the next hop C is returned.

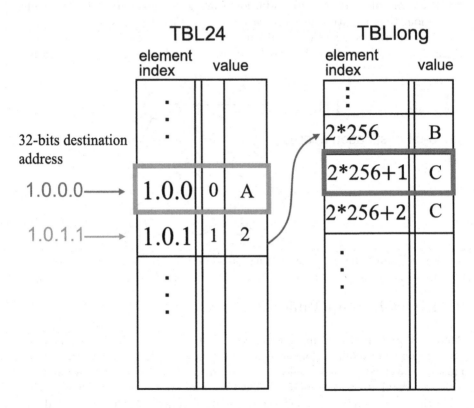

Fig. 5. Two searches with a 32-bit destination address in DIR-24-8 basic.

3.1   Level Pushing

A clear description of applying this concept to tries is presented in [16]. First, the trie corresponding to the router table is constructed. Second, nodes in level $< \delta$ are pushed to level δ, and the next hops stored by all nodes in level δ are stored in a direct lookup table with 2^{δ} elements. If the trie is searched for the next hop corresponding to an LPM before level $delta+1$, the direct lookup table is queried by extracting the most significant δ bits of the destination address as an index to obtain the result, reducing the number of memory accesses from the root to level δ. For example, Fig. 6(b) presents the binary trie corresponding

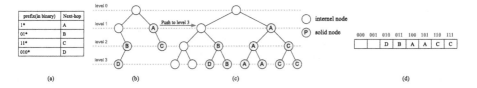

Fig. 6. (a) FIB table. (b) Corresponding Binary trie. (c) Push to level 3. (d) Corresponding direct lookup table for level 3.

to the forwarding information base (FIB) table in Fig. 6(a). To obtain a direct lookup table for $\delta = 3$, all nodes (both solid and internal) in levels 1 and 2 to are pushed to level 3. After level pushing, all node values in level 3 can be stored to the direct lookup array with 8 (2^3) elements from index 0 (000_2) to 7 (111_2). To look up the IP address 110*, the most significant $\delta = 3$ bits of the address are used to fetch index 6 ($= 110_2$), obtaining the next hop C.

3.2 Priority Table

To store a next hop with prefix length $\leq \delta$ in the direct lookup table, recursive level pushing from level 0 to level δ must be used. However, this process creates numerous unused internal nodes, thus wasting memory space. To avoid this situation, next hops can be directly stored in the direct lookup table by expanding prefixes, as described in [18]. For example, to store the prefix 1* in the direct lookup table in Fig. 6, the prefix 1* with length 1 must be expanded to a prefix with length 3; thus, the prefix 1* is left shifted by two bits, and all possible combinations of two bits ({00,01,10,11}) are added to it to obtain four corresponding prefixes: 100*, 101*, 110*, 111*. The corresponding next hop A is then stored in index 4 (100_2), 5 (101_2), 6 (110_2), and 7 (111_2). The process for prefix 01* is similar; however, when prefix 11* is stored in the direct lookup table, prefix 11* is expanded to obtain the corresponding indexes 6 (110_2) and 7 (111_2). The next hop C cannot be stored in these indexes directly because the the next hop A has already been stored in these indexes. The storage of the next hop A in index 6 (110_2) indicates that a corresponding prefix that may be 1*, 11*, or 110* exists. If the corresponding prefix length is ≤ 2, then the next hop A can be changed to C; otherwise, it cannot. Because information on only the next hop is stored in the direct lookup table, information on the original prefix length has been lost, and whether a next hop with an existing index should be stored cannot be determined. To store the corresponding prefix length for each index, a priority table for the direct lookup table can be included.

The priority table has the same number of elements as the direct lookup table. The initial value of the priority table is 0, and when a next hop is stored in an index (e.g., 6), the value in that index in the priority table is checked. If the prefix length is greater than or equal to the value in the priority table, the next hop can be stored to the direct lookup table, and the value in the priority table is changed to the prefix length. Otherwise, no change is made. Figure 7 presents the same level pushing steps as those in Fig. 6 but with a priority table. When the prefix 11* is expanded and collides with the prefixes 110* and 111*, the priority values can be checked. All are 1 (< 2); thus, the next hop is changed to C, and the priority value is changed to 2. The same steps are performed for the prefix 010*.

This storage method can be summarized into two cases as follows:

- Prefix length $l < \delta$: Expand the prefix length to δ and derive the prefix expansion set ($\{P_l \ll (\delta - l)$ to $(P_l + 1) \ll (\delta - l) - 1\}$). Use this set to assess the priority values in the corresponding index individually. If the priority value $\leq l$, store the indexed next hop in the direct lookup table and modify the priority value to l. Otherwise, take no action.
- Prefix length $l = \delta$: Store the next hop in the corresponding index in the direct lookup table. Modify the corresponding indexed priority value to δ in the priority table.

The level pushing algorithm for the priority table is presented in Algorithm 1.

Algorithm 1. LEVEL_PUSH(p, l, n, δ)

Input: Prefix p, length l, next-hop n, push to level δ
Output: Direct lookup table D
We initiate the direct lookup table D and priority table *priority* before performing this algorithm.

```
1 /* extend 0                                                       */
2 Start ← p ≪ (δ − l)
    /* extend 1                                                     */
3 End ← (p + 1) ≪ (δ − l) − 1
    /* Change the storage of the next hop depending on the priority
      value                                                         */
4 for i ← Start to End do
5    if l ≥ priority[i] then
6       D[i] ← n
        priority[i] ← l
```

---

4   C-index

When the direct lookup table is searched and the corresponding next hop is obtained, the next hop may not correspond to the LPM. It only corresponds to the LPM before the $\delta + 1$ level; thus, a trie search must still be performed to check whether longer prefixes exist after the level δ. If the absence of such matching prefixes in the trie can be ascertained, then the search can be avoided,

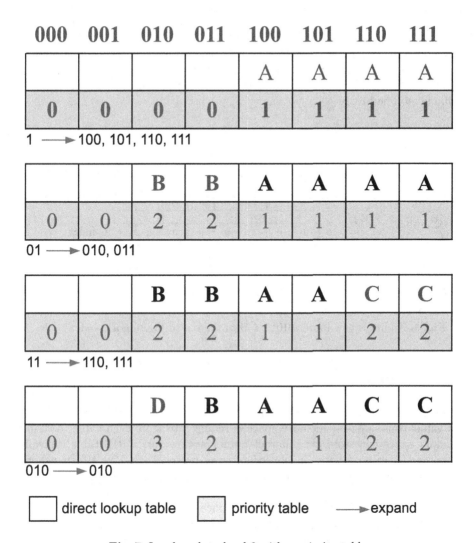

000	001	010	011	100	101	110	111
				A	A	A	A
0	0	0	0	1	1	1	1

1 ⟶ 100, 101, 110, 111

		B	B	A	A	A	A
0	0	2	2	1	1	1	1

01 ⟶ 010, 011

		B	B	A	A	C	C
0	0	2	2	1	1	2	2

11 ⟶ 110, 111

		D	B	A	A	C	C
0	0	3	2	1	1	2	2

010 ⟶ 010

☐ direct lookup table   ▨ priority table   ⟶ expand

Fig. 7. Level push to level 3 with a priority table.

thus saving the trie lookup time. A study [16] proposed an additional flag table that indicates whether longer prefixes exist after the δ level; this table is called the C-index. The C-index table has the same number of elements as the direct lookup table. If a string longer than δ exists, the most significant δ bits of this prefix are extracted as the index to the C-index table, and the corresponding value in the C-index table is set to 1. For an incoming destination address, the most significant δ bits are used as the index for searching the direct lookup table and the C-index table. If the indexed value is 0, the trie search is unnecessary, and the result derived for the direct lookup table is returned. Otherwise, the trie search is performed to determine whether a longer LPM exists.

Figure 8 presents an example of a search process for a prefix with length $> \delta$ in a C-index table. First, the C-index values are initialized to 0. When the new router 0101*/4 D in Fig. 6 is added, the router information is stored in the corresponding binary trie. Because the prefix length $4 > \delta = 3$, the most significant 3 bits 010 are extracted as the index to the C-index, and the indexed value is modified to 1.

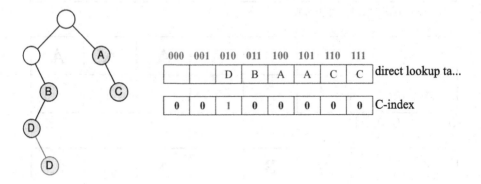

Fig. 8. Adding a new router 0101*/4 D to the trie in Fig. 6 in a C-index table.

5   Next-hop Table

The next-hop value in an IPv4 routing information base (RIB) table is a 32-bit value; thus, a 32-bit memory space is required to store each value. A 32-bit memory space can store 2^{32} different numbers; however, a RIB table typically stores far fewer next hops. In border gateway protocol (BGP) [19] snapshots, approximately 2^{10} different next hops are typically stored. Therefore, a next-hop table [6,15] with a 32-bit memory space for each element can be constructed to store the next hops, and a 10-bit memory space can be used to store the index of each element. The original RIB next-hop table of can be modified in accordance with this index to reduce the memory required to store the next hops.

For example, as indicated in Fig. 9, a 5-bit memory space is required to store each next hop in the original RIB table, and storing all seven routers requires 35 bits of memory. A next-hop table with four routers with 5-bit addresses requires 20 bits of memory space. The original RIB next-hop indexes are modified to the next-hop table indexes. Indexes 0 to 3 require only two bits of memory space; thus, storing all seven next-hop indexes requires only 14 bits of memory space. This strategy requires only 34 bits of total memory space, representing a 1-bit reduction.

We present an algorithm for next-hop table construction in Algorithm 2. The next hop n is used as the input. If n is not in the next-hop table, the next-hop table is resized, n is added to it, and the index is returned. Otherwise, the corresponding next-hop index is found and returned.

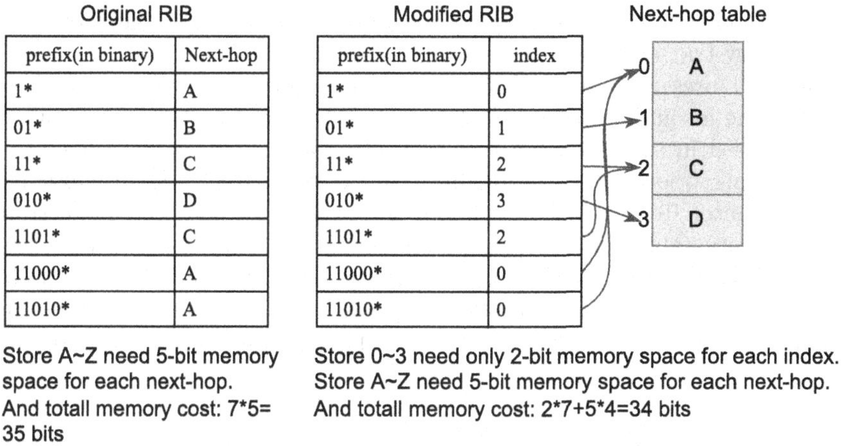

Original RIB			Modified RIB			Next-hop table
prefix(in binary)	Next-hop		prefix(in binary)	index		

Original RIB

prefix(in binary)	Next-hop
1*	A
01*	B
11*	C
010*	D
1101*	C
11000*	A
11010*	A

Modified RIB

prefix(in binary)	index
1*	0
01*	1
11*	2
010*	3
1101*	2
11000*	0
11010*	0

Next-hop table

0	A
1	B
2	C
3	D

Store A~Z need 5-bit memory space for each next-hop. And totall memory cost: 7*5= 35 bits

Store 0~3 need only 2-bit memory space for each index. Store A~Z need 5-bit memory space for each next-hop. And totall memory cost: 2*7+5*4=34 bits

Fig. 9. Reduction in memory consumption by using a next-hop table.

6 Synthetic Method

We also propose a synthetic binary trie method combining the aforementioned algorithms (direct lookup table, C-index, and next-hop table), and Fig. 10 presents its architecture. First, when an IP packet arrives, a next-hop table is used to convert the next hop to a next-hop index (Nidx). Second, the prefix length is detected, and if the length $l \le \delta$, then the corresponding Nidx is stored in the direct lookup table. Finally, the remaining prefixes with length $l > \delta$ that

---

Algorithm 2. NEXTHOP_TABLE (n)
Input: Next-hop n
Output: Corresponding next-hop index idx
We initialize the next-hop table with N elements and size $size$ of 0 before performing this algorithm.

```
1 /* Check all elements in the next-hop table and find the
      corresponding next-hop index.                              */
2 for i ← 0 to size − 1 do
3    if n = N[i] then
4       idx ← i
        return idx

5 /* If n is not in next-hop table, add n to the table, resize the
      table, and return the corresponding index.                 */
6 N[size] ← n
   idx ← size
   size ← size + 1
   return idx
```

are not included in the direct lookup table have their corresponding Nidx stored in the binary trie, and the corresponding C-index value is modified.

Figure 11 presents a method of inserting a router in the synthetic architecture. For the incoming router 1*/1 A, the next hop A is set to Nidx 0, and the Nidx is stored in the expansion indexes 2 (10_2) and 3 (11_2). The value of the corresponding priority table is modified to prefix length 1. For a subsequent incoming router 10*/2 B, the next hop B is set to Nidx 1 and the Nidx is stored in the priority table. This next hop collides with the index for A in index 2 (10_2) of the direct lookup table. In the priority table, the priority value is 1 < prefix length 2; therefore, the indexed value is changed to Nidx 1 in the direct lookup table, and the indexed value in the priority table is changed to prefix

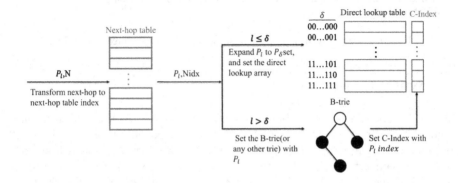

Fig. 10. Synthetic binary trie architecture.

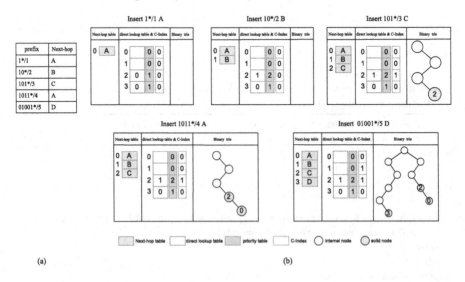

(a)   (b)

Fig. 11. (a) Router table. (b) Example of updating (inserting) routers in the synthetic architecture.

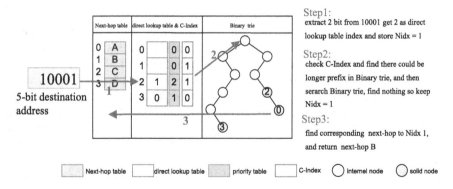

Fig. 12. Example of a lookup for a 5-bit destination address in the synthetic architecture.

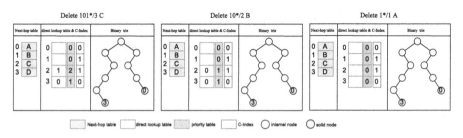

Fig. 13. Example of updating (deleting) a router in the synthetic architecture with $\delta = 2$.

length 2. For a third incoming router 101*/3 C, the next hop C is set to Nidx 2. Because the prefix length $3 > \delta = 2$, the Nidx is stored in the binary trie, and 2 bits of 101* are extracted. These bits indicate index 2 (10_2) of the direct lookup table, which already contains Nidx 1. Therefore, the indexed value in the C-index table is modified to 1. For a fourth incoming router 1011*/4 A, the next hop A is already set to Nidx 0. Because the prefix length $4 > \delta = 2$, Nidx 0 is also stored in the binary trie, and the first 2 bits of 1011* are extracted as index 2 (10_2) in the C-index, which is again set to 1. For a fifth incoming router 01001*/5 D, the next hop D is set to Nidx 3. Because the prefix length $5 > \delta = 2$, Nidx 3 is stored in the binary trie. Two bits of 01001* are extracted, indicating index 1 (01_2) in the C-index; the value in this index is set to 1.

Figure 12 presents a search for an incoming 5-bit destination address 10001. The first 2 bits of 10001 are extracted as 10; the value 2 (10_2) is used as the priority table index to obtain Nidx 1. However, the C-index value in this index is 1, indicating that another suitable Nidx corresponding to a longer matched prefix may exist in the binary trie. However, the binary trie search returns no matches. Finally, Nidx 1 is determined to be the LPM and is used to look up the next hop, which is B in the next-hop table.

Figure 13 presents the deletion of a router in the synthetic method. The deletion rules are similar to insert rules. If router 101*/3 C is to be deleted, the prefix length 3> δ = 2. Therefore, the stored information in the binary trie can be simply modified by changing the corresponding solid node to an internal node. However, the value of the C-index cannot be modified because another prefix may correspond to this index in the C-index. Second, if router 10*/2 B is to be deleted, the prefix length 2 ≤ δ. Thus, the priority table and C-index value should be modified to contain only 1*/1 A. However, the router information is not stored, and the previous information is overwritten after the insertion of 10*/2 B. Therefore, the delete operation in the direct lookup table requires storing all routers in the binary trie. By referencing the trie, we can change the indexed value to 0 in the direct lookup table and to 1 in the C-index. Third, deleting router 1*/1 A is similar to the deletion of 10*/2 B. The binary trie is referenced, the indexed value is changed to the initial value in the direct lookup table, and the C-index value is set to 0.

7   Parallel Data Processing Method

For any software LPM algorithm, the lookup time of an IP packet cannot be reduced to less than one cycle time. The lookup time is limited by the speed of the processor; that is, the lookup throughput of a processor has an upper bound. To overcome this limitation, multiple processors can be used to simultaneously process multiple incoming IP packets.

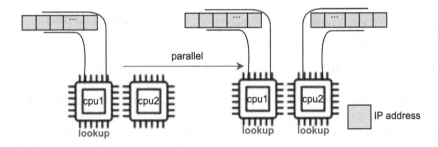

Fig. 14. Parallel LPM lookup with 2 CPU cores.

As illustrated in Fig. 14, only one processor initially performs LPM lookups for incoming IP packets. If two processors are used, the throughput can be duplicated if the execution time for each IP packet is constant. Increasing the number of processors should increase the theoretical throughput; however, memory resources still limit throughput in practice. If an excessive number of processors simultaneously run LPM lookup processes, a memory race condition is produced, which reduces throughput.

8   Experiment

We performed simulations using real data acquired from BGP router snapshots by using the C programming language on a computer with an AMD Ryzen 7

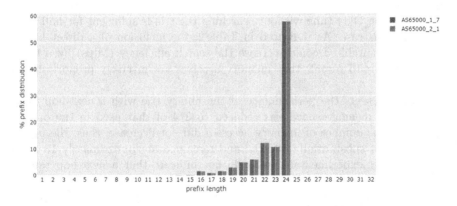

Fig. 15. IPv4 prefix length distribution.

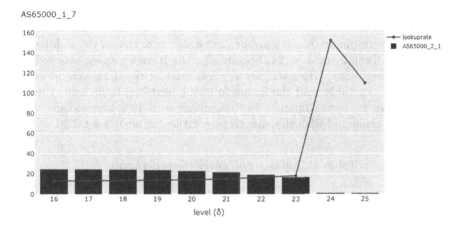

Fig. 16. Relationship between lookup rate and memory accesses on AS65000_1_7

4800H CPU with Radeon integrated graphics and 15.4 GB of memory. Two datasets were used, namely AS65000_1_7 and AS65000_2_1 with 855,997 and 876,489 active prefixes, respectively. Figure 15 presents the prefix length distribution for these two datasets.

We used five metrics to evaluate each algorithm: memory consumption, trie height, average lookup rate (Mlps), average memory accesses, and average update (insert/delete) time.

Table 1 presents the performance of the binary trie. Table 2 presents the performance of the binary trie with a direct lookup table and C-index. A comparison of the data in Tables 1 and 2 revealed that the inclusion of the direct lookup table could not reduce the trie height but could reduce memory access. According to Fig. 15, prefixes of length 24 constituted more than half of the router table. Therefore, a direct lookup table with $\delta = 24$ might minimize the average number of memory accesses and the maximum Mlps because querying the direct lookup table in O(1) time without searching the trie is sufficient for half of all lookups in this case. As indicated in Table 2, the inclusion of a direct lookup table with a suitable δ could increase the search efficiency (Mlps) by a factor of 11.83. Figure 16 reveals that memory accesses are inversely proportional to Mlps.

Table 3 presents the performance of the binary trie with a next-hop table. Although the memory space was reduced to 3/4 of that used in the original binary trie, the number of memory accesses did not decrease; thus, the performance was not substantially affected and remained at approximately 13 Mlps. However, these experimental results do not indicate that a next-hop table is useless; this table is simply not suitable for use with an original binary trie. Because the binary trie requires little memory, reducing memory usage with a next-hop table is not effective. However, the inclusion of a next-hop table is useful for alleviating memory consumption in the synthetic architecture because the direct lookup table substantially increases memory consumption.

Table 4 presents the lookup performance corresponding to the architecture in Fig. 10. The performance was determined to be similar to that of the architecture presented in Table 2 for $\delta < 24$. Specifically, the memory space was reduced by approximately 25%. However, for $\delta = 24$, most of the data were stored in the direct lookup table, and the inclusion of the next-hop table helped reduce memory usage by approximately 50%, resulting in a 10% increase in overall performance compared with the architecture without a next-hop table.

Table 1. Evaluation of binary trie performance

AS65000_1_7					AS65000_2_1				
Memory consumption [MiB]	Trie height	Avg. Mlps	Avg. memory accesses	Avg. update time (s)	Memory consumption [MiB]	Trie height	Avg. Mlps	Avg. memory accesses	Avg. update time (s)
26.84	29	12.67	24.96	0.353	26.84	29	13.03	24.97	0.362

Table 2. Evaluation of binary trie performance with direct lookup and C-index tables for different δ values

δ	AS65000_1_7					AS65000_2_1				
	Memory consumption [MiB]	Trie height	Avg. Mlps	Avg. memory accesses	Avg. update time (s)	Memory consumption [MiB]	Trie height	Avg. Mlps	Avg. memory accesses	Avg. update time (s)
16	30.64	29	12.47	24.76	0.182	31.32	29	13.32	24.77	0.182
17	31.04	29	12.81	24.63	0.183	31.72	29	13.37	24.64	0.186
18	31.86	29	12.78	24.38	0.181	32.54	29	13.24	24.40	0.184
19	33.54	29	13.31	23.93	0.178	34.22	29	12.80	23.95	0.181
20	36.89	29	14.38	23.02	0.223	37.54	29	13.56	23.05	0.179
21	44.16	29	15.08	21.78	0.183	44.79	29	15.08	21.81	0.180
22	58.62	29	16.50	19.32	0.179	89.18	29	17.06	19.33	0.179
23	89.82	29	18.22	16.85	0.196	90.32	29	17.33	16.85	0.205
24	134.31	29	150.52	1.04	0.142	134.32	29	181.58	1.04	0.180
25	268.43	29	143.76	1	0.237	268.43	29	143.21	1	0.257

Table 3. Performance of a binary trie with a next-hop table

AS65000_1_7					AS65000_2_1				
Memory consumption [MiB]	Trie height	Avg. Mlps	Avg. memory accesses	Avg. update time (s)	Memory consumption [MiB]	Trie height	Avg. Mlps	Avg. memory accesses	Avg. update time (s)
20.13	29	12.70	24.96	0.353	20.13	29	13.05	24.97	0.362

Table 5 presents the lookup performance of the architecture displayed in Fig. 10 at $\delta = 24$ and n threads. As mentioned in Sect. 7, lookup throughput theoretically grows linearly with the number of processors. However, as listed in Table 5, increasing n from 1 to 2 increased the performance by a factor of only 1.8; doubling n to 4 increased the performance by a further factor of only 1.3. The improvement in theoretical throughput can be attributed to the memory race condition. However, parallel data processing is an effective option for increasing the throughput of an effective LPM algorithm. In our environment, parallel data processing achieved 501 Mlps on average at $n = 8$, reaching the standard speed of a wired connection.

Table 4. Performance of a binary trie with the synthetic method

δ	AS65000_1_7					AS65000_2_1				
	Memory consumption [MiB]	Trie height	Avg. Mlps	Avg. memory accesses	Avg. update time (s)	Memory consumption [MiB]	Trie height	Avg. Mlps	Avg. memory accesses	Avg. update time (s)
16	22.98	29	13.57	24.76	0.183	23.49	29	13.91	24.77	0.186
17	23.28	29	13.55	24.63	0.183	23.79	29	13.97	24.64	0.186
18	23.89	29	13.78	24.38	0.181	24.405	29	13.60	24.40	0.182
19	25.15	29	13.80	23.93	0.177	25.67	29	13.72	23.95	0.178
20	27.66	29	13.89	23.02	0.223	28.15	29	14.96	23.05	0.179
21	33.12	29	15.40	21.78	0.183	33.59	29	15.22	21.81	0.183
22	40.96	29	15.96	19.32	0.179	50.88	29	17.03	19.33	0.179
23	55.36	29	18.83	16.85	0.196	55.74	29	19.02	16.85	0.205
24	71.73	29	178.28	1.04	0.142	71.74	29	195.57	1.04	0.180
25	135.32	29	149.4	1	0.237	136.32	29	145.21	1	0.257

Table 5. Performance (Mlps) of a binary trie with level pushing to $\delta = 24$, a C-index, and a next-hop table with n threads (IPv4)

n	AS65000_1_7		AS65000_2_1	
	Avg.	Worst	Avg.	Worst
1	177.28	169.76	179.57	175.69
2	311.04	244.59	310.97	244.03
4	429.94	282.94	464.88	365.88
8	501.35	328.77	501.02	341.77
16	453.27	264.06	450.80	247.46

9   Conclusion

In this paper, we briefly introduce state-of-the-art lookup algorithms. We also conducted experiments to explore how they can increase the efficiency of IP lookup processes. State-of-the-art algorithms focus on reducing memory access and usage. The use of direct lookup tables can reduce memory accesses, which is the factor with the greatest effect on lookup performance. However, the effectiveness of this technology varies with the choice of δ. Because IPv4 router prefixes typically have a length of 24, we observed that setting $\delta = 24$ could produce a direct lookup table with the best performance; the average lookup rate exceeded 150 Mlps. In addition to trie memory accesses, reducing memory usage is critical. Our experimental results reveal that decreasing memory usage by half increased performance by 10%. Moreover, the average lookup rate exceeded 170 Mlps. These algorithms can be used to enhance the performance of binary trie methods, which initially could not achieve sufficient connection speeds. Furthermore, in addition to reducing the lookup time, parallel data processing can be used to increase the lookup throughput. In this study, the use of parallel data processing increased the average lookup rate to 450 Mlps, which is an excellent performance level.

References

1. Hayes, B.: Cloud computing. Commun. ACM **51**(7), 9–11 (2008). https://doi.org/10.1145/1364782.1364786
2. Fuller, T.V., Yu, J.L., Varadhan, K.: Classless inter-domain routing (CIDR): an address assignment and aggregation strategy, RFC 1519, Sept (1993)
3. Postel, J.: Internet protocol DARPA internet program protocol specification, RFC791, Sept. (1981)
4. Zheng, K., Hu, C., Lu, H., Liu, B.: A TCAM-based distributed parallel IP lookup scheme and performance analysis. IEEE/ACM Trans. Netw. **14**(4), 863–875 (2006)
5. Cui, C., Deng, H., Telekom, D., Michel, U., Damker, H.: Network functions virtualisation
6. Zec, M., Rizzo, L., Mikuc, M.: DXR: towards a billion routing lookups per second in software. ACM SIGCOMM Comput. Commun. Rev. **42**(5), 29–36 (2012)
7. Jain, R.: A comparison of hashing schemes for address lookup in computer networks. IEEE Trans. Commun. **40**(10), 1570–1573 (1992)
8. Dharmapurikar, S., Krishnamurthy, P., Taylor, D.E.: Longest prefix matching using bloom filters. In: Proceedings of the 2003 Conference on Applications, Technologies, Architectures, and Protocols for Computer Communications, pp. 201–212 (2003)
9. Fan, B., Andersen, D.G., Kaminsky, M., Mitzenmacher, M.D.: Cuckoo filter: practically better than bloom. In: Proceedings of the 10th ACM International on Conference on emerging Networking Experiments and Technologies, pp. 75–88 (2014)
10. Lim, H., Lee, N.: Survey and proposal on binary search algorithms for longest prefix match. IEEE Commun. Surv. Tutorials **14**(3), 681–697 (2011)
11. Lim, H., Yim, C., Swartzlander, E.E.: Priority tries for IP address lookup. IEEE Trans. Comput. **59**(6), 784–794 (2010)

12. Sahni, S., Kim, K.S.: Efficient construction of fixed-stride multibit tries for IP lookup. In: Proceedings Eighth IEEE Workshop on Future Trends of Distributed Computing Systems. FTDCS 2001, pp. 178–184 (2001)
13. Nilsson, S., Karlsson, G.: IP-address lookup using lC-tries. IEEE J. Selected Areas Commun. **17**(6), 1083–1092 (1999)
14. Sklower, K.: A tree-based packet routing table for Berkeley unix. USENIX Winter Citeseer **1991**, 93–99 (1991)
15. Asai, H., Ohara, Y.: Poptrie: a compressed trie with population count for fast and scalable software IP routing table lookup. ACM SIGCOMM Comput. Commun. Rev. **45**(4), 57–70 (2015)
16. Islam, M.I., Khan, J.I.: CP-TRIE: Cumulative popcount based trie for ipv6 routing table lookup in software and ASIC. In: Proceedings of the 2021 IEEE 22nd International Conference on High Performance Switching and Routing (HPSR), pp. 1–8. IEEE (2021)
17. Gupta, P., Lin, S., McKeown, N.: Routing lookups in hardware at memory access speeds. In: Proceedings of the IEEE INFOCOM 1998, the Conference on Computer Communications. Seventeenth Annual Joint Conference of the IEEE Computer and Communications Societies. Gateway to the 21st Century (Cat. No. 98, vol. 3, pp. 1240–1247. IEEE (1998)
18. Srinivasan, V., Varghese, G.: Fast address lookups using controlled prefix expansion. ACM Trans. Comput. Syst. **17**(1), 1–40 (1999). https://doi.org/10.1145/296502.296503
19. BGP. https://bgp.potaroo.net/

Social Networks and Learning

Equilibrium Strategies and Social Welfare in Cognitive Radio Networks with Imperfect Spectrum Sensing

Jinting Wang[1]($^{\boxtimes}$) (iD), Wei Wayne Li[2] (iD), and Zhongbin Wang[3] (iD)

[1] Department of Management Science, School of Management Science and Engineering, Central University of Finance and Economics, Beijing 100081, China
`jtwang@cufe.edu.cn`

[2] Department of Computer Science and the NSF Center for Research on Complex Networks, Texas Southern University, Houston, TX 77004, USA
`wei.li@tsu.edu`

[3] College of Management and Economics, Tianjin University, Tianjin 300072, China
`zhongbin_wang@tju.edu.cn`

Abstract. Spectrum sensing is essential in opportunistic cognitive radio (CR) systems for detecting primary users' (PUs') activities and protecting the PUs against harmful interference. By extending the perfect spectrum sensing in the literature to more realistic situations, a new random sensing error framework of secondary users (SUs) is proposed to study the SUs' behavior so as to make the best benefit for the CR system in this paper. A novel queueing-game theoretical model is formulated first and then various system stationary performance measures are procured. Furthermore, the SU's equilibrium joining strategies are obtained, the throughput of SUs is derived, and the CR system's social welfare's monotonous in terms of the sensing error and the SU's request frequency are characterized. Particularly, three interesting but counterintuitive results are observed as below: (i) the expected delay for joining SUs can be non-monotone in their effective arrival rate; (ii) multiple equilibrium joining strategies of SUs can always exist; and (iii) the spectrum sensing error does not necessarily worsen the CS system's social welfare, i.e., some sensing error in the system may possibly lead to more efficient outcomes in terms of throughput and social welfare. The results and observations offered in this paper are expected to extend spectrum sensing research in a more efficient way to better provide CR system services to various users.

Keywords: Cognitive radio · Queueing game · Sensing error · Equilibrium strategy · Social welfare

Supported in part by the National Natural Science Foundation of China (Grant Nos. 71871008,72001118), the US National Science Foundation (Grant No. 1827940) and the Emerging Interdisciplinary Project of CUFE (Grant No. 21XXJC010).

Z. J. Haas et al. (Eds.): WiCON 2022, LNICST 464, pp. 179–200, 2023.
https://doi.org/10.1007/978-3-031-27041-3_13

1 Introduction

Cognitive radio (CR) technology has been shown to be prevalent in utilizing the wireless spectrum resources [6] and [20]. In CR systems, SUs are allowed to use the unoccupied spectrum in an opportunistic way without affecting the primary user (PU), which can significantly improve the efficiency of networks. In principle, CR systems are mainly classified as two classes: underlay CR and opportunistic (or interweave) CR systems. The former does not require spectrum sensing to detect PUs' activities, they need coordination between PUs and SUs to obtain channel state information (CSI). While opportunistic CR systems do not require coordination between PUs and SUs to acquire CSI corresponding to SU-PU link, they necessitate spectrum sensing to monitor and detect PUs' activities.

In opportunistic CR systems, SUs decide to access the spectrum band if they sense the spectrum is idle or the system is not so congested to some extent. Otherwise, when the system is sensed to be congested, SUs may choose to balk upon arrival. That is, the spectrum sensing for SUs plays an important role in the CR networks. In most previous works investigating the spectrum sharing problem, the SUs are believed to be capable in distinguishing the exact state of spectrum and a perfect sensing assumption is made, in which no collision happens. Nevertheless, owing to the inherent feedback delays, estimation errors, quantization errors caused by the unreliable channel or signal interferences, there are inevitable sensing errors in practice, which lead to heavy interference to the PUs and negatively impact the performance of CR networks. It is for these indispensable reasons, there has been a great deal of related work in the research of CR system so far. We summarize several recent publications that are closely related to our research in this paper as follows:

Devarajan et al. [1] studied the strategic behaviour of users in an Internet of Things (IoT) system that is impeded by an unreliable server, and equilibrium joining probabilities for individual strategies and optimum joining probabilities for social welfare were obtained. Ni et al. [7] investigated a general situation wherein a datacenter can determine the cost of using resources and a Cloud service user can decide whether it will pay the price for the resource or not for an incoming task, and verified that the optimal policy for admitting tasks is a threshold policy. Toma et al. [11] provided a detailed analysis of a broad range of primary channel statistics under Imperfect Spectrum Sensing (ISS) and found a set of closed-form expressions for the calculated statistics under ISS as a function of the original primary channel statistics, probability of error, and the employed sensing period. Wang et al. [13] carried out an extensive analysis of the non-cooperative and cooperative joining behaviors of SUs in a CR system with a single PU band, which is the first time that the strategic behavior of SUs has been studied with a retrial phenomenon in the system from an economics point of view. Furthermore, Wang et al. [12] considered the SUs' joining behavior in cognitive radio network with a single bandwidth under imperfect spectrum sensing by using retrial queueing system formulation with server breakdowns. Wang et al. [14] conducted the game-theoretic analysis of the behavior of SUs in a cognitive radio system with a single primary user band and sensing failures, and the equilibrium behavior of SUs as well as the socially optimal strategies of SUs were obtained. Wang et al. [16] investigated joining strategies and admission control policy for SUs with retrial behavior in a CR system where a single PU coexists with multiple SUs. Wang et al. [15] discussed the decentralized and centralized behavior of SUs with retrial phenomenon under two situations in which SUs have no information or partially observable information. Wang et al. [18] investigated a CR system with two classes of service requests (PU and SU requests). Equilibrium probability strategies of PUs and SUs in no queue length information, and equilibrium Nash balance thresholds for PUs and SUs in partial queue length information and full queue length information cases are obtained, respectively. Yazdani et al. [19] considered an opportunistic cognitive radio system in which secondary transmitter is equipped with a reconfigurable antenna (RA), and established a lower bound on the achievable rates of opportunistic cognitive radio systems using RAs With imperfect sensing and channel estimation. Zhang et al. [21] investigated the price-based spectrum access control policy that characterizes the network operator's provision to heterogeneous and delay-sensitive SUs through pricing strategies. Under different information levels, Zhu et al. [23] investigated the equilibrium strategic behaviors of PU and SUs and attained the optimal service rates of PU under different information structures from the perspective of the service provider. Zhu et al. [22] employed a two-server preemptive priority queue to study CR systems with multiple spectrums, and they obtained a joint optimal pricing strategy to maximize profit for the service provider as well as an optimal pricing strategy to maximize social welfare from the social administrator's viewpoint. For more details on the topic, we refer to the survey paper by Palunčíć et al. [8] and the references therein.

To characterize the underlying data transmission mechanism of CR systems, various queueing models have been established extensively which are beneficial for analyzing the CR systems. In particular, queueing models are recently applied to study the performance of CR systems with interruptions when the system congestion is considered, see [4,5]. In the single spectrum setting, the effect of PU on SUs was investigated in [2], in which SUs make a decision based on the average delay measurement that takes into account the presence of PU. In that work, the visiting of PU is regarded as a kind of breakdown, which stops the processing service of SUs. The interrupted SU can continue her service at the leaving of PU till her service is completed, and the quality-of-service experienced by PU will not be affected by SUs. However, in practice, the channels are not perfectly reliable due to the hardware or environmental issues. As a result, the imperfect sensing can exist, and the PU will inevitably be affected by the speculating SUs because of the unreliability of channels. That is to say, it is necessary to consider the sensing failures in the derivation of system performance.

In general, in CR systems there exist two kinds of spectrum sensing errors (misdetections) for arriving SUs, see [9,10]. The first spectrum sensing error, called Class-A misdetection, may occur to both PU and SU during transmission (i.e., during service) when an arriving SU senses the PU band incorrectly and miss-senses that the PU band is idle. When it happens, a collision is resulted in, and both the arriving SU and job (PU/SU) in service will be deleted. The second spectrum sensing error, called Class-B error or disruption, is a type of disruption events to a PU and may occur when an ongoing SU transmits through the PU band and it incorrectly detects the presence of an arriving PU and assesses there is no PU accessing to the PU band. Wang et al. [14] conducted the game-theoretic analysis of the behavior of SUs in a cognitive radio system with class-B misdetection. They formulated the problem as a retrial queueing system for characterizing SUs' retrying transmission due to the interruptions by PUs and the spectrum sensing failure. The equilibrium and socially optimal strategies for all SUs were derived. An appropriate admission fee on SUs who decide to join the system was imposed to eliminate the gap between equilibrium strategy and socially optimal strategy. Nevertheless, the class-A misdetection is often ignored in the literature because it has the following difficulties in tractability: (1) the throughput of SUs does not equal to its effective arrival rate in steady state due to the loss of jobs; and (2) the SUs who decide to join the system does not necessarily obtain the service reward eventually, that is, the received service reward of SUs is random. In this paper, we focus on the class-A misdetection, and investigate its impact on the CR system.

To our best knowledge, it is the first work to study the strategic behavior of SUs in CR systems with class-A misdetection. Comparing to the existing related works in CR networks, our major contributions are as follows. First, we consider the negative effect of SUs on both SUs and PU. In particular, when the collision probability is 0, our model degenerates to that in [2]. In comparison, Do et al. [2] studied a similar problem for queueing control by formulating it as an M/M/1 queueing-game with server breakdowns where each customer wants to optimize their benefit in a selfish distributed manner. To improve the service efficiency, an admission fee was proposed to correct the gap between individually optimal strategy and socially optimal strategy. However, it is evident that the issue of imperfect sensing has not been considered in Do et al. [2]. Second, we investigate the equilibrium joining strategy as well as the expected utility of SUs under different levels of sensing errors. Last but not least, we find that, interestingly, the system throughput and overall social welfare is not monotonically decreasing in the sensing error probability. That is to say, a higher sensing error does not necessarily worsen the system throughput and social welfare. And the social welfare can be maximized at a certain level of sensing error.

To summarize, the contribution of our study to the literature is three-fold and described as follows:

- A new random spectrum sensing error framework of secondary users (SUs) is proposed to study the SUs' behavior so as to make the best benefit for the CR system and by overcoming the perfect spectrum sensing in the literature. A novel queueing-game theoretical model is formulated and various system stationary performance measures are derived
- The equilibrium strategy of SUs under the unobservable situation by considering imperfect sensing is firstly identified and then obtained. Obviously, such

an imperfect sensing formulation is not only more realistic to real-world practices, but also increases the complexity of the research problem. For games without sensing error, it is well-known that avoid-the-crowd (ATC) typically leads to a unique symmetric equilibrium, while follow-the-crowd (FTC) (see [3] for the definitions of ATC and FTC) leads to multiple equilibria. However, in our setting, we firstly observed that both ATC and FTC behavior can exist, which depends on the level of sensing error and leads to multiple equilibria.

– The system throughput and social welfare are first verified to be non-monotone in the level of sensing error, respectively. These results further surprisingly disclose that some amount of sensing error (but not all) in the system can lead to more efficient outcomes in terms of throughput and social welfare.

The reminder of paper is organized as follows. Section 2 introduces the problem formulation considered in this paper. The system performance analysis is provided in Sect. 3. The equilibrium joining strategies of SUs are derived in Sect. 4. Section 5 is devoted to the SUs throughput analysis. In Sect. 6, the system's social welfare characteristics are investigated and the performance evaluations are illustrated accordingly. The conclusion and future works are provided in Sect. 7.

2   Problem Formulation

We focus on a cognitive radio system with a single PU band that opportunistically used by SUs, which means that the PU band can transmit either one PU packet or one SU packet at one time. This PU band can be regarded as a server. As PU packets have a preemptive priority over the SUs, an arriving PU packet can get the service immediately even if the service area is occupied by an SU job. The server resumes to be shared by SUs until the PU completes transmissions.

We construct this service system as a classic $M/M/1$ queue, in which potential arrival rate of SUs is Λ_s, and the corresponding service rate is μ_s. The service of an SU packet can be interrupted at the arrival of a primary user. A PU packet will access the system only when the PU band is not occupied by another PU packet. The arrival rate of primary user is λ_p, and its service time is exponentially distributed with rate μ_p. The probability of sensing error for SUs is denoted by $\epsilon \in [0, 1]$. Specifically, if the spectrum is occupied, but the arriving SUs sense (*mistakenly*) that the channel is idle, she will try to access to the spectrum, then a collision happens, and the two jobs will be cleared. On the other hand, as mentioned in the previous section, the SUs can also mistakenly sense an idle channel to be a busy one. This kind of sensing error is referred to as a false alarm and we do not consider it in this paper.

The SUs are strategic in the sense that every arriving SU who wants to get service at the CR base station has the right to decide whether to join the system or not. In this work we consider the unobservable case that SUs do not know the system information. That is, an arriving SU has no knowledge of whether

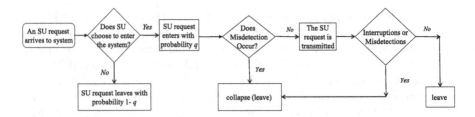

Fig. 1. Strategic behavior of SUs with imperfect sensing in a CR system

the PU band is available or not and the total number of SUs in the system. To characterize the economic structure of the decision process, we assume that at the completion of service, SUs and PU can receive a service reward R_s and R_p, respectively. During the sojourn time in system, including waiting time in queue and service time by the PU band, the SUs will suffer a waiting cost c per time unit. Note that the collision can only be caused by an arriving SU. And the primary user will definitely preempt the SUs on service. We do not consider the waiting cost of PU because its expected waiting time is constant, which equals to its service time, thus it can be subtracted from R_p. It is irrevocable for SUs' decisions on joining or balking according to their assessment on the reward against the costs. For convenience, Table 1 lists some important notations used in this paper.

Methodologically we adopt a queueing-game approach (see [3]) to study the SUs' strategic behavior, which is characterized by $q \in [0, 1]$ that is the probability an SU decides to enter the system. Equivalently, with probability $1 - q$ the SU decides to leave the system. Therefore, the effective entering probability for SUs is $\lambda_s \equiv \Lambda_s q$. The model is presented in Fig. 1. Since all SUs have the right to take their own decisions, we model this system as a non-cooperative queueing-game problem and aim to derive the symmetric Nash equilibria. In the sequel, we will give some results about SUs' equilibrium behavior and socially optimal strategies in the unobservable situation under the impact of sensing failures.

3   System Performance Analysis

In this section, we derive the system performance (i.e., the expected delay and the stationary probability) under a fixed effective arrival rate of SUs. The major results are given in the Theorem 1 as below:

Theorem 1. *When the sensing error probability is $\epsilon \in [0, 1]$,*

- *the system is stable if and only if $\lambda_s < \bar{\lambda}(\epsilon)$, where*

$$\bar{\lambda}(\epsilon) = \begin{cases} \frac{\sqrt{\vartheta^2 + 4\mu_p\mu_s\epsilon(1-2\epsilon)} - \vartheta}{2\epsilon(1-2\epsilon)}, & if\ \epsilon < 1/2; \\ \infty, & if\ \epsilon \geq 1/2, \end{cases}$$

and $\vartheta = \lambda_p(1 - \epsilon) + \mu_p - \epsilon(2\mu_p + \mu_s)$.

Table 1. Important notations in this paper.

Notation	Meaning
R_p	Reward for each service of PU
R_s	Reward for each service of SU
c	Waiting cost per time unit of SUs
Λ_s	Potential arrival rate for SUs
λ_s	Effective arrival rate for SUs
λ_p	Arrival rate for PU's packets
μ_s	Transmission rate for SUs
μ_p	Transmission rate for PUs
ϵ	The probability of misdetection
q	The probability an SU decides to join
$U(\lambda_s; \epsilon)$	Expected utility of a joining SUs with λ_s and ϵ

- The stationary probability that the system is occupied by PU or not is given by

$$\Pi_0 = \frac{\beta}{\lambda_p + \beta} \quad and \quad \Pi_1 = \frac{\lambda_p}{\lambda_p + \beta}. \tag{1}$$

- The expected number of SUs in system is

$$N_s = \frac{\lambda_s \xi((\lambda_p + \beta)^2 - \lambda_p[(\lambda_p + \beta)\epsilon - (1 - \epsilon)(\xi + \lambda_s\epsilon)])}{(\lambda_p + \beta)(\xi + \lambda_s\epsilon)(\beta\xi - (\lambda_p + \beta)\lambda_s(1 - \epsilon))}. \tag{2}$$

- The expected waiting time for each joining SU is

$$\bar{w}_s = \frac{\xi((\lambda_p + \beta)^2 - \lambda_p[(\lambda_p + \beta)\epsilon - (1 - \epsilon)(\xi + \lambda_s\epsilon)])}{(\lambda_p + \beta)(\xi + \lambda_s\epsilon)[\beta\xi - (\lambda_p + \beta)\lambda_s(1 - \epsilon)]}. \tag{3}$$

Proof. We define $I(t)$ and $N(t)$ as the spectrum state and the number of SUs in the system, respectively, where $I(t) = 0, 1$ corresponds to that the service area is occupied by $I(t)$ primary users. Thus $\{(I(t), N(t)), t \geq 0\}$ forms a two-dimensional Markov chain. The transition diagram is illustrated in Fig. 1, where $\xi = \mu_s + \epsilon\lambda_s$, $\beta = \mu_p + \epsilon\lambda_s$ (Fig. 2).

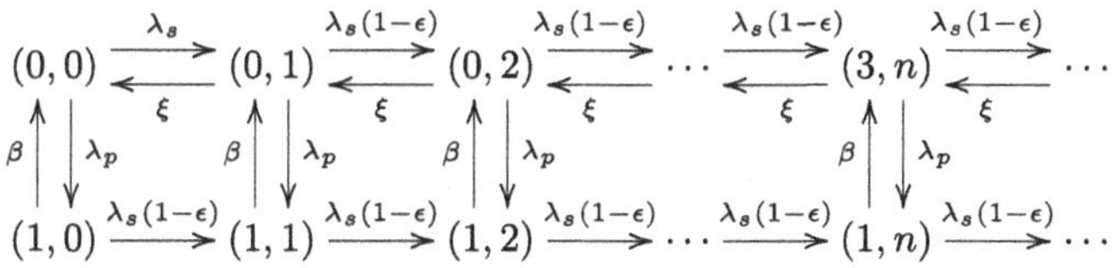

Fig. 2. Transition rate diagram.

Denote by $\pi_{i,j}$ the stationary probability at state (i,j), then we can have the following transition equations.

$$\pi_{0,0}(\lambda_p + \lambda_s) = \pi_{1,0}\beta + \pi_{0,1}\xi, \tag{4}$$

$$\pi_{0,1}(\lambda_p + \lambda_s + \mu_s) = \pi_{1,1}\beta + \pi_{0,0}\lambda_s + \pi_{0,2}\xi, \tag{5}$$

$$\pi_{0,i}(\lambda_p + \lambda_s + \mu_s) = \pi_{1,i}\beta + \pi_{0,i-1}\lambda_s(1-\epsilon) + \pi_{0,i+1}\xi, \tag{6}$$

$$\pi_{1,0}(\beta + \lambda_s(1-\epsilon)) = \pi_{0,0}\lambda_p, \tag{7}$$

$$\pi_{1,j}(\beta + \lambda_s(1-\epsilon)) = \pi_{1,j-1}\lambda_s(1-\epsilon) + \pi_{0,j}\lambda_p, \tag{8}$$

where $i \geq 2$ and $j \geq 1$. Define $\Pi_k(z) = \sum_{i=0}^{\infty} \pi_{k,i} z^i$ as the generating functions and $\Pi_k = \Pi_k(1)$ for $k = 0, 1$.

By combining (4)–(8), we can have the following equations:

$$\left[\lambda_p + (1-z)\left(\lambda_s - \frac{\mu_s}{z} - \frac{(1+z)\lambda_s \epsilon}{z} \right) \right] \Pi_0(z)$$

$$= \frac{z-1}{z}\pi_{0,0}[\xi + z\lambda_s\epsilon] + \beta\Pi_1(z), \tag{9}$$

$$[\beta + \lambda_s(1-\epsilon)(1-z)]\Pi_1(z) = \lambda_p\Pi_0(z). \tag{10}$$

By letting $z = 1$ in Eq. (10), we can get $\lambda_p\Pi_0 = \beta\Pi_1$. As $\Pi_0 + \Pi_1 = 1$, it gives the result (1). By taking the deviation of z on the both sides of (9) and (10), and letting $z = 1$, we have

$$\lambda_p\Pi_0' + [\xi - \lambda_s(1-\epsilon)]\Pi_0 = (\xi + \lambda_s\epsilon)\pi_{0,0} + \beta\Pi_1', \tag{11}$$

$$\beta\Pi_1' = \lambda_p\Pi_0' + \lambda_s(1-\epsilon)\Pi_1. \tag{12}$$

Combining (11)–(12), we can obtain that

$$\pi_{0,0} = \frac{\beta[\xi - \lambda_s(1-\epsilon)] - \lambda_s(1-\epsilon)\lambda_p}{(\lambda_p + \beta)(\xi + \lambda_s\epsilon)}.$$

Then the system can be stable if and only if $\pi_{0,0} > 0 \Leftrightarrow \lambda_s(1-\epsilon) < \frac{\beta\xi}{\lambda_p+\beta}$. By plugging the $\Pi_0(z)$ in (9) into (10), we have

$$\left(\left[\lambda_p + (1-z)\left(\lambda_s - \frac{\mu_s}{z} - \frac{(1+z)\lambda_s\epsilon}{z} \right) \right] (\beta + \lambda_s(1-\epsilon)(1-z)) - \lambda_p\beta \right) \Pi_1(z)$$

$$= \lambda_p \frac{z-1}{z} \cdot \frac{(\beta[\xi - \lambda_s(1-\epsilon)] - \lambda_s(1-\epsilon)\lambda_p)(\xi + z\lambda_s\epsilon)}{(\lambda_p + \beta)(\xi + \lambda_s\epsilon)}.$$

By eliminating $(1-z)$ on the both sides above, we can get

$$\left[\lambda_p\lambda_s(1-\epsilon) + \left(\lambda_s - \frac{\mu_s}{z} - \frac{(1+z)\lambda_s\epsilon}{z} \right) \times (\beta + \lambda_s(1-\epsilon)(1-z)) \right] \Pi_1(z)$$

$$= -\frac{\lambda_p}{z} \cdot \frac{(\beta[\xi - \lambda_s(1-\epsilon)] - \lambda_s(1-\epsilon)\lambda_p)(\xi + z\lambda_s\epsilon)}{(\lambda_p + \beta)(\xi + \lambda_s\epsilon)}. \tag{13}$$

By taking the deviation of (13) with respect to z, and letting $z = 1$, we can derive that

$$\Pi_1' = \frac{\lambda_p}{\lambda_p + \beta}\left[\frac{\beta\xi - (\lambda_s(1-\epsilon) - \xi)\lambda_s(1-\epsilon)}{\beta\xi - (\lambda_p + \beta)\lambda_s(1-\epsilon)} - \frac{\xi}{\xi + \lambda_s\epsilon}\right].$$

Combining (12) and (1), we can get

$$\Pi_0' = \frac{\beta}{\lambda_p + \beta}\left[\frac{\beta\xi - (\lambda_s(1-\epsilon) - \xi)\lambda_s(1-\epsilon)}{\beta\xi - (\lambda_p + \beta)\lambda_s(1-\epsilon)} - \frac{\xi}{\xi + \lambda_s\epsilon}\right] - \frac{\lambda_s(1-\epsilon)}{\lambda_p + \beta}.$$

Therefore, the expected number of SUs in system is

$$N_s = \Pi_0' + \Pi_1' = \frac{\lambda_s\xi((\lambda_p + \beta)^2 - \lambda_p[(\lambda_p + \beta)\epsilon - (1-\epsilon)(\xi + \lambda_s\epsilon)])}{(\lambda_p + \beta)(\xi + \lambda_s\epsilon)(\beta\xi - (\lambda_p + \beta)\lambda_s(1-\epsilon))}.$$

Notice that the actual joining rate of SUs is $\lambda_s(1 - \sum_{i=1}^{\infty}\epsilon\pi_{0,i} - \sum_{i=0}^{\infty}\epsilon\pi_{1,i})$, based on the Little's law, the expected sojourn time of a joining SUs who are not rejected (i.e., no collision happens upon arrival) is given by

$$w_s = \frac{N_s}{\lambda_s(1 - \sum_{i=1}^{\infty}\epsilon\pi_{0,i} - \sum_{i=0}^{\infty}\epsilon\pi_{1,i})}.$$

And the overall expected delay is

$$\bar{w}_s = (1 - \sum_{i=1}^{\infty}\epsilon\pi_{0,i} - \sum_{i=0}^{\infty}\epsilon\pi_{1,i})w_s + (\sum_{i=1}^{\infty}\epsilon\pi_{0,i} + \sum_{i=0}^{\infty}\epsilon\pi_{1,i}) \cdot 0$$

$$= \frac{N_s}{\lambda_s} = \frac{\xi((\lambda_p + \beta)^2 - \lambda_p[(\lambda_p + \beta)\epsilon - (1-\epsilon)(\xi + \lambda_s\epsilon)])}{(\lambda_p + \beta)(\xi + \lambda_s\epsilon)[\beta\xi - (\lambda_p + \beta)\lambda_s(1-\epsilon)]}.$$

Finally, notice that the stability condition

$$\lambda_s(1-\epsilon) < \frac{\beta\xi}{\lambda_p + \beta} \Leftrightarrow \lambda_s(1-\epsilon) < \frac{(\mu_p + \lambda_s\epsilon)(\mu_s + \lambda_s\epsilon)}{\lambda_p + \mu_p + \lambda_s\epsilon}.$$

If $\epsilon < 1/2$, then it holds if and only if

$$\lambda_s < \frac{\sqrt{(\lambda_p(1-\epsilon) + \mu_p - \epsilon(2\mu_p + \mu_s))^2 + 4\mu_p\mu_s\epsilon(1-2\epsilon)} + \lambda_p(\epsilon - 1) - \mu_p + (\mu_s + 2\mu_p)\epsilon}{2\epsilon(1-2\epsilon)}.$$

When $\epsilon \geq 1/2$, it is readily seen that the stability condition holds for any $\lambda_s > 0$. This completes the proof. ∎

Remark 1. It should be noted that by considering the error probability of imperfect spectrum sensing, the stability condition of the underlying system is quite different from the previous works such as Do et al. [2], in which the stability condition is $\lambda_s < \frac{\mu_p\mu_s}{\mu_p+\lambda_p}$ by our notations. We find that the system can be stable if $\lambda_s < \bar{\lambda}(\epsilon)$, when ϵ is relatively large, the system can be stable for any effective arrival rate of SUs because each arriving SU who finds an occupied PU band will be deleted due to the definite sensing error. In particular, when $\epsilon = 0$, our model can degenerate to the situation in [2] which considered the perfect spectrum sensing mechanism.

Theorem 2. *For any given λ_s, the overall expected delay of an SU request is decreasing in the service rate of SU request, i.e., $\bar{w}_s$ is decreasing in μ_s for any $\epsilon \in [0,1]$.*

Proof. To show that $\bar{w}_s$ is decreasing in μ_s, it is sufficient to prove that $\bar{w}_s$ is decreasing in $\xi = \mu_s + \epsilon\lambda_s$. Notice that $\bar{w}_s$ can be rewritten as

$$\bar{w}_s = \frac{((\lambda_p + \beta)(\lambda_p + \beta - \lambda_p\epsilon)/(\xi + \lambda_s\epsilon) - (1 - \epsilon)])}{(\lambda_p + \beta)[\beta - (\lambda_p + \beta)\lambda_s(1 - \epsilon)/\xi]},$$

which is obviously decreasing in ξ. Next, we will prove that $\bar{w}_s$ is decreasing in ϵ. Notice that $\bar{w}_s$ can be rewritten as $\bar{w}_s(\beta, \xi, \epsilon)$, where $\beta(\epsilon)$ and $\xi(\epsilon)$ are both increasing in ϵ. Then we use three steps to complete this proof.

(1) We need to show that $\partial\bar{w}_s(\beta, \xi, \epsilon)/\partial\beta < 0$. It is sufficient to show that

$$\frac{(\lambda_p + \beta)[\beta + \lambda_p(1 - \epsilon)]}{(\lambda_p + \beta)[\beta\xi - (\lambda_p + \beta)\lambda_s(1 - \epsilon)]} + \frac{\lambda_p(1 - \epsilon)(\xi + \lambda_s\epsilon)}{(\lambda_p + \beta)[\beta\xi - (\lambda_p + \beta)\lambda_s(1 - \epsilon)]}$$

is decreasing in β. The second term is obviously decreasing in β because $\xi > \lambda_s(1 - \epsilon)$. Then it suffices to prove that $\phi(\beta) = \frac{\beta + \lambda_p(1-\epsilon)}{\beta[\xi - \lambda_s(1-\epsilon)] - \lambda_s(1-\epsilon)\lambda_p}$ is decreasing in β. And it can be verified directly because

$$\frac{d\phi(\beta)}{d\beta} = \frac{\lambda_p(\epsilon - 1)(\epsilon\lambda_s + \xi)}{[\beta(\xi - (1 - \epsilon)\lambda_s) - \lambda_p(1 - \epsilon)\lambda_s]^2} < 0.$$

(2) We need to show that $\partial\bar{w}_s(\beta, \xi, \epsilon)/\partial\xi < 0$. As $\bar{w}_s$ can be rewritten as

$$\bar{w}_s = \frac{\frac{(\lambda_p+\beta)(\lambda_p+\beta-\lambda_p\epsilon)}{\xi+\lambda_s\epsilon} + \lambda_p(1 - \epsilon)}{(\lambda_p + \beta)[\beta - \frac{(\lambda_p+\beta)\lambda_s(1-\epsilon)}{\xi}]}. \tag{14}$$

Then it is not difficult to verify that $\frac{(\lambda_p+\beta)(\lambda_p+\beta-\lambda_p\epsilon)}{\xi+\lambda_s\epsilon}$ and $\beta - \frac{(\lambda_p+\beta)\lambda_s(1-\epsilon)}{\xi}$ are decreasing and increasing in ξ, respectively. Thus we can get that $\bar{w}_s$ is decreasing in ξ.

(3) We need to show that $\partial\bar{w}_s(\beta, \xi, \epsilon)/\partial\epsilon < 0$. By 14, we can verify that $\frac{(\lambda_p+\beta)(\lambda_p+\beta-\lambda_p\epsilon)}{\xi+\lambda_s\epsilon} + \lambda_p(1 - \epsilon)$ and $\beta - \frac{(\lambda_p+\beta)\lambda_s(1-\epsilon)}{\xi}$ are decreasing and increasing in ϵ, respectively. Thus we can get that $\partial\bar{w}_s(\beta, \xi, \epsilon)/\partial\epsilon < 0$. So far, we can establish the monotonicity of $\bar{w}_s$ because

$$\frac{d\bar{w}_s(\beta, \xi, \epsilon)}{d\epsilon} = \frac{\partial\bar{w}_s(\beta, \xi, \epsilon)}{\partial\beta} \cdot \frac{\partial\beta}{\partial\epsilon} + \frac{\partial\bar{w}_s(\beta, \xi, \epsilon)}{\partial\xi} \cdot \frac{\partial\xi}{\partial\epsilon} + \frac{\partial\bar{w}_s(\beta, \xi, \epsilon)}{\partial\epsilon} < 0$$

by combining the three results derived above, which completes this proof. ■

Remark 2. Theorem 2 shows that the expected waiting time is decreasing in the error probability. It is intuitive because when ϵ increases, more SUs are blocked or squeezed by the collisions. Thus the system congestion is reduced, which results in a lower expected waiting time. Similarly, the expected waiting time is decreasing in the service rate of SUs because a shorter service time is needed.

4   Equilibrium Strategy

In this section, we will investigate the equilibrium strategy of SUs. First of all, we tend to determine the monotonicity of $\bar{w}_s$ in the effective arrival rate λ_s. Different from the results derived before, counter to our intuition, the expected delay of SUs is not always increasing in λ_s. Let denote by

$$
\begin{aligned}
A = {} & (\lambda_p + \mu_p + \epsilon\lambda_s)(2\epsilon\lambda_s + \mu_s)(\lambda_p(\epsilon - 1)\lambda_s + (\mu_p + \epsilon\lambda_s)((2\epsilon - 1)\lambda_s + \mu_s)) \times \\
& [(\epsilon\lambda_s + \mu_s)(2\lambda_s(\lambda_p + \mu_p + \epsilon\lambda_s) - \lambda_p(\lambda_p + \mu_p - 2\lambda_s + 6\epsilon\lambda_s + \mu_s)) \\
& + \lambda_s\left((\lambda_p + \mu_p + \epsilon\lambda_s)^2 - \lambda_p(\epsilon(\lambda_p + \mu_p + \epsilon\lambda_s) + (\epsilon - 1)(2\epsilon\lambda_s + \mu_s))\right)],
\end{aligned}
\tag{15}
$$

$$
\begin{aligned}
B = {} & \lambda_s(\epsilon\lambda_s + \mu_s)\left[(\lambda_p + \mu_p + \epsilon\lambda_s)^2 - \lambda_p(\epsilon(\lambda_p + \mu_p + \epsilon\lambda_s) + (\epsilon - 1)(2\epsilon\lambda_s + \mu_s))\right] \times \\
& [(\lambda_p + \mu_p + \epsilon\lambda_s)(2\epsilon\lambda_s + \mu_s)(\lambda_p + 2\mu_p - \lambda_s + 4\epsilon\lambda_s + \mu_s) \\
& + 2(\lambda_p + \mu_p + \epsilon\lambda_s)(\lambda_p(\epsilon - 1)\lambda_s + (\mu_p + \epsilon\lambda_s)((2\epsilon - 1)\lambda_s + \mu_s)) \\
& + (2\epsilon\lambda_s + \mu_s)(\lambda_p(\epsilon - 1)\lambda_s + (\mu_p + \epsilon\lambda_s)((2\epsilon - 1)\lambda_s + \mu_s))],
\end{aligned}
\tag{16}
$$

we will have the following result:

Theorem 3. *The monotonicity of overall expected delay of an SU request with regards to the service rate of the SUs are characterized through following three situations:*

- *When $\epsilon \in (0, 1)$, the overall expected delay of an SU request is decreasing in the service rate of SU request, i.e., $\bar{w}_s$ is increasing in λ_s if and only if $A > B$, where A and B are given in the following Eq. (15)–(16).*
- *In case if $\epsilon = 0$, $\bar{w}_s$ is increasing in λ_s;*
- *In case if $\epsilon = 1$, $\bar{w}_s$ is decreasing in λ_s.*

Proof. For any $\epsilon \in [0, 1]$, by taking the deviation of $\bar{w}_s$ with respect to λ_s, one can check that $d\bar{w}_s/d\lambda_s > 0 \Leftrightarrow A > B$, where A and B are given in (15)–(16), respectively. If $\epsilon = 0$, we have that $\bar{w}_s = \frac{(\lambda_p + \mu_p)^2 + \lambda_p\mu_s}{(\lambda_p + \mu_p)[\mu_p\mu_s - (\lambda_p + \mu_p)\lambda_s]}$, then

$$
\frac{\partial \bar{w}_s}{\partial \lambda_s} = \frac{(\lambda_p + \mu_p)[(\lambda_p + \mu_p)^2 + \lambda_p\mu_s]}{(\lambda_p + \mu_p)[\mu_p\mu_s - (\lambda_p + \mu_p)\lambda_s]^2} > 0,
$$

which implies that $\bar{w}_s$ is increasing in λ_s. If $\epsilon = 1$, we can get that $\bar{w}_s = \frac{1}{\mu_s + 2\lambda_s}$, which is obviously decreasing in λ_s. This completes our proof. ∎

When $\epsilon \in (0, 1)$, it is hard to obtain the exact monotonicity of $\bar{w}_s$. However, we can still investigate its property numerically. Figure 3 illustrates the $\bar{w}_s$ for different λ_s under three error probabilities (i.e., $\epsilon = 0.1$, $\epsilon = 0.45$ and $\epsilon = 0.8$). From Fig. 3, we can observe that if ϵ is small (large), $\bar{w}_s$ is increasing (decreasing) in λ_s, which is consistent with our Theorem 3. Otherwise, if ϵ drops into the intermediate interval, $\bar{w}_s$ decreases in λ_s firstly and then increases in λ_s. That is to say, the monotonicity of $\bar{w}_s$ in λ_s is quite sensitive to ϵ.

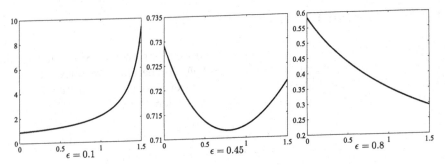

Fig. 3. The $\bar{w}_s$ vs. λ_s when $\mu_s = \mu_p = 2$ and $\lambda_p = 1$.

So far, we have derived the expected waiting times of the SUs, next, we aim to characterize the expected utilities of SUs. Define $U(\lambda_s; \epsilon)$ as the expected utility of a joining SUs when the effective arrival rate is λ_s and the error probability is ϵ. We also define the probability that the SUs who are already in system can be served successfully as P_s. Because such collision can happen only when the tagged user is in the service area, we have that

$$P_s = \frac{\mu_s}{\mu_s + \lambda_s + \lambda_p} \cdot 1 + \frac{\lambda_s(1-\epsilon)}{\mu_s + \lambda_s + \lambda_p} \cdot P_s$$
$$+ \frac{\lambda_p}{\mu_s + \lambda_s + \lambda_p} \cdot P_s + \frac{\lambda_s \epsilon}{\mu_s + \lambda_s + \lambda_p} \cdot 0,$$

which gives $P_s = \frac{\mu_s}{\xi}$. Then $U(\lambda_s; \epsilon)$ can be divided into three parts in (17).

Lemma 1. *The expected utility of a joining SU, i.e., $U(\lambda_s; \epsilon)$, is increasing in* μ_s.

Proof. Because $U(\lambda_s; \epsilon) = \frac{R_s \mu_s}{\xi}[1 - (1 - \pi_{0,0})\epsilon] - c\bar{w}_s$. It is not difficult to verify that $\mu_s/\xi = \mu_s/(\mu_s + \lambda_s \epsilon)$ and $\pi_{0,0}$ are both increasing in μ_s, then $\frac{R_s \mu_s}{\xi}[1 - (1 - \pi_{0,0})\epsilon]$ is increasing in μ_s. On the other hand, we have shown that $\bar{w}_s$ is decreasing in μ_s (see Theorem 2), thus $U(\lambda_s; \epsilon)$ is increasing in μ_s. ∎

To characterize the equilibrium joining strategy for SUs, we need to investigate the property of $U(\lambda_s; \epsilon)$. At the first sight, we can observe that the expected service reward is decreasing in λ_s because of the collisions become to be more frequently. But as we have shown that, the expected delay can be non-monotone in λ_s. Then the monotonicity of $U(\lambda_s; \epsilon)$ is equivocal. Denote by q_e the equilibrium joining probability of SUs. Next, we study the equilibrium strategy for SUs under two special cases to give some insights. Since it is very difficult to determine the monotonicity of $\bar{w}_s$ for the case $\epsilon \in (0,1)$ and thus it is still an open problem to get the equilibrium joining probability in general. However, we have figured out the following two equilibrium joining probabilities in a popular situations for the case when $\epsilon = 0$ or $\epsilon = 1$.

Theorem 4. *The two equilibrium joining probabilities for the case when $\epsilon = 0$ or $\epsilon = 1$ are:*

$$U(\lambda_s; \epsilon) = \quad \underbrace{0 \cdot [\sum_{i=1}^{\infty} \epsilon\pi_{0,i} + \sum_{i=0}^{\infty} \epsilon\pi_{1,i}]}_{collision\ happens\ upon\ arrival} \quad \underbrace{- cw_s \cdot [(1 - \sum_{i=1}^{\infty} \epsilon\pi_{0,i} - \sum_{i=0}^{\infty} \epsilon\pi_{1,i})](1 - P_s)}_{collision\ happens\ during\ service}$$

$$+ \underbrace{(R_s - cw_s) \cdot P_s[(1 - \sum_{i=1}^{\infty} \epsilon\pi_{0,i} - \sum_{i=0}^{\infty} \epsilon\pi_{1,i})]}_{collision\ never\ happens} \tag{17}$$

$$= R_s \cdot P_s[(1 - \sum_{i=1}^{\infty} \epsilon\pi_{0,i} - \sum_{i=0}^{\infty} \epsilon\pi_{1,i})] - c\bar{w}_s$$

$$= \frac{R_s\mu_s}{\xi}[1 - (1 - \pi_{0,0})\epsilon] - c\bar{w}_s$$

$$= \frac{[(\lambda_p + \beta)[\xi + 2\lambda_s\epsilon(1 - \epsilon)] - \lambda_p\xi\epsilon]\mu_s R_s}{(\lambda_p + \beta)(\xi + \lambda_s\epsilon)\xi}$$

$$- \frac{c\xi((\lambda_p + \beta)^2 - \lambda_p[(\lambda_p + \beta)\epsilon - (1 - \epsilon)(\xi + \lambda_s\epsilon)])}{(\lambda_p + \beta)(\xi + \lambda_s\epsilon)[\beta\xi - (\lambda_p + \beta)\lambda_s(1 - \epsilon)]}$$

$$= \frac{[(\lambda_p + \beta)[\xi + 2\lambda_s\epsilon(1 - \epsilon)] - \lambda_p\xi\epsilon]\mu_s}{(\lambda_p + \beta)(\xi + \lambda_s\epsilon)\xi}$$

$$\cdot \left(R_s - \frac{c\xi^2((\lambda_p + \beta)^2 - \lambda_p[(\lambda_p + \beta)\epsilon - (1 - \epsilon)(\xi + \lambda_s\epsilon)])}{\mu_s((\lambda_p + \beta)[\xi + 2\lambda_s\epsilon(1 - \epsilon)] - \lambda_p\xi\epsilon)[\beta\xi - (\lambda_p + \beta)\lambda_s(1 - \epsilon)]}\right).$$

– When $\epsilon = 0$, the equilibrium strategy is given by

$$q_e = \begin{cases} 1, & if\ \Lambda_s < \frac{\beta\mu_s}{\lambda_p + \beta}\ and\ U(\Lambda_s; 0) > 0; \\ 0, & if\ U(0; 0) \le 0; \\ \frac{\left(\mu_p\mu_s - \frac{c[(\lambda_p + \mu_p)^2 + \lambda_p\mu_s]}{R_s(\lambda_p + \mu_p)}\right)}{\Lambda_s(\lambda_p + \mu_p)}, & otherwise. \end{cases}$$

– When $\epsilon = 1$, the equilibrium strategy is given by

$$q_e = \begin{cases} 1, & if\ U(0; 1) \ge 0; \\ \frac{(\lambda_p + \mu_p)c - \mu_p R_s\mu_s}{\mu_p R_s\mu_s - c}, & if\ U(\Lambda_s; 1) \ge 0 > U(0; 1); \\ 0, & if\ U(\Lambda_s; 1) < 0, \end{cases}$$

Proof. (1) When $\epsilon = 0$, we have that $U(\lambda_s; 0) = R_s - c\frac{(\lambda_p + \mu_p)^2 + \lambda_p\mu_s}{(\lambda_p + \mu_p)[\mu_p\mu_s - (\lambda_p + \mu_p)\lambda_s]}$, which is decreasing in λ_s because $\frac{(\lambda_p + \mu_p)^2 + \lambda_p\mu_s}{(\lambda_p + \mu_p)[\mu_p\mu_s - (\lambda_p + \mu_p)\lambda_s]}$ is increasing in λ_s (see Theorem 3). Therefore, when all other SUs adopt joining strategy $q = \lambda_s/\Lambda_s$, the best response for the tagged one is

$$q_{\lambda_s} = \underset{\hat{q} \in [0,1]}{\arg\max}\ \hat{q} \cdot U(\lambda_s; 0).$$

• When $\Lambda_s < \frac{\beta\mu_s}{\lambda_p + \beta}$, we consider the following three cases:

If $U(0;0) < 0$, then $q_{\lambda_s} = 0$ for all $\lambda_s \in [0, \Lambda_s]$. Similarly, if $U(\lambda_s;0) \geq 0$, then $q_{\lambda_s} = 1$. Otherwise, if $U(0;0) \geq 0 > U(\Lambda_s;0)$, there exists unique λ_s' such that $U(\lambda_s;0) \geq 0$ and $U(\lambda_s;0) < 0$ for $\lambda_s \in [0, \lambda_s']$ and $\lambda_s \in (\lambda_s', \Lambda_s]$, respectively. Then we have $q_{\lambda_s} = 1$ and $q_{\lambda_s} = 0$ for $\lambda_s \in [0, \lambda_s']$ and $\lambda_s \in (\lambda_s', \Lambda_s]$, accordingly. In summary, we have that q_{λ_s} is weakly decreasing in $\lambda_s \in [0, \Lambda_s]$, which characterizes an ATC type behavior. And the equilibrium strategy is

$$q_e = \begin{cases} 1, & \text{if } U(\Lambda_s;0) > 0; \\ \dfrac{\mu_p\mu_s - \frac{c[(\lambda_p+\mu_p)^2+\lambda_p\mu_s]}{R_s(\lambda_p+\mu_p)}}{\Lambda_s(\lambda_p+\mu_p)}, & \text{if } U(\Lambda_s;0) \leq 0 < U(0;0); \\ 0, & \text{if } U(0;0) \leq 0. \end{cases}$$

- When $\Lambda_s \geq \frac{\beta\mu_s}{\lambda_p+\beta}$, from the same argument, we have

$$q_e = \begin{cases} \dfrac{1}{\Lambda_s(\lambda_p+\mu_p)} \cdot \left(\mu_p\mu_s - \dfrac{c[(\lambda_p+\mu_p)^2+\lambda_p\mu_s]}{R_s(\lambda_p+\mu_p)}\right), & \text{if } U(0;0) > 0; \\ 0, & \text{if } U(0;0) \leq 0. \end{cases}$$

And the same ATC type behavior can be justified.

(2) When $\epsilon = 1$, we can get that $U(\lambda_s;1) = \frac{1}{\mu_s+2\lambda_s}\left[\frac{(\mu_p+\lambda_s)\mu_s R_s}{(\lambda_p+\mu_p+\lambda_s)} - c\right]$. By taking the deviation of $(\mu_s + 2\lambda_s)U(\lambda_s;1)$ with respect to λ_s, we have

$$\frac{\partial(\mu_s + 2\lambda_s)U(\lambda_s;1)}{\partial\lambda_s} = \frac{\lambda_p\mu_s R_s}{(\lambda_s+\lambda_p+\mu_p)^2} > 0.$$

Therefore, if $U(0;1) \geq 0$, then $q_{\lambda_s} = 1$ for all $\lambda_s \in [0, \Lambda_s]$. If $U(\lambda_S;0) < 0$, then $q_{\lambda_s} = 0$ for all $\lambda_s \in [0, \Lambda_s]$. Otherwise, if $U(0;0) < 0 \leq U(\Lambda_s;0)$, there exists unique λ_s' such that $U(\lambda_s;0) < 0$ and $U(\lambda_s;0) \geq 0$ for $\lambda_s \in [0, \lambda_s']$ and $\lambda_s \in (\lambda_s', \Lambda_s]$, respectively.

Thus we have $q_{\lambda_s} = 0$ and $q_{\lambda_s} = 1$ for $\lambda_s \in [0, \lambda_s']$ and $\lambda_s \in (\lambda_s', \Lambda_s]$, accordingly. That is, q_{λ_s} is weakly increasing in $\lambda_s \in [0, \Lambda_s]$, which characterizes an FTC type behavior. And the equilibrium joining strategy is given by

$$q_e = \begin{cases} 1, & \text{if } U(0;1) \geq 0; \\ \dfrac{(\lambda_p+\mu_p)c-\mu_p R_s\mu_s}{\mu_p R_s\mu_s - c}, & \text{if } U(\Lambda_s;1) \geq 0 > U(0;1); \\ 0, & \text{if } U(\Lambda_s;1) < 0, \end{cases}$$

which completes this proof. ∎

Remark 3. Theorem 4 discloses that customers present different behaviors at two extreme cases $\epsilon = 0$ and $\epsilon = 1$. In particular, when ϵ is small, the expected utility of SUs is decreasing in ϵ, then SUs are more hesitate to join the system when others do. Thus an ATC type behavior can be observed. However, when ϵ is large, the decreased amount of delay is higher than that of reduced service value. Thus, the SUs are more inclined to join when others do, which presents an FTC type behavior, and multiple equilibria can exist. That is to say, both FTC and ATC joining behavior can exist in the system, which depends on the level of misdetection. More discussions on the ATC and FTC can be found in [3].

5   Throughput of the Secondary Users

In this part, we tend to investigate how the throughput of SUs (denote by T_s) changes with the sensing error level. Notice that when the sensing error is considered, the throughput of SUs is given by $T_s = \frac{\lambda_s[(\lambda_p+\beta)[\xi+2\lambda_s\epsilon(1-\epsilon)]-\lambda_p\xi\epsilon]\mu_s}{(\lambda_p+\beta)(\xi+\lambda_s\epsilon)\xi}$. Then we can have the following result.

Theorem 5. *The monotonic properties of the throughput of SUs regard to the reward for completing the service of a SU are characterized by the following results:*

- *If $\epsilon \in (0,1)$, the throughput of SUs is not monotonically increasing in the reward for completing the service of a SU, i.e., T_s is not monotonically increasing function of R_s;*
- *If $\epsilon = 0$, the throughput of SUs is increasing in the reward for completing the service of a SU, i.e., T_s is an increasing function of R_s;*
- *If $\epsilon = 1$, the throughput of SUs is decreasing in the reward for completing the service of a SU, i.e., T_s is an decreasing function of R_s;*

Proof. When $\epsilon = 0$, we have $T_s = \lambda_s$. By Theorem 4, the equilibrium λ_s is determined by $\max\{\lambda_s|U(\lambda_s;0) \geq 0\}$, which increases in R_s. Then T_s is increasing in R_s. On the other hand, when $\epsilon = 1$, $T_s = \frac{\lambda_s}{\mu_s+2\lambda_s}$. Because $U(\lambda_s;1) = \frac{1}{\mu_s+2\lambda_s}\left[\frac{(\mu_p+\lambda_s)\mu_s R_s}{(\lambda_p+\mu_p+\lambda_s)} - c\right]$, which implies that the equilibrium λ_s is decreasing in R_s. Then T_s is decreasing in R_s by noticing that T_s increases in λ_s, which completes this proof.   ∎

Remark 4. Theorem 5 discloses that, under the equilibrium strategy of SUs, the throughput of SUs is not necessarily increasing in their service reward. Specifically, when the error probability is large, the throughput T_s can be even decreasing in R_s. That is to say, when the service reward of SUs increases, a lower throughput can be resulted in, which is led by the decrease of equilibrium joining rate.

Denote by λ_s^e and T_s^e the effective arrival rate and throughput of SUs in equilibrium. Next, we compare the effective arrival rate λ_s and throughput T_s in equilibrium for different sensing error level in Fig. 4.

By Fig. 4, we can observe that the throughput is always lower than the effective arrival rate when $\epsilon > 0$ because of the possible collisions. In addition, the effective arrival rate is weakly increasing in the sensing error level. It is intuitive by recalling that the expected waiting time of SUs is decreasing in ϵ by Theorem 2. Interestingly, the throughput is non-monotone in the sensing error level. To explain this phenomenon, we need to understand the essential characteristics when the sensing error is considered. On the positive side, increasing the sensing error level can help SUs crowd out the PU in service, which cut down their expected waiting time greatly, thus more SUs could be served. On the negative side, it should be noted that sensing error can also happen to the SUs themselves, which lowers the probability of SUs to complete this service. In particular, when

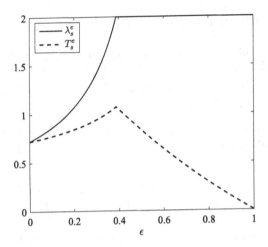

Fig. 4. The comparison of λ_s^e and throughput T_s^e for different ϵ when $R_s = \mu_s = \mu_p = \mu_p = 2$ and $\lambda_p = 1$

ϵ is small, the PU is less affected by the arriving SUs, thus increasing sensing error level can efficiently access the PU band by deleting the PU in service. By contrast, when ϵ is large, the expected service reward received by SUs decreases greatly, which outperforms the amount of reduced waiting time of them, thus the negative effect plays a dominant role, and a lower throughput is resulted in.

6   System Social Welfare

In this section, we investigate how the sensing error affects the social welfare. Recall that the benefit of SUs and PU generated per time unit is $\lambda_s U(\lambda_s; \epsilon)$ and $\Pi_1 R_p \mu_p = \frac{R_p \lambda_p \mu_p}{\lambda_p + \beta} = \frac{R_p \lambda_p \mu_p}{\lambda_p + \mu_s + \epsilon \lambda_s}$, respectively. Then the social welfare is $SW(\lambda_s; \epsilon) = \lambda_s U(\lambda_s; \epsilon) + \frac{R_p \lambda_p \mu_p}{\lambda_p + \mu_p + \epsilon \lambda_s}$. The following results provides the property of social welfare.

Theorem 6. *The system's social welfare is not monotonically decreasing in either the effective arrival rate for SUs or the spectrum error probability, i.e., the function $SW(\lambda_s; \epsilon)$ is not monotonically decreasing in either λ_s or ϵ.*

Proof. Notice that the expected utility of SUs is given by

$$U(\lambda_s; \epsilon) = \frac{[(\lambda_p + \beta)[\xi + 2\lambda_s \epsilon(1 - \epsilon)] - \lambda_p \xi \epsilon]\mu_s}{(\lambda_p + \beta)(\xi + \lambda_s \epsilon)\xi}.$$
$$\left(R_s - \frac{c\xi^2((\lambda_p + \beta)^2 - \lambda_p[(\lambda_p + \beta)\epsilon - (1 - \epsilon)(\xi + \lambda_s \epsilon)])}{\mu_s((\lambda_p + \beta)[\xi + 2\lambda_s \epsilon(1 - \epsilon)] - \lambda_p \xi \epsilon)[\beta \xi - (\lambda_p + \beta)\lambda_s(1 - \epsilon)]} \right).$$

Denote by $\bar{\lambda}_s$ the unique solution of

$$R_s - \frac{c\xi^2((\lambda_p + \beta)^2 - \lambda_p[(\lambda_p + \beta)\epsilon - (1 - \epsilon)(\xi + \lambda_s \epsilon)])}{\mu_s((\lambda_p + \beta)[\xi + 2\lambda_s \epsilon(1 - \epsilon)] - \lambda_p \xi \epsilon)[\beta \xi - (\lambda_p + \beta)\lambda_s(1 - \epsilon)]},$$

we have $U(\lambda_s; \epsilon) > 0$ for any $\lambda_s \in [0, \bar{\lambda}_s)$. Then it gives $SW(\bar{\lambda}_s; \epsilon) = \frac{R_p \lambda_p \mu_p}{\lambda_p + \mu_s + \lambda_s + \epsilon}$.
Also, we have $SW(0; \epsilon) = \frac{R_p \lambda_p \mu_p}{\lambda_p + \mu_s}$. It immediately follows that $SW(0; \epsilon) > SW(\bar{\lambda}_s; \epsilon)$. Thus $SW(\lambda_s; \epsilon)$ is not monotonically decreasing in λ_s.

On the other hand, when $\epsilon = 0$, we have that

$$SW(\lambda_s; 0) = \lambda_s \left[R_s - c \frac{(\lambda_p + \mu_p)^2 + \lambda_p \mu_s}{(\lambda_p + \mu_p)[\mu_p \mu_s - (\lambda_p + \mu_p)\lambda_s]} \right] + \frac{R_p \lambda_p \mu_p}{\lambda_p + \mu_p}.$$

When $\epsilon = 1$, we have that $SW(\lambda_s; 1) = \frac{\lambda_s}{\mu_s + 2\lambda_s} \left[\frac{(\mu_p + \lambda_s)\mu_s R_s}{(\lambda_p + \mu_p + \lambda_s)} - c \right] + \frac{R_p \lambda_p \mu_p}{\lambda_p + \mu_p + \lambda_s}$.
Notice that

$$SW(\lambda_s; 1) - SW(\lambda_s; 0) > 0$$

$$\Leftrightarrow R_p < \left(\frac{1}{\lambda_p} + \frac{1}{\mu_p} \right) (\lambda_p + \mu_p + \lambda_s) \cdot$$

$$\left(\frac{c((\lambda_p + \mu_p)^2 + \lambda_p \mu_s)}{(\lambda_p + \mu_p)(\mu_p \mu_s - \lambda_s(\lambda_p + \mu_p))} - \frac{(c + 2R_s \lambda_s)(\lambda_p + \mu_p + \lambda_s) + \lambda_p \mu R_s}{(\mu + 2\lambda_s)(\lambda_p + \mu_p + \lambda_s)} \right).$$

Thus, when R_p is small, a higher social welfare can be obtained when $\epsilon = 1$. That is, $SW(\lambda_s; \epsilon)$ is not monotonically decreasing in ϵ. ∎

Theorem 6 indicates that a higher congestion level of SUs and a higher level of sensing error do not necessarily worsen the social welfare. The first result in intuitive since the SUs is also a part of society, which can bring positive benefit to the system. Even though it puts a negative effect on the PU when sensing error happens, it could improve the social welfare by carefully controlling its arrival rate. In addition, the second result reveals that some amount of occurrence of sensing error can indeed induce a higher social welfare than that without sensing error. It is because that increasing the level of sensing error allows the SUs to crowd out the users in service, which reduce the system congestion and in turn, improves the total benefits of SUs. When R_p is small, the social welfare generated by PU is less sensitive to the sensing error, where the marginal loss of PU's benefit is lower than the marginal benefit of SUs, then a higher social welfare can be reached. The following corollary is a follow-up result of Theorem 6.

Corollary 1. When $\epsilon = 0$, $SW(\lambda_s; 0)$ is unimodal in λ_s. When $\epsilon = 1$, if $\mu_s \geq 2\lambda_p$, $SW(\lambda_s; 1)$ is unimodal in λ_s.

Proof. (i) When $\epsilon = 0$, then we have that

$$SW(\lambda_s; 0) = \lambda_s \left[R_s - c \frac{(\lambda_p + \mu_p)^2 + \lambda_p \mu_s}{(\lambda_p + \mu_p)[\mu_p \mu_s - (\lambda_p + \mu_p)\lambda_s]} \right] + \frac{R_p \lambda_p \mu_p}{\lambda_p + \mu_p}.$$

By taking the deviation of λ_s with respect to $SW(\lambda_s; 0)$, we can get

$$\frac{dSW(\lambda_s; 0)}{d\lambda_s} = R_s - c \frac{[(\lambda_p + \mu_p)^2 + \lambda_p \mu_s]\mu_p \mu_s}{(\lambda_p + \mu_p)[\mu_p \mu_s - (\lambda_p + \mu_p)\lambda_s]^2},$$

which is decreasing in λ_s. If $\frac{dSW(\lambda_s;0)}{d\lambda_s}\big|_{\lambda_s=0} = R_s - c\frac{(\lambda_p+\mu_p)^2+\lambda_p\mu_s}{(\lambda_p+\mu_p)\mu_p\mu_s} < 0$, $SW(\lambda_s;0)$ is decreasing in λ_s. Otherwise, $SW(\lambda_s;0)$ is increasing first and then decreasing in λ_s. In summary, $SW(\lambda_s;0)$ is unimodal in λ_s.

(ii) When $\epsilon = 1$, then we have that $SW(\lambda_s;1) = \frac{\lambda_s}{\mu_s+2\lambda_s}\left[\frac{(\mu_p+\lambda_s)\mu_s R_s}{(\lambda_p+\mu_p+\lambda_s)} - c\right] +$ $\frac{R_p\lambda_p\mu_p}{\lambda_p+\mu_p+\lambda_s}$. Let $x = \frac{\lambda_p}{\lambda_p+\mu_p+\lambda_s}$ and $f(x) = \frac{\lambda_s}{\mu_s+2\lambda_s} = \frac{x(\lambda_p+\mu_p)-\lambda_p}{x(2\lambda_p+2\mu_p-\mu_s)-2\lambda_p}$, where $x \in \left(0, \frac{\lambda_p}{\mu_p+\lambda_p}\right]$. Then $SW(\lambda_s;1)$ can be rewritten as $F(x) = f(x)[\mu_s R_s(1-x) - c] + \lambda_p R_p x$. It is not difficult to verify that

$$f'(x) = -\frac{\lambda_p\mu_s}{[x(2\lambda_p+2\mu_p-\mu_s)-2\lambda_p]^2} < 0,$$
$$f''(x) = \frac{2\lambda_p(2\lambda_p+2\mu_p-\mu_s)\mu_s}{[x(2\lambda_p+2\mu_p-\mu_s)-2\lambda_p]^3}.$$

If $\mu_s \geq 2(\lambda_p + \mu_p)$, we have $f''(x) > 0$, which implies that $F''(x) = f''(x)[\mu_s R_s(1-x) - c] - 2\mu_s R_s f'(x) > 0$ because $\frac{\mu_p\mu_s R_s}{\mu_p+\lambda_p} > c$. Otherwise, if $\mu_s < 2(\lambda_p + \mu_p)$, notice that

$$F''(x) > 0 \Leftrightarrow f''(x)[\mu_s R_s(1-x) - c] - 2\mu_s R_s f'(x) > 0$$
$$\Leftrightarrow (2\lambda_p + 2\mu_p - \mu_s)[\mu_s R_s(1-x) - c]$$
$$< -\mu_s R_s[x(2\lambda_p + 2\mu_p - \mu_s) - 2\lambda_p]$$
$$\Leftrightarrow (2\mu_p - \mu_s)\mu_s R_s < c(2\lambda_p + 2\mu_p - \mu_s).$$

If $2\mu_p \leq \mu_s < 2(\lambda_p + \mu_p)$, we still have $F''(x) > 0$. Therefore, for $\mu_s \geq 2\lambda_p$, $F'(x)$ is increasing in $x \in \left(0, \frac{\lambda_p}{\mu_p+\lambda_p}\right]$. In this case, if $F'(0) \geq 0$, then $F(x)$ is increasing in $x \in \left(0, \frac{\lambda_p}{\mu_p+\lambda_p}\right]$, i.e., $SW(\lambda_s;1)$ is decreasing in λ_s. If $F'(\frac{\lambda_p}{\mu_p+\lambda_p}) \leq 0$, i.e., $SW(\lambda_s;1)$ is increasing in λ_s. Otherwise, we can obtain that $SW(\lambda_s;1)$ is increasing first and then decreasing in λ_s.

In summary, $SW(\lambda_s;1)$ is unimodal in λ_s if $\mu_s \geq 2\lambda_p$. ∎

Corollary 1 presents the property of social welfare in λ_s under two special cases (i.e., $\epsilon = 0$ and $\epsilon = 1$), under which the unique social welfare maximizer $\hat{\lambda}_s$ can be derived.

Figure 5 illustrates how the social welfare changes with the effective arrival rate for different ϵ. We can observe that the social welfare shows a different trend when ϵ varies. In particular, when ϵ is small, the social welfare is unimodal in the arrival rate of SUs (i.e., λ_s). When ϵ is intermediate, it is increasing in λ_s. However, when ϵ is large, the social welfare becomes to be decreasing in λ_s. Denote by $\hat{\lambda}_s$ the effective arrival rate of SUs that maximizes the social welfare. Obviously, $\hat{\lambda}_s$ is non-monotone in ϵ by Fig. 5.

To have a better understanding for the impacts of ϵ on the social welfare, we examine the socially optimal effective arrival rate of SUs $\hat{\lambda}_s$ and the

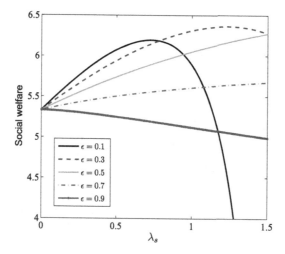

Fig. 5. The social welfare vs. λ_s for different ϵ when $R_s = 3$, $R_p = 8$, $\mu_s = \mu_p = 2$ and $\lambda_p = 1$

corresponding social welfare for different levels of sensing error ϵ in 6. Figure 6/(a) indicates that $\hat{\lambda}_s$ is unimodal in the level of sensing error. When the sensing error level is low, the negative impact of SUs on PU is small, thus increasing the arrival rate of SUs can efficiently improve the social welfare. By contrast, when the sensing error level is high, the frequent visiting of SUs can lead to large amount of sensing errors, which greatly reduce the benefit of PU. As a result, the SUs should be forbidden. Interestingly, we can observe that by Fig. 6/(b) that the optimal social welfare is non-monotone in the error probability ϵ. When ϵ is small, optimal social welfare can be increasing in ϵ because it can reduce the delay of SUs, which increases the expected utility of SUs, which results in a higher social welfare. On the other hand, when ϵ is large, the increased welfare of SUs cannot compensate for the decreased utility of PU, which worsens the social welfare. In sum, combining Fig. 4 and Fig. 6 discloses that some amount of sensing error can lead to a higher throughput and social welfare. The similar result can be found in Wang and Wang [18], which reveals that some amount of lack of information (but not all) in the population can lead to more efficient outcomes in retrial queues.

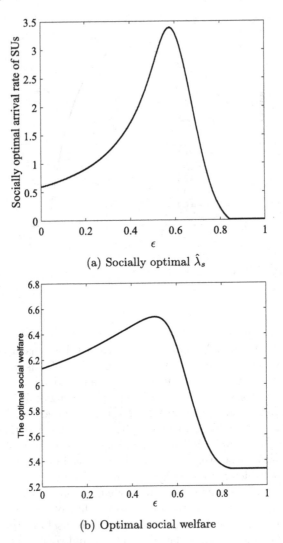

(a) Socially optimal $\hat{\lambda}_s$

(b) Optimal social welfare

Fig. 6. The socially optimal throughput and welfare for different ϵ when $R_s = 3$, $R_p = 8$, $\mu_s = \mu_p = 2$ and $\lambda_p = 1$

7   Conclusion

This paper conducted a theoretical investigation of equilibrium joining behavior of SUs in CR system when the spectrum sensing error is taken into account. The sensitivity of both SUs' behavior and system performance to the error rate were studied, and some major performance insights were provided accordingly. By adopting the queueing-game approach, the equilibrium strategy of SUs was firstly derived by considering the spectrum sensing error. It is more realistic and also more difficult than the scenario without sensing error in the literature.

In our setting, both ATC and FTC behavior exist (depending on the level of sensing error) which lead to multiple equilibria of the queueing-game model. It is observed that when the sensing error is considered, the system throughput and social welfare are non-monotone in the level of sensing error. It is pretty interesting to disclose the fact that some amount of sensing error (but not all) in the system can lead to more efficient outcomes in terms of throughput and social welfare. For the future work, it would be quite meaningful to incorporate both class-A and class-B sensing errors, as well as a non-linear reward-cost structure.

Acknowledgment. The authors would like to thank three anonymous referees for their valuable comments and suggestions which greatly improved the presentation and the quality of this paper.

References

1. Devarajan, K., Senthilkumar, M.: Strategic access in a Green IoT (Internet of Things) system with an unreliable server. Perform. Eval. **157**, 102314 (2022)
2. Do, C.T., Tran, N.H., Nguyen, M.V., Hong, C.S., Lee, S.: Social optimization strategy in unobserved queueing systems in cognitive radio networks. IEEE Commun. Lett. **16**(12), 1944–1947 (2012)
3. Hassin, R., Haviv, M.: To Queue Or Not to Queue: Equilibrium Behavior In Queueing Systems. Kluwer Academic Publishers, Boston (2003)
4. Jagannathan, K., Menache, I., Modiano, E., Zussman, G.: Non-cooperative spectrum access - the dedicated vs. free spectrum choice. Sel. Areas Commun. IEEE J. **30**(11), 2251–2261 (2011)
5. Li, H., Han, Z.: Socially optimal queuing control in CR networks subject to service interruptions: to queue or not to queue? IEEE Trans. Wireless Commun. **10**, 1656–1666 (2011)
6. Mitola, J.: Cognitive radio for flexible mobile multimedia communications. In: 1999 IEEE International Workshop on Mobile Multimedia Communications (MoMuC 1999) (Cat. No.99EX384), pp. 3–10 (1999). https://doi.org/10.1109/MOMUC.1999.819467
7. Ni, W., Zhang, Y., Li, W.W.: An optimal strategy for resource utilization in cloud data centers. IEEE ACCESS **7**, 158095–158112 (2019)
8. Palunčić, F., Alfa, A.S., Maharaj, B.T., Tsimba, H.M.: Queueing models for cognitive radio networks: a survey. IEEE ACCESS **6**, 50801–50823 (2018)
9. Suliman, I., Lehtomaki, J., Braysy, T., Umebayashi, K.: Analysis of cognitive radio networks with imperfect sensing. In: Proceedings IEEE Personal Indoor Mobile Radio Communications, pp. 1616–1620 (2009)
10. Tang, S., Mark, B.L.: Modeling and analysis of opportunistic spectrum sharing with unreliable spectrum sensing. IEEE Trans. Wireless Commun. **8**(4), 1934–1943 (2009)
11. Toma, O.H., López-Benítez, M., Patel, D.K., Umebayashi, K.: Estimation of primary channel activity statistics in cognitive radio based on imperfect spectrum sensing. IEEE Trans. Commun. **68**(4), 2016–2031 (2020). https://doi.org/10.1109/TCOMM.2020.2965944
12. Wang, F., Wang, J., Li, W.W.: Game-theoretic analysis of opportunistic spectrum sharing with imperfect sensing. EURASIP J. Wireless Commun. Networking (EJWCN) **2016**(141), 1–12 (2016). https://doi.org/10.1186/s13638-016-0637-x

13. Wang, J., Li, W.W.: Non-cooperative and cooperative joining strategies in cognitive radio networks with random access. IEEE Trans. Veh. Technol. **65**(7), 5624–5636 (2016). https://doi.org/10.1109/TVT.2015.2470115

14. Wang, J., Wang, F., Li, W.W.: Strategic behavior and admission control of cognitive radio systems with imperfect sensing. Comput. Commun. **113**, 53–61 (2017)

15. Wang, J., Wang, F., Li, W.W.: Strategic spectrum occupancy for secondary users in cognitive radio networks with retrials. Nav. Res. Logist. **64**(7), 599–609 (2017)

16. Wang, J., Zhang, Y., Li, W.W.: Strategic joining and optimal pricing in the cognitive radio system with delay-sensitive secondary users. IEEE Trans. Cogn. Commun. Networking **3**(3), 298–312 (2017)

17. Wang, J., Zhu, S., Li, W.W.: Strategic behavior of cognitive radio networks with different information. IEEE Trans. Veh. Technol. **68**(5), 4810–4823 (2019)

18. Wang, Z., Wang, J.: Information heterogeneity in a retrial queue: throughput and social welfare maximization. Queueing Syst. **92**, 131–172 (2019). https://doi.org/10.1007/s11134-019-09608-z

19. Yazdani, H., Vosoughi, A., Gong, X.: Achievable rates of opportunistic cognitive radio systems using reconfigurable antennas with imperfect sensing and channel estimation. In: IEEE Transactions on Cognitive Communications and Networking. Early Access (2021). https://doi.org/10.1109/TCCN.2021.3056691

20. Zhao, Q.: A survey of dynamic spectrum access: signal processing, networking, and regulatory policy. IEEE Signal Process. Mag. **24**(3), 79–89 (2007)

21. Zhang, Y., Wang, J., Li, W.W.: Optimal pricing strategies in cognitive radio networks with heterogeneous secondary users and retrials. IEEE ACCESS **7**, 30937–30950 (2019)

22. Zhu, S., Wang, J., Li, W.W.: Optimal pricing strategies in cognitive radio networks with multiple spectrums. IEEE Syst. J. **15**(3), 4210–4220 (2020)

23. Zhu, S., Wang, J., Li, W.W.: Optimal service rate in cognitive radio networks with different queue length information. IEEE ACCESS **6**, 51577–51586 (2018). https://doi.org/10.1109/ACCESS.2018.2867049

Spatial Temporal Graph Convolutional Network Model for Rumor Source Detection Under Multiple Observations in Social Networks

Xihao Wu[1], Hui Chen[1], Rong Jin[2], and Qiufen Ni[1(✉)]

[1] School of Computer Science and Technology, Guangdong University of Technology,
GuangZhou, China
niqiufen@gdut.edu.cn

[2] Department of Computer Science, California State University, Fullerton, USA

Abstract. Rumor source detection has long been an important but difficult problem. Most existing methods only rely on the limit observation of a single batch of single snapshot during the propagation process in the spatial graph networks, which neglects temporal dependency and temporal features of the rumor propagation process. Taking multiple batches of multiple snapshots as input can reveal the temporal dependency. Inspired by the traditional spatial-temporal graph convolution network (STGCN), which is a model can combine the spatial and temporal feature. In this paper, we propose an STGCN based model called Spatio-Temporal Approximate Personalized Propagation of Neural Predictions (STAPPNP), which firstly learns both the spatial and temporal features automatically from multiple batches of multiple snapshots to locate the rumor source. As there are no input algorithms which are suitable for multiple batches of multiple snapshots to capture the feature of nodes' connectivity in STAPPNP, we develop an input algorithm to generate a 4-dimensional input matrix from the multiple batches of multiple snapshots to feed the proposed model. Nonetheless, for deep learning models, such input of multiple batches of multiple snapshots results in a long training time as the number of model layers gets large. To address these issues, we improve the Spatio-Temporal-Convolutional(ST-Conv) block, in which we adopt the approximate personalized propagation of neural predictions in the spatial convolutional layer of STAPPNP. Our experimental results show that the accuracy of the source detection is improved by using STAPPNP, and the speed of the training process of STAPPNP outperforms state-of-the-art deep learning approaches under the popular epidemic susceptible-infected (SI) and susceptible-infected-recovery (SIR) model in social networks.

Keywords: Rumor source detection · Deep learning · Spatio-temporal graph convolutional networks · Social network

© ICST Institute for Computer Sciences, Social Informatics and Telecommunications Engineering 2023
Published by Springer Nature Switzerland AG 2023. All Rights Reserved
Z. J. Haas et al. (Eds.): WiCON 2022, LNICST 464, pp. 201–212, 2023.
https://doi.org/10.1007/978-3-031-27041-3_14

1 Introduction

Social networks have undergone rapid growth during the past a decade and have dramatically changed people's lifestyle. In social networks, people share information easily, which has the advantage that people can communicate and learn through it at a low cost. But there are also disadvantages, the information can be false. Misinformation such as rumor can be spread rapidly and exponentially in social networks, which may lead to destructive consequences to individuals, organizations, and even society [1,2]. Consequently, the problem of rumor control via computational approaches has been studied by many researchers [3,4].

There are a variety of approaches to control the rumor propagation. In general, most research can be divided into two kinds of methods for this problem. One is content-based rumor identification and the other is rumor source detection. The major computational technique for content-based rumor identification [5] is the binary classification, which uses some machine learning model to classify whether a given text is a rumor or not. These models can be trained to classify the text by capturing the content features, sentiment features and user features from input texts. Detecting the rumor source in social networks is the second kind of method for controlling rumors. The rumor can be controlled if the rumor source is detected at an early stage of the rumor spread. The problem of rumor source detection has attracted lots of attentions in a decade ago [6]. In the past, most existing research on the rumor source detection problem only take a single snapshot observation of the rumor diffusion graph as input to estimate the source nodes, which neglects the temporal feature of rumor propagation. Due to the development of location technology, we can obtain multiple snapshots observed at different stages of the rumor propagation, and these independent snapshots can help reveal the temporal dynamics of the rumor propagation. Therefore, the research using multiple snapshots [4] has begun to appear recently. This fact motivates us to adopt a spatial-temporal graph convolutional network (STGCN) [7] framework that can combine temporal and spatial information at the same time in the multiple rumor propagation snapshots. However, the traditional STGCN model still suffers from shortcoming that the input of these models is either using original infection state as node label or one-dimensional one-hot encoded vector of the infection states, which limits observation in the underlying connectivity of nodes in the social network, and thus restricts the precision of source detection. Dong et al. [3] introduce an input algorithm instead of one-hot encoded to capture the feature of rumor centrality and source prominence based on connectivity of nodes in the social network, However, the input algorithm in reference [3] only for a single batch of single snapshot. For this problem, we introduce an input algorithm in our propose model Spatio-Temporal Approximate Personalized Propagation of Neural Predictions (STAPPNP), STAPPNP is a STGCN based model, in which the input algorithm is applied to multiple batches of multiple snapshots to generate a 4-dimensional vector for the input of node states in our proposed model. The 4-dimensional vector can capture the feature of rumor centrality and source prominence for each node. However, taking the multiple batches of multiple snapshots as STAPPNP input requires a long training time. To address these issues, our propose model adopts the approximate personalized propagation of neural predictions (APPNP) [8] in the spatial layer that requires less training parameters than Graph convolutional network (GCN) based model, which enables much faster training speed. In this paper, we use the infection model [9] to describe our rumor propagation model in the social network. Additionally, we conduct extensive experiments on several real world social networks. The main contributions of this paper are summarized as follows:

- We firstly propose an input algorithm which is applicable to multiple batches of multiple snapshots input, which can capture the feature of rumor centrality and source prominence for each node.
- We use the approximate personalized propagation of neural predictions instead of graph convolutional network in spatial layers, which speeds up model training.

The rest of the paper is distributed as follows: Sect. 2 discusses the related work. Section 3 shows the structure and details of the proposed model, followed by the experiment and analysis in Sect. 4. Section 5 concludes the paper.

2   Related Work

2.1   Graph Convolutional Networks

GCN is a burgeoning deep learning model on graph. The earliest GCN is proposed by Duvenaud et al. [10], literature [10] introduce convolutional-like propagation rule on graphs. Defferrard et al. [11] use chebyshev polynomials to optimize the propagation rule, and the model achieved satisfactory experimental results. Kipf and Welling. [12] further approximate the propagation rule to a 1-order approximation, which reducing the computational complexity to linearity. However, 1-order approximation GCN still has the problem that training time becomes longer as the size of convolutional layers increases. Hence, Klicpera et al. [8] propose the Approximate Personalized Propagation of Neural Predictions (APPNP) algorithm to reduce the size of training parameters so as to improve the time of training.

2.2   Rumor Source Detection

Shah et al. [13] firstly study on the rumor source detection problem a decade ago. Wang et al. [14] investigate the problem of locating multiple source nodes, and propose the Label Propagation based Source Identification (LPSI) algorithm to identify them without knowledge of the underlying propagation model. Li et al. [15] then attempt to apply the deep learning model named Graph Convolutional Networks (GCN). However, Sha et al. [7] prove that the prediction precision of GCN based approach does not outperform the simple label propagation algorithm in literature [14] for a single snapshot. Hence, Sha et al. [7]

adopt a spatial temporal graph convolutional network (STGCN) to detect the source based on the multiple snapshots. But STGCN uses one-hot encoded as input algorithm which ignores the connectivity of nodes in social network. Dong et al. [3] introduce an input algorithm instead of one-hot encoded to capture the features of rumor centrality and source prominence based on connectivity of nodes in the social network.

3   Proposed Model

3.1   Input Algorithm for Multiple Batches of Multiple Snapshots

Inspired by literature [3], we propose our input algorithm to capture the feature of rumor centrality [14] and source prominence [16] from multiple batches of multiple snapshots. The process of our input algorithm is illustrated in Algorithm 1. Firstly, we concatenate the infection states of all nodes of multiple snapshots as the infection state matrix X. The shape of the matrix X is $Q \times T \times N$, and Q is the number of batches of multiple snapshots, T is the number of snapshots, N is the number of nodes on each snapshot. Each snapshot contains the infection states of all nodes in social network graph at different times. Infection state of random node $v = +1$ means the node is infected and $v = -1$ means the node is not infected for the SI model or SIR model (note that $v = -1 \in \{susceptible(S)state, recovery(R)state\}, v = +1 \in \{infected(I)state\}$). Next, from step 2 to step 16, we need to generate some matrix that can capture the feature of rumor centrality and source prominence. We reduce the dimensionality of X to a new 2-D matrix $X_1 \in R^{(Q \times T) \times N}$, where $R^{(Q \times T) \times N}$ denotes the matrix X_1 shape as $(Q \times T) \times N$, $(Q \times T)$ denotes the result of $Q \times T$. P and O are defined and initialized, they are used to generate c and d. The dimensions of a, b, c and d are same as X_1, literature [3] proves that b can capture the source prominence, c and d can capture the features of rumor centrality. In step 14 to 16, the $\alpha \in (0, 1)$ is a hyperparameter, α denotes the percentage of label information aggregated from neighboring nodes. At step 17, a, b, c and d are concatenated into a high dimensional vector corresponding to each snapshot. Finally, in step 18, we obtain a 4-D output matrix Y^0 by reshaping the 3-D matrix Y', where Y^0 denotes the infection state matrix for all nodes under the observation of multiple snapshots in $(Q \times T)$. The infection label of each node is a 4-dimensional vector, which contains the feature of rumor centrality and source prominence.

3.2   Spatio-Temporal-Convolutional Block

Inspired by [8], we propose an improved Spatio-Temporal-Convolutional (ST-Conv) block, which adopts the Approximate Personalized Propagation of Neural Predictions (APPNP) as the spatial convolutional layer to extract the spatial features of the nodes. We use APPNP instead of GCN as spatial layer can speed up the model training. As illustrated in Fig. 1, we take the output Y^0 of the Algorithm 1 as the first ST-Conv block input, and Y^0 is in the shape of

Algorithm 1. Input algorithm for multiple batches of multiple snapshots.

Require: Infection State Matrix $X \in R^{Q \times T \times N}$; degree matrix D; adjacency matrix A; hyperparameter α;

Ensure: Four-Dimension infection state input matrix $Y \in R^{Q \times T \times N \times 4}$;

1: Defined the normalized matrix $U = D^{-\frac{1}{2}} A D^{-\frac{1}{2}}$, Q is the batch size, T is the number of snapshots, N is the number of nodes, Identity matrix I;
2: $X_1 = reshape(X) \in R^{(Q \times T) \times N}$
3: define $P = X_1, O = X_1$;
4: **for** $i = 0 \rightarrow len(Q \times T)$ **do**
5:    **for** $j = 0 \rightarrow len(N)$ **do**
6:       **if** $X_{1_{i,j}} == -1$ **then**
7:          $P_{i,j} = 0$;
8:       **else**
9:          $O_{i,j} = 0$;
10:       **end if**
11:    **end for**
12: **end for**
13: $a = X_1$;
14: $b = (1 - \alpha)(I - \alpha U)^{-1} X_1$;
15: $c = (1 - \alpha)(I - \alpha U)^{-1} P$;
16: $d = (1 - \alpha)(I - \alpha U)^{-1} O$;
17: $Y' = concatenate(a, b, c, d) \in R^{(Q \times T) \times N \times 4}$;
18: $Y^0 = reshape(Y') \in R^{Q \times T \times N \times 4}$;
19: **return** Y^0;

$R^{Q \times T \times N \times C_{in}}$, where C_{in} denotes the number of input channels. As Algorithm 1 expands the label vector of each node to 4 dimensions, thus, the value of C_{in} in the first ST-Conv block is equal to 4. The details of our ST-Conv block are described as follows:

Temporal Gated-Convolution. The temporal convolutional layer contain a 1-D convolutional neural network (CNN) with a width-K_t kernel followed by gated linear unit (GLU) as activation function. Since the convolutional kernel size is K_t, the time series will be reduced by $K_t - 1$ after passing through a temporal convolutional layer. The temporal convolutional layer can be represented as follows:

$$Y_1 = GLU(CNN(Y^0)) \in R^{Q \times (T - K_t + 1) \times N \times C_h} \tag{1}$$

we use Eq. (1) to capture the temporal feature, in which Y^0 is the input of the temporal layer, C_h is the output dimension of the temporal layer, and Y_1 is the output matrix of the temporal layer, GLU is a gated linear unit and CNN is a convolutional neural network layer.

Spatial Approximate Personalized Propagation of Neural Predictions. In the spatial layer we use APPNP instead of GCN to capture spatial features. The rules of spatial feature extraction are designed as follows:

$$H^{(0)} = Z = f_\theta(Y_1) \tag{2}$$

$$H^{(l+1)} = (1 - \delta)\widetilde{A}H^{(l)} + \delta Z \in R^{Q \times (T - K_t + 1) \times N \times C_h} \tag{3}$$

$$Y^2 = H^{(L)} = softmax((1 - \delta)\widetilde{A}H^{(L-1)} + \delta Z) \in R^{Q \times (T - K_t + 1) \times N \times C_h}. \tag{4}$$

The Eq. (2) using neural networks to predict the class of nodes, f_θ is a neural network with a parameter set θ. Y_1 represents the input of the spatial layer and corresponds to the output of the first temporal layer. The Eq. (3) is the message propagation rule, we use this equation to aggregate information about neighboring nodes. $H^{(l+1)}$ is the matrix of activations in the $(l+1)^{th}$. $\delta \in (0, 1]$ is a hyperparameter, which represents the restart probability (i.e., the percentage of label information aggregated from root nodes). In Eq. (4), L denotes the number of power iteration steps, and $l \in [0, L - 2]$ in Eq. (3). The APPNP uses $softmax$ as the activation function, with the spatial layer kernel size K_s. Through APPNP, the spatial information of each node can be extracted and then integrated with its neighbors within the area of K_s layers. As shown in Fig. 1. After passing the spatial layer, we set the output Y_2 of the spatial layer as the input to the following temporal layer, the following temporal layer is the same as the first temporal layer in the ST-Conv block. Due to an ST-Conv block contains two gated sequential convolution layers and one spatial convolution layer, the time series will be subtracted by $(2K_t - 2)$ after passing through an ST-Conv block. Assume that we have L_1 ST-Conv blocks for feature extractions, then the time series of the final output matrix will be subtracted by $(2L_1K_t - 2L_1)$. Thus the final output dimension is $Y_3 \in R^{Q \times (T - 2L_1K_t + 2L_1) \times N \times C_{out}}$, where C_{out} denotes the output dimension of the last gated sequential convolution layer.

3.3 Spatio-Temporal Approximate Personalized Propagation of Neural Predictions

Our STAPPNP is built on the STGCN construction. The construction of STAPP NP is illustrated in Fig. 1. At first, the input is an infection state matrix X of the shape $Q \times T \times N$, which is generated based on multiple batches of multiple snapshots. The multiple batches of multiple snapshots are observations of the rumor propagation processes on social network graph. Next, we take X as the input of Algorithm 1, and the output is a new matrix Y^0 of the shape $Q \times T \times N \times 4$. Then, the matrix Y^0 flows via two ST-Conv blocks where each block contains a spatial layer and two temporal gated-convolutional layers to capture the spatial and temporal features of each node. Note that the number of ST-Conv blocks is not necessarily fixed. In practice, multiple ST-Conv blocks can be stacked together to extract the features of nodes. Finally, the output of the last ST-Conv block Y_3 is sent to the output layer. The temporal convolution layer attached with one fully connected layer to output the probability of each node contains the rumor source node. The activation of the fully connected layer is $softmax$. The output layer can be written as:

$$Y = Softmax(FC(GLU(CNN(Y_3)))) \in R^{Q \times N} \tag{5}$$

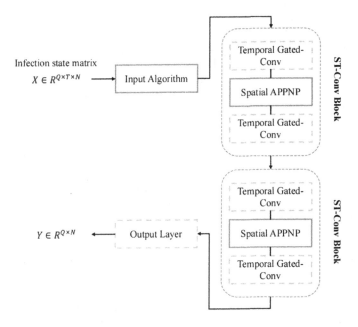

Fig. 1. Construct of STAPPNP.

the output of STAPPNP is a matrix Y, the shape of Y is $Q \times N$, which represents the probabilities that each node in Q batch graphs is the rumor source, and FC is a fully connected layer.

4 Experiment

4.1 Datasets

Our model is suitable for small or medium social networks. Datasets are divided into two types. The first type are ER and BA social networks [17]. The second type is empirical contact social network adopted from High school [18] and SFHH conference [19], both of which are generated on the dynamic contact sequences. The statistics of the datasets are listed in Table 1.

Table 1. Statistics of four datasets.

Datasets	Nodes	Edges
BA	2000	19900
ER	1000	9953
High School	774	7792
SFHH	403	9565

4.2   Parameter Setting

Common Settings. In our experiment, we generate 2000 rumor propagation processes for each social network based on SI and SIR infection propagation models. 80%, 10% and 10% of rumor propagation processes are used as the training dataset, the validation set, and the test set, respectively. The batch size is set to be 50. All the deep learning models are trained for 50 epochs using RMSProp optimizer, and the learning rate starts from 0.001 and decays with rate 0.7 every 5 epochs. Since the RSD problem is a multi-classification problem, cross-entropy is used as the loss function. As shown in Fig. 1, we use two ST-Conv blocks to capture features of nodes. The input channels and output channels for the first temporal layer and spatial layer and last temporal layer in first ST-Conv block are {4, 64}, {64, 64}, {64, 128}. The input channels and output channels for the second ST-Conv block are {128, 64}, {64, 64}, {64, 72}.

Parameter Setting Under Two Infection Propagation Models. Under the SI model, the infection rate is set to be 0.05, each rumor propagation process simulates 15 iterations of rumor propagations to generate 15 snapshots. Then, we randomly choose 10 rumor propagation infection snapshots. For a small batch of snapshots under the SI model, we set temporal kernel size (K_t) from set {2,3} and spatial kernel size (K_s) from set {2,3,4,5}, we find that STAPPNP achieves the best performance with $K_t = 2$ and $K_s = 5$. Under the SIR model, we set the infection rate and the recovery rate to be 0.25 and 0.1, respectively. We simulate the rumor propagation process with 30 iterations to generate the 30 rumor propagation infection snapshots, and then we randomly select 16 snapshots as the inputs as well as we set temporal kernel size from set {2,3,4} and spatial kernel size from set {2,3,4,5}. For the SIR model, the STAPPNP achieves the best performance with $K_t = 3$ and $K_s = 5$. In the following experiments, we adhere to this setup.

4.3   Comparison and Evaluation

We compare our STAPPNP with three popular baseline models in terms of two types of evaluation metrics, as shown in Table 2. All models are trained on NVIDIA GeForce RTX 2080 Ti GPU servers.

Evaluation Metrics. We evaluate the performance of the model with the following metrics:

- **Detection accuracy.** Detection accuracy is the percentage of true rumor sources being detected correctly. In this paper, we take the average of the detection accuracy based on the test set as evaluation metrics.
- **Temporal evaluation.** The performance of temporal evaluation is usually compared to the model training time. To verify the temporal superiority, for each neural, we train 50 epochs based on the same dataset to compare the training time.

Table 2. Comparison of STAPPNP and baseline.

Models	Training time	Detection accuracy
STAPPNP	✓	✓
STGCN(1ST-order approximation) [12]	✓	✓
STGCN(Chebyshev polynomials approximation) [11]	✓	✓
LPSI [14]	×	✓

✓ indicates participation in the corresponding comparison trial and × represents no participation in the corresponding comparison trial, e.g., we compare the detection accuracy but not the training time of LPSI with other models. Since the LPSI algorithm performs rumor source detection in a single snapshot, the input type of LPSI is different from STAPPNP. Therefore, we do not include LPSI in the comparison of training time comparison. In the following, we use STGCN (Cheb) to represent the STGCN (Chebyshev polynomials approximation), and STGCN (1ST-order) represents the STGCN (1ST-order approximation).

Comparison of the Training Time. Table 3 summarizes the results for the training speed of the comparative models. In the experiment, we set the batch size to 50 and compare the training time under the same social network graph. For each neural network model, to ensure input algorithms are the same, we use the one-hot encoding instead of Algorithm 1 as the STAPPNP input algorithm. The results show that the extent of improvement in training speed of STAPPNP increases with the scale of the graph and the complexity of the infection model. STAPPNP achieves the best results in BA networks under both of the two infection models. It improves the training speed by 57s in SI model and 71s in SIR model compare to STGCN (Cheb), which is a significant improvement. STAPPNP also achieves faster training speed than comparing models under all datasets based on two different infection models. Overall, the results show that using APPNP instead of traditional GCN as the spatial layer can improve the training speed under the model significantly. The results demonstrate the effectiveness of our improvements to the ST-Conv block in improving the training speed.

Table 3. Comparisons of training time under two propagation models.

Model	SI				SIR			
	BA	ER	HighSchool	SFHH	BA	ER	HighSchool	SFHH
STGCN (1st-order)	821 s	364 s	289 s	177 s	949 s	670 s	551 s	273 s
STGCN (Cheb)	861 s	369 s	285 s	178 s	951 s	668 s	549 s	275 s
STAPPNP	804 s	353 s	282 s	173 s	880 s	652 s	521 s	267 s

Comparison of Source Detection Accuracy. Since rumor propagation is consistent with the SI infection model, we only verify the superiority of the source detection accuracy under the SI infection model. For the STGCN (1st-order) and STGCN (Cheb), we adopt the one-hot encoding of the node state matrix as input algorithm. LPSI uses 2000 rumor propagation infection graphs without dividing the training set, test set, validation set. The LPSI is not a deep learning model, only deep learning models need to divide the datasets into training, test and validation sets. Thus we use 2000 rumor propagation infection graphs without dividing the training set, test set, validation set and take the last infection result snapshot of each infection graph as LPSI inputs.

As shown in Table 4, which summarizes the result of detection accuracy of deep learning models and LPSI. We divide the test set into four groups and take the average of these four groups as the accuracy result. In the BA network, each deep learning model achieves the best performance. For example, the accuracy of STAPPNP in BA network compared with ER, HighSchool and SFHH networks, rumor source detection accuracy performance increases of 9.5%, 15.5% and 29%, respectively. The results show that for deep learning models, the accuracy of rumor source detection increases with the scale of social networks graph. And we notice that the STGCN (Cheb) outperforms STGCN (1st-order) in a small size graph, but in the large social network BA, STGCN (1st-order) achieves a higher detection accuracy rate than STGCN (Cheb), as stated in [12], the extent of improvement of 1ST-order approximation GCN over chebyshev polynomials approximation GCN increases with the size of the social network graph. Furthermore, to verify that using Algorithm 1 as input algorithm can improve the detection accuracy of STAPPNP, we compare the detection accuracy of STAPPNP to all baselines and find that STAPPNP outperforms all the baseline methods in terms of detection accuracy under all types of networks. STAPPNP achieves the best performance in ER network, the detection accuracy of STAPPNP is 3.5% higher than STGCN (1st-order) in ER network. The results show that taking Algorithm 1 as input algorithm can improve the accuracy of the rumor source detection. The results demonstrate the effectiveness of taking Algorithm 1 as the input algorithm to expresses the relationship between nodes for multiple batches of multiple snapshots.

As shown in Table 4, we notice that STAPPNP significantly outperforms LPSI. For example, in the ER network, the detection accuracy of STAPPNP is 66.45% higher than LPSI. In the BA, High school and SFHH networks, detection accuracy of STAPPNP increases 64.70%, 60.56% and 46.35% over LPSI, respectively. For our experiments, LPSI performs rumor source detection based on a single snapshot and STAPPNP performs rumor source detection based on multiple snapshots. Therefore, we conclude that the better detection performance of STAPPNP is related to much more information obtained from multiple snapshots.

Table 4. Accuracy comparison.

Model	BA	ER	HighSchool	SFHH
LPSI	11.80%	0.55%	0.44%	1.15%
STGCN (1st-order)	76.00%	63.50%	58.50%	43.50%
STGCN (Cheb)	75.00%	65.00%	59.50%	46.00%
STAPPNP	76.50%	67.00%	61.00%	47.50%

5   Conclusion

In this paper, we investigate the problem of rumor source detection (RSD) under multiple batches of multiple snapshots in the social networks. We propose a modified spatial-temporal convolutional neural network model called STAPPNP. For the RSD problem, we find that taking multiple batches of multiple snapshots as input can improve the detection accuracy. As there is no input algorithm that is suitable for our observation on multiple batches of multiple snapshots, we firstly propose an input algorithm to capture node connectivity features of the multiple batches of multiple snapshots. Our STAPPNP significantly improves the detection accuracy. Meanwhile, to solve the problem of long training time caused by taking the multiple batches of multiple snapshots as input, we improve the ST-Conv block by replacing GCN with APPNP to further increase the training speed. We conduct the experiments on the real world social networks datasets. The results indicate the effectiveness of STAPPNP, which outperforms the 1ST-order approximation STGCN models by about 3.5% in accuracy of rumor source detection, and outperforms the Chebyshev polynomials approximation STGCN 8% in terms of training speed, and even by 66.45% in accuracy of rumor source detection comparing to the LPSI. Since our model is based on the infection model, in the future, we plan to apply STAPPNP in the influence model, filling the gap in the influence model where there are no deep learning models that can aggregate spatio-temporal features.

Acknowledgment. This work is supported in part by the National Natural Science Foundation of China under Grant No. 62202109, and in part by the Guangdong Basic and Applied Basic Research Foundation under Grant No. 2021A1515110321 and No. 2022A1515010611 and in part by Guangzhou Basic and Applied Basic Research Foundation under Grant No. 202201010676.

References

1. Wang, H., Qiao, C., Guo, X., Fang, L., Sha, Y., Gong, Z.: Identifying and evaluating anomalous structural change-based nodes in generalized dynamic social networks. ACM Trans. Web **15**(4), 1–22 (2021)
2. Ni, Q., Guo, J., Weili, W., Wang, H., Jigang, W.: Continuous influence-based community partition for social networks. IEEE Trans. Netw. Sci. Eng. **9**(3), 1187–1197 (2021)

3. Dong, M., Zheng, B., Quoc Viet Hung, N., Su, H., Li, G.: Multiple rumor source detection with graph convolutional networks. In: Proceedings of the 28th ACM International Conference on Information and Knowledge Management, pp. 569–578 (2019)

4. Wang, Z., Dong, W., Zhang, W., Tan, C.W.: Rumor source detection with multiple observations: fundamental limits and algorithms. ACM SIGMETRICS Perform. Eval. Rev. **42**(1), 1–13 (2014)

5. Zhao, Z., Resnick, P., Mei, Q.: Enquiring minds: early detection of rumors in social media from enquiry posts. In: Proceedings of the 24th International Conference on World Wide Web, pp. 1395–1405 (2015)

6. Jin, R., Wu, W.: Schemes of propagation models and source estimators for rumor source detection in online social networks: a short survey of a decade of research. Discrete Math. Algorithms Appl. **13**(04), 2130002 (2021)

7. Sha, H., Al Hasan, M., Mohler, G.: Source detection on networks using spatial temporal graph convolutional networks. In: 2021 IEEE 8th International Conference on Data Science and Advanced Analytics, pp. 1–11 (2021)

8. Klicpera, J., Bojchevski, A., Gunnemann, S.: Predict then propagate: graph neural networks meet personalized pagerank. In: Proceedings of the 7th International Conference on Learning Representations (ICLR), pp. 1–15 (2019)

9. Allen, L.J.: Some discrete-time SI, SIR, and SIS epidemic models. Math. Biosci. **124**(1), 83–105 (1994)

10. Duvenaud, D.K., et al.: Convolutional networks on graphs for learning molecular fingerprints. In: Advances in Neural Information Processing Systems, vol. 28, no. 9, pp. 2224–2232 (2015)

11. Defferrard, M., Bresson, X., Vandergheynst, P.: Convolutional neural networks on graphs with fast localized spectral filtering. In: Advances in Neural Information Processing Systems, vol. 29, pp. 3844–3852 (2016)

12. Kipf, T.N., Welling, M.: Semi-supervised classification with graph convolutional networks. In: Proceedings of the 5th International Conference on Learning Representations (ICLR), pp. 1–14 (2017)

13. Shah, D., Zaman, T.: Rumors in a network: who's the culprit? IEEE Trans. Inf. Theory **57**(8), 5163–5181 (2011)

14. Wang, Z., Wang, C., Pei, J., Ye, X.: Multiple source detection without knowing the underlying propagation model. In: Proceedings of the AAAI Conference on Artificial Intelligence, vol. 31, pp. 217–223 (2017)

15. Li, L., Zhou, J., Jiang, Y.: Propagation source identification of infectious diseases with graph convolutional networks. J. Biomed. Inform. **116**, 103720 (2021)

16. Shah, D., Zaman, T.: Rumor centrality: a universal source detector. In: Proceedings of the 12th ACM SIGMETRICS/PERFORMANCE Joint International Conference on Measurement and Modeling of Computer Systems, vol. 40, pp. 199–210 (2012)

17. Albert, R., Barabasi, A.L.: Statistical mechanics of complex networks. Rev. Mod. Phys. **74**(1), 47–92 (2002)

18. Salathe, M., Kazandjieva, M., Lee, J.W., Levis, P., Feldman, M.W., Jones, J.H.: A high-resolution human contact network for infectious disease transmission. Proc. Nat. Acad. Sci. **107**(51), 22020–22025 (2010)

19. Genois, M., Barrat, A.: Can co-location be used as a proxy for face-to-face contacts? EPJ Data Sci. **7**(1), 1–18 (2018). https://doi.org/10.1140/epjds/s13688-018-0140-1

Addressing Class Imbalance in Federated Learning via Collaborative GAN-Based Up-Sampling

Can Zhang[1], Xuefeng Liu[1(✉)], Shaojie Tang[2], Jianwei Niu[1], Tao Ren[1], and Quanquan Hu[1]

[1] Beihang University, Beijing, China
{can_zhang,liu_xuefeng,niujianwei,nebulau}@buaa.edu.cn
[2] The University of Texas at Dallas, Richardson, USA
shaojie.tang@utdallas.edu

Abstract. Federated learning (FL) is an emerging learning framework that enables decentralized devices to collaboratively train a model without leaking their data to each other. One common problem in FL is class imbalance, in which either the distribution or quantity of the training data varies in different devices. In the presence of class imbalance, the performance of the final model can be negatively affected. A straightforward approach to address class imbalance is up-sampling, by which data of minority classes in each device are augmented independently. However, this up-sampling approach does not allow devices to help each other and therefore its effectiveness can be greatly compromised. In this paper, we propose FED-CGU, a collaborative GAN-based up-sampling strategy in FL. In FED-CGU, devices can help each other during up-sampling via collaboratively training a GAN model which augments data for each device. In addition, some advanced designs of FED-CGU are proposed, including dynamically determining the number of augmented data in each device and selecting complementary devices that can better help each other. We test FED-CGU with benchmark datasets including Fashion-MNIST and CIFAR-10. Experimental results demonstrate that FED-CGU outperforms the state-of-the-art algorithms.

Keywords: Federated learning · Class imbalance · Collaborative up-sampling · Generative adversarial networks

1 Introduction

Federated learning (FL) is a popular distributed learning framework that allows a large number of mobile devices to collaboratively train a global model without sharing their local data [16]. However, one phenomenon that can degrade the performance of FL is class imbalance. Class imbalance, defined as the disproportionate ratio of observations in each class, is a concept originally defined for traditional centralized machine learning. In FL, class imbalance can happen

© ICST Institute for Computer Sciences, Social Informatics and Telecommunications Engineering 2023
Published by Springer Nature Switzerland AG 2023. All Rights Reserved
Z. J. Haas et al. (Eds.): WiCON 2022, LNICST 464, pp. 213–227, 2023.
https://doi.org/10.1007/978-3-031-27041-3_15

either within a device (an individual device is class-imbalanced) or among multiple devices (the overall class distribution across devices is imbalanced). The phenomenon of class imbalance happens frequently in practical scenarios of FL. For example, when multiple mobile devices collaboratively train a image classification model using their own photos, the number of photos with different themes can vary greatly both within each device and across all devices according to users' interests. Class imbalance can slow down the convergence and even degrade the performance of the obtained global model [12,25].

How to address the class imbalance has been studied extensively in centralized machine learning. Methods for handling class imbalance can be largely grouped into algorithm-level techniques and data-level methods [6]. A widely used data-level method is up-sampling, which augments samples in minority classes in order to decrease the level of imbalance. Experimental results show that up-sampling generally displays a good performance on various datasets [15]. To implement the up-sampling technique in FL, a straightforward approach is to let each device augment enough number of samples in minority classes until class balance is achieved. However, as up-sampling is implemented independently in each device, samples augmented in one device do not exploit information from others.

Therefore, a collaborative up-sampling strategy in FL that allows devices to help each other without leaking their private data is greatly desired. To address this issue, one strategy is to utilize a Generative Adversarial Network (GAN). In particular, devices first collaboratively train a GAN in the framework of FL. Then the GAN is utilized to augment minority classes for each device. As the GAN is trained collaboratively by all devices, up-sampling for one device leverages information from others.

Although the above idea of using a GAN for collaborative up-sampling is simple, implementing such an idea, however, entails substantial challenges.

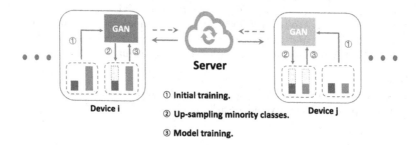

Fig. 1. Collaborative GAN-based up-sampling to address class imbalance in FL.

First, we find that the GAN model generally cannot be well trained in the presence of class imbalance. Therefore, a better approach is to let the two tasks (i.e. training the GAN and up-sampling minority classes) be implemented alternately in an iterative manner. As shown in Fig. 1, a GAN is firstly trained using the original data of all devices. Then the GAN is utilized for augmenting data in all devices. Afterwards, the GAN is updated again based on the updated data. This process alternates in an iterative manner until the model converges.

Another challenge is for each round of the above process, how to determine the number of augmented data in each device. We find that GAN is generally not well trained initially, and generating a large number of low-quality samples can have a negative effect on the convergence, which may further lead to lower quality augmented samples. The intuition is that the number of augmented data by GAN should be dynamically determined by their quality. To implement this idea, we utilize a genetic algorithm, which utilizes the performance of the target training task as a guidance to dynamically determine the number of augmented data for each device. In addition, we incorporate prior knowledge, which states that the number of augmented data is increased, into the genetic algorithm to reduce the searching rounds of the genetic algorithm.

Another issue is how to select devices in each round of the above process. In the traditional FL framework, devices are generally selected uniformly at random. However, we find that in the presence of class imbalance, choosing devices with complementary classes can often accelerate the convergence of the GAN model. We utilize the Kullback-Leibler Divergence (KLD) distance as a measure to select complementary devices in each communication round of FL. Implementing this strategy, we can reduce the computation and communication cost for the devices.

In view of all the above issues, we propose FED-CGU, the first collaborative GAN-based up-sampling strategy to address class imbalance in FL. In FED-CGU, devices can help each other during up-sampling via collaboratively training a GAN model. In addition, FED-CGU has some advanced designs, including alternately implementing GAN training and up-sampling in an iterative manner, dynamically determining the number of augmented data in each device, and selecting the complementary devices in each round of FL. We test FED-CGU with benchmark datasets including Fashion-MNIST and CIFAR-10, and the experimental results demonstrate that FED-CGU outperforms the state-of-the-art algorithms.

Our contributions are listed as follows:

- We propose the first collaborative up-sampling strategy in FL that allows devices to help each other without leaking their private data.
- We design a strategy that can dynamically determine the number of augmented data for each device.
- We design a device sampling strategy which selects complementary devices to accelerate the convergence of the GAN model.
- We test FED-CGU with benchmark datasets including Fashion-MNIST and CIFAR-10. Experimental results indicate that FED-CGU outperforms the state-of-the-art algorithms.

2   Related Work

Class imbalance can make the overall accuracy of machine learning biased to the majority classes which leads to misclassifying the minority class samples or furthermore treats them as noise [6]. Prior approaches to address this problem in centralized learning can be grouped into algorithm-level methods and data-level methods [6]. Algorithm-level methods punish classification mistakes on the minority classes [21,26]. Such methods make the model focus more on minority classes. On the other hand, data-level methods modify the class distributions to decrease the level of class imbalance. Data-level methods include down-sampling and up-sampling. Down-sampling methods only selects partial data in majority classes [19], and up-sampling methods augment data in minority classes (e.g. rotation, scaling or translation) [1,13]. Experimental results on some large datasets show that up-sampling generally displays better performance than down-sampling [15]. However, all the above methods implement common up-sampling (e.g. flipping, rotation), which are designed for a single device. When these methods are implemented in FL, they can not exploit information from other devices. Although using Generative Adversarial Networks (GAN) [5] and its improved versions [17,18] for up-sampling can leverage other devices' information, training a GAN model in is a challenging task with the presence of class imbalance.

In addition to centralized methods, approaches to address class imbalance in FL are also widely studied. We classify these approaches into several categories. The first category is to optimize the loss function of FL. L. Wang et al. [23] leverages the global imbalance and Q. Li et al. [11] aligns representation learned by the local models to address class imbalance. The second category is personalized federated learning [4,20]. Personalized strategies train a personalized model for each device with the help from other devices. Another category is the aggregation scheme. Aggregation schemes modify the aggregation function of FL to faster the convergence in non-IID data [2,9,14]. Recently, Astraea [3] and FAVOR [22] apply device sampling to deal with class imbalance in FL. Astraea and FAVOR choose the devices to participate in FL to counterbalance the bias introduced by class imbalance. Our proposed FED-CGU is perpendicular to the above approaches and can improve their performance.

3   Algorithm Design

3.1   FED-CGU Overview

The overview of FED-CGU framework is shown in Fig. 2. We choose training a classifier as the target task. In FED-CGU, we also train an extra GAN model and up-sample minority classes alternately in an iterative manner. We propose a complementary device sampling strategy to accelerate the convergence of GAN, and design a genetic algorithm to determine the number of up-sampled data. The workflow of FED-CGU is as follows:

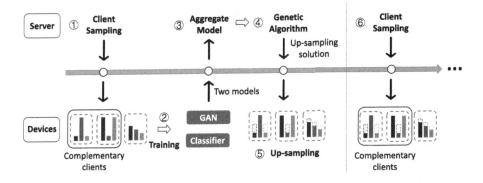

Fig. 2. Overview of FED-CGU framework.

- *Step* 1 : The server selects a few devices whose data distributions are complementary.
- *Step* 2 : The selected devices update the classifier and GAN on their local data and augmented data, and then upload the models.
- *Step* 3 : The server aggregates the uploaded models.
- *Step* 4 : After multiple rounds' training and aggregation, the server utilizes a genetic algorithm to generate up-sampling solutions based on the evaluation of the classifier.
- *Step* 5 : Devices download the solutions and then implement GAN for up-sampling according to the solutions.
- *Step* 6 : Go to *step* 1 and repeat the whole procedure.

3.2   Detailed Design of FED-CGU

We introduce the detailed designs of FED-CGU in this subsection. The content is organized as follows. First, we discuss the complementary device sampling strategy. Then we introduce the design of our up-sampling method. Finally, we introduce how we utilize the genetic algorithm to determine the number of augmented data.

Design of Device Sampling. We observe that in the presence of class imbalance, complementary devices can accelerate each other's training. The key point to leverage this observation is to explore complementary devices. If the overall class distribution of a group of devices is similar to a balanced distribution, the devices in this group are complementary. In this paper, we utilize the Kullback-Leibler Divergence of devices' class distribution to select complementary devices and the optimization function is as follows:

$$\min \sum_{c_i \subset C} D_{KL}(P_{c_i} \| P_{balance}) \tag{1}$$

where C denotes the set of all involved devices, $\{c_1, c_2, \ldots | c_1 \cup c_2 \cup \ldots = C\}$ are independent subsets of C. P_{c_i} denotes the class distribution of clients in c_i and $P_{balance}$ denotes the balanced class distribution. Based on the above function, we can divide devices into complementary subsets and devices in each subset are complementary to each other. In the process of each round's training, we randomly select a subset of devices to participate.

Design of Up-Sampling. Common up-sampling methods (flipping, rotation, etc.) are widely utilized in centralized training. However, since common up-sampling methods are based on devices' local data, they cannot exploit the information from other devices to improve the effects of up-sampling. In addition, simply using local data can also make devices easy to cause over-fitting. If a device does not have data in specific classes, we are even unable to supplement such classes.

To solve the above issues, we utilize a GAN model to perform up-sampling. Since the GAN model is collaboratively trained by all devices, it can leverage the information of all devices' data and prevent over-fitting. A straightforward strategy to implement up-sampling with GAN is to first train a GAN model and then utilize the GAN to augment data. However, since class imbalance can make the model treat the minority classes as noise, directly training a GAN model is a challenging task.

To address this challenge, we propose to train the GAN model and up-sample minority classes alternately in an iterative manner. We initially leverage the original data of all devices to train a GAN model. Then we implement the GAN for augmenting minority classes on all devices. Afterwards, we again train the GAN based on the updated data. We iteratively alternate the above process until the model converges.

Design of Determining the Number of Augmented Data. The number of augmented data is an important variable in FED-CGU. Since the GAN model cannot be well trained initially, mass up-sampled data may lead to the accuracy degradation of the training model. Given insufficient up-sampled data, it cannot adequately exploit all devices' data. Therefore, we need to find the optimal up-sampling quantity. In this paper, we adopt the nondominated sorting genetic algorithm II (NSGA-II), a widely used multi-objective evolutionary algorithm to search for the up-sampling solution.

In our settings, the objectives of the searching are the optimal up-sampling quantities of different classes in each device. We denote S^* as the optimal up-sampling quantities and the chromosomes of S^* are shown as follows:

$$S^* = (Q, p_1, p_2, \ldots, p_n) \tag{2}$$

where Q denotes the number of augmented data and p_i denotes the proportion of the i-th device. The number Q and p_i are both a one-dimensional array with c parameters, where c is the number of classes.

To optimize the searching, we set the validation accuracy as the evaluating indicator. The objective function of the genetic algorithm is:

$$\arg\max_{S^*} \sum_{D^i \in D^*} E(w - \eta \nabla_w l(w; D^i \cup Aug^i(S^*))) \tag{3}$$

where D^i and Aug^i denote the local data and augmented data based on S^* in the i-th device, respectively. The parameter of w is the target classifier model, η is the learning rate and l is the loss function. We update w on the up-sampled data and evaluate the model on the validation data with the evaluation function E.

The Computational Cost of the Genetic Algorithm. The computational cost of the genetic algorithm consists of server-side and device-side cost. The largest cost on the server-side is fast non-dominated sorting, which has a time complexity of $O(N^2)$. In our experimental settings (in the evaluation section), it takes less than 3s in each round using NVIDIA GeForce GTX 1660. The computation on the device-side is the calculation of the solutions' fitness. The computation time on the device-side for each device is less than 10s in each round with NVIDIA GeForce GTX 1660.

In addition, to accelerate the searching, we also incorporate prior knowledge, which is gradually increasing the number of augmented data, into the genetic algorithm. At the beginning of training, we just augment a small amount of data as the GAN model is not well trained. When the performance of the GAN model gets better, We gradually increase the amount of up-sampling. Applying this prior knowledge, we reduce the searching rounds of the genetic algorithm and thus save the computational power of the devices.

4   Evaluation

In this section, we empirically evaluate the proposed FED-CGU framework on benchmark data classification with general multi-class datasets. We first compare FED-CGU with FedAvg, Astraea and FAVOR. Then we validate the performance of different up-sampling methods. In addition, the effects of device sampling and the iterative GAN training strategy are also evaluated.

4.1   Experimental Setup

Datasets. The experiments are performed on the widely used Fashion-MNIST [24] and CIFAR-10 [10] datasets. We hold out 10% of the original training data as the validation dataset. The remaining training data are partitioned to the devices according to the following class imbalance settings.

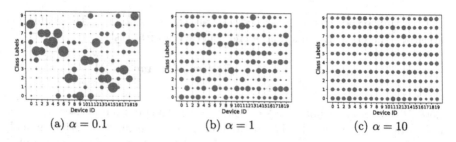

(a) $\alpha = 0.1$ (b) $\alpha = 1$ (c) $\alpha = 10$

Fig. 3. The above figures visualize how data are distributed among 20 devices on different α values. The horizontal axis represents the device ID and the vertical axis represents the class labels. The sizes of circles indicate the number of samples per class allocated to each device. The smaller the α is, the more likely the devices hold samples from only one class.

Class Imbalance Settings. The total number of devices N is set to 20. We use the Dirichlet distribution to create the distribution of devices' training data, which is proposed by [14]. A hyper-parameter α is utilized to denote the level of class imbalance. As shown in Fig. 3, the smaller α is, the higher the level of class imbalance is.

Models. We modify the popular ResNet-18 [7] for CIFAR-10. The modified model consists of a 7×7 convolutional layer followed by a 3×3 max-pooling layer, four convolutional layers with 3×3 kernel size followed by a 2×2 average-pooling layer, a 512 fully connected layer, and finally a 10 class softmax output layer. The model for Fashion-MNIST consists of two convolutional layers with 5×5 kernel size followed by a fully connected layer.

4.2   Results of FED-CGU

Table 1. Results of FED-CGU.

Test Accuracy on Fashion-MNIST and CIFAR-10							
Fashion-MNIST				CIFAR-10			
	$\alpha = 0.1$	$\alpha = 1$	$\alpha = 10$		$\alpha = 0.1$	$\alpha = 1$	$\alpha = 10$
FedAvg	64.63%	72.14%	78.26%	FedAvg	60.24%	67.51%	73.10%
FAVOR	77.60%	82.91%	85.64%	FAVOR	64.74%	76.49%	78.58%
Astraea	78.69%	82.17%	85.15%	Astraea	70.34%	76.78%	80.31%
two-step	70.40%	76.07%	81.35%	two-step	65.12%	72.21%	78.34%
FED-CGU	81.04%	83.31%	85.79%	FED-CGU	75.74%	80.45%	82.81%

We compare our proposed FED-CGU with FedAvg, FAVOR, and Astraea on Fashion-MNIST and CIFAR-10 datasets. We also compare FED-CGU with a proposed two-step baseline, in which we first train a GAN model and then utilize the GAN to augment data once. Table 1 shows the results on Fashion-MNIST after 40 training rounds and CIFAR-10 after 60 training rounds.

According to the results, our proposed FED-CGU reaches the highest accuracy on the Fashion-MNIST and CIFAR-10 datasets on various α settings. In addition, FED-CGU gets even better results than FAVOR and Astraea when $\alpha = 0.1$ (achieves up to 11% higher accuracy). The reason is that, compared with the two strategies, FED-CGU utilizes the up-sampling to release class imbalance in each device during the training. Since the level of the class imbalance is reduced through up-sampling, the convergence of GAN can be accelerated. Therefore, FED-CGU outperforms FAVOR and Astraea. FED-CGU also outperforms the two-step strategy. Since the class imbalance can affect the performance of training, the GAN of the two-step strategy cannot be well trained simply on original data. Thus using such a GAN model in the two-step strategy for up-sampling introduces much noise to the devices. In the ablation experiments of Sect. 4.5, we deeply discuss the two-step strategy (train the GAN once) and iterative strategy.

4.3 Performance of Different Up-sampling Methods

In this subsection, we compare the performance of using a global GAN model for up-sampling with using local up-sampling methods in FL. We evaluate the effects of different up-sampling methods under various levels of class imbalance.

In this experiment, we first utilize up-sampling to supplement the devices' data and then train the model in federated learning. We compare 6 up-sampling methods (i.e. using global GAN for up-sampling, using local GAN for up-sampling, flipping, scale, rotation and shifting). Since common local up-sampling methods (flipping, scale, rotation and shifting) rely on original data, we set the minimum number of each class to 50. With regard to the GAN-based up-sampling, we pretrain a GAN model and use the trained GAN model to perform up-sampling. The local GAN is trained on every single device's local data and the global GAN is trained on all devices' data. The results are shown in Table 2.

Table 2. Test accuracy of different up-sampling methods.

Test Accuracy on CIFAR-10							
	$\alpha = 0.1$	$\alpha = 1$	$\alpha = 10$		$\alpha = 0.1$	$\alpha = 1$	$\alpha = 10$
Global GAN	67.2%	73.3%	75.5%	Scale	59.1%	70.9%	75.7%
Local GAN	60.1%	70.4%	74.6%	Rotation	58.1%	71.2%	74.2%
Flipping	58.7%	70.6%	74.7%	Shifting	57.1%	71.0%	73.8%

We first compare the effects of using a global GAN for up-sampling with other up-sampling approaches. Under various levels of class imbalance, using the global GAN model for up-sampling achieves the highest effect. When the level of class imbalance is high ($\alpha = 0.1$), using global GAN for up-sampling performs significantly better than other methods (accuracy is 7.1%–10.1% higher than other methods). The significant difference between global GAN and other approaches is that the data generated by the global GAN model leverages information from other devices. Using the global GAN model for up-sampling can introduce information of other devices' data to the local device. When the data are nearly balanced, we only need to augment fewer data to balance the class distribution, and less information is introduced by the global GAN. This can explain the results of $\alpha = 10$. When the degree of imbalance increases, more up-sampled data are needed and more information is introduced. Therefore, using the global GAN for up-sampling obtains the maximum advantage over local methods at $\alpha = 0.1$.

We then discuss the results of common up-sampling methods (such as rotation, flip, etc.) and using local GAN for up-sampling. When $\alpha = 0.1$, the performance of the local GAN is slightly higher than that performed by other local up-sampling methods. This is because common up-sampling methods only utilize the information of data with a certain label when augmenting the data with a such label. In this extreme imbalanced case ($\alpha = 0.1$), common up-sampling methods need to supplement a large amount of data, which can easily make the model overfit. On the other hand, the training of the GAN model utilizes all the data with various labels. As information of data with all the labels is utilized, data generated by the GAN model is better than that by common up-sampling methods.

4.4   Effects of Device Sampling

In this subsection, we verify the opinion that applying device sampling can improve the performance of up-sampling. We first compare directly implementing up-sampling, with implementing both up-sampling and device sampling. We regard the gradients of centralized learning as the ground truth and calculate the similarity between gradients of federated learning with centralized ones. The detailed experimental results are shown in Fig. 4. We find that, with device sampling, the similarity between centralized gradients and federated gradients is smaller than that without device sampling under the same level of class imbalance.

We also compare the communication cost for our complementary sampling and random sampling to reach a target accuracy rate. Experimental results in Fig. 5 show the communication cost of different up-sampling curves on Fashion-MNIST and CIFAR-10. Results show that complementary sampling is actually more communication-efficient than random sampling. When $\alpha = 0.1$, the communication consumption of training a CNN on CIFAR-10 using random sampling to reach 70% accuracy is 1795.5 MB whereas complementary sampling uses merely 215 MB. Our complementary sampling also achieves a 57.83% reduction to reach 75% accuracy on Fashion-MNIST when $\alpha = 0.1$.

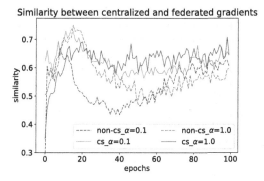

Fig. 4. Comparison of directly sampling devices and sampling devices after up-sampling on CIFAR-10. The curves of 'non-cs' and 'cs' show the results of directly using up-sampling and using both up-sampling and device sampling, respectively.

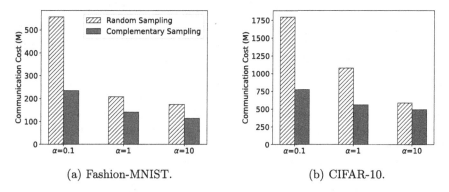

Fig. 5. Communication cost to reach a target accuracy for complementary sampling and random sampling.

We then adjust the proportion of selected devices in each round. As shown in Fig. 6, our complementary sampling achieves better performance, especially when the proportion equals 30%–40%. Since complementarϴy devices have information that other devices do not have, they can better help each other. This is the reason why our method is superior to random sampling. When all devices participate in each round, our method is the same as random sampling in practice. It should be noted that if there are very few devices selected in each round, the accuracy of complementary sampling is sometimes not as good as random sampling. This is because if only few devices are selected in each round, it can be difficult for some devices to find complementary devices.

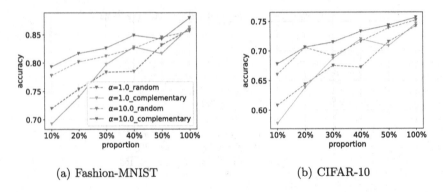

(a) Fashion-MNIST   (b) CIFAR-10

Fig. 6. Effects of the sampling proportions on Fashion-MNIST and CIFAR-10

4.5   Comparison of the Two-Step and Iterative Strategies

In this part, we compare the two strategies of up-sampling: (1) the two-step strategy: train the GAN first and then perform up-sampling once; (2) the iterative strategy: simultaneously perform up-sampling and train the GAN in an iterative manner.

Performance of Iteratively Training GAN. We first validate the assumption that training GAN and up-sampling alternately in an iterative manner can improve the performance of GAN. We utilize the Frechet Inception Distance score [8] of GAN to show the GAN's performance.

$$FID = \|\mu_x - \mu_g\|_2^2 + TR(\Sigma_x + \Sigma_g - 2(\Sigma_x \Sigma_g)^{\frac{1}{2}}) \tag{4}$$

The Frechet Inception Distance score calculates the distance between the real data distribution x and the generated distribution g based on the mean and covariance matrix. Lower scores indicate that the generated data are closer to the original data. We validate the GAN during the training by the FID score [8]. As shown in Fig. 7, the quality of data generated by the GAN models is getting better after each iteration in all scenarios.

Test Accuracy of Using GAN Trained in Different Strategies. We then compare the test accuracy of the classifier with the two-step baseline and our iterative strategy. According to the results shown in Fig. 8, it is better to iteratively perform up-sampling and train the GAN. When the level of class imbalance is high ($\alpha = 0.1$), iteratively performing up-sampling and training the GAN achieves significantly higher accuracy than the two-step strategy. The reason is that, in the two-step strategy, the GAN model cannot be well trained in the presence of class imbalance. Data generated by the GAN of the two-step strategy may have much noise that can degrade the accuracy. In the iterative strategy, the class imbalance is gradually balanced during training, and finally, the GAN model is trained in the IID scene.

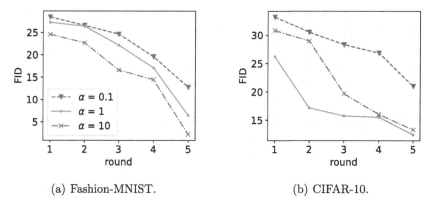

(a) Fashion-MNIST.   (b) CIFAR-10.

Fig. 7. Performance of GAN during the training on Fashion-MNIST and CIFAR-10.

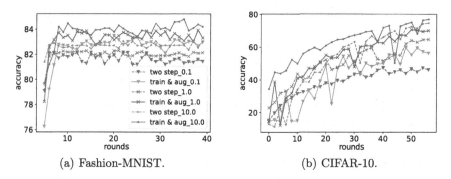

(a) Fashion-MNIST.   (b) CIFAR-10.

Fig. 8. Test accuracy with different GAN training strategies on Fashion-MNIST and CIFAR-10. The numbers at the end of the legend $(0.1, 1.0, 10)$ are the values of α, which indicates the level of class imbalance.

Note that the initial training process of the iterative strategy is more oscillatory than that of the two-step strategy when the level of class imbalance is high. Since the GAN is not well trained at the beginning of training, the iterative strategy does not augment much data. As the training process proceeds, the iterative strategy augments more and gets better performance.

5   Conclusion

Class imbalance, one of the challenges in FL, can degrade the performance of the final model. To address this problem, we propose the first collaborative GAN-based up-sampling strategy in FL that allows devices to help each other without leaking their private data. To accelerate the convergence of the GAN model, we design a device sampling strategy that selects complementary devices. In addition, we adopt a genetic algorithm to dynamically determine the number of augmented data for each device. Experimental results on Fashion-MNIST and CIFAR-10 indicate that FED-CGU outperforms the state-of-the-art algorithms.

Acknowledgements. This work was supported in part by National Natural Science Foundation of China under Grant No. 61976012.

References

1. Chawla, N.V., Lazarevic, A., Hall, L.O., Bowyer, K.W.: SMOTEBoost: improving prediction of the minority class in boosting. In: Lavrač, N., Gamberger, D., Todorovski, L., Blockeel, H. (eds.) PKDD 2003. LNCS (LNAI), vol. 2838, pp. 107–119. Springer, Heidelberg (2003). https://doi.org/10.1007/978-3-540-39804-2_12
2. Dinh, C.T., Tran, N.H., Nguyen, T.D.: Personalized federated learning with moreau envelopes. In: Advances in Neural Information Processing Systems, vol. 33: Annual Conference on Neural Information Processing Systems 2020, NeurIPS 2020, 6–12 December 2020, virtual (2020)
3. Duan, M., Liu, D., Chen, X., Liu, R., Tan, Y., Liang, L.: Self-balancing federated learning with global imbalanced data in mobile systems. IEEE Trans. Parallel Distrib. Syst. **32**(1), 59–71 (2021). https://doi.org/10.1109/TPDS.2020.3009406
4. Fallah, A., Mokhtari, A., Ozdaglar, A.E.: Personalized federated learning with theoretical guarantees: a model-agnostic meta-learning approach. In: Advances in Neural Information Processing Systems, vol. 33: Annual Conference on Neural Information Processing Systems 2020, NeurIPS 2020, 6–12 December 2020, virtual (2020)
5. Goodfellow, I.J., et al.: Generative adversarial nets. In: Advances in Neural Information Processing Systems, vol. 27: Annual Conference on Neural Information Processing Systems, Montreal, Quebec, Canada 2014, 8–13 December 2014, pp. 2672–2680 (2014)
6. He, H., Garcia, E.A.: Learning from imbalanced data. IEEE Trans. Knowl. Data Eng. **21**(9), 1263–1284 (2009). https://doi.org/10.1109/TKDE.2008.239
7. He, K., Zhang, X., Ren, S., Sun, J.: Deep residual learning for image recognition. In: 2016 IEEE Conference on Computer Vision and Pattern Recognition, CVPR 2016, Las Vegas, NV, USA, 27–30 June 2016, pp. 770–778. IEEE Computer Society (2016)
8. Heusel, M., Ramsauer, H., Unterthiner, T., Nessler, B., Hochreiter, S.: GANs trained by a two time-scale update rule converge to a local nash equilibrium. In: Advances in Neural Information Processing Systems, vol. 30: Annual Conference on Neural Information Processing Systems 2017, Long Beach, CA, USA, 4–9 December 2017, pp. 6626–6637 (2017)
9. Karimireddy, S.P., Kale, S., Mohri, M., Reddi, S.J., Stich, S.U., Suresh, A.T.: SCAFFOLD: stochastic controlled averaging for federated learning. In: Proceedings of the 37th International Conference on Machine Learning, ICML 2020. Proceedings of Machine Learning Research, 13–18 July 2020, Virtual Event, vol. 119, pp. 5132–5143. PMLR (2020)
10. Krizhevsky, A.: Learning multiple layers of features from tiny images. Technical report (2009)
11. Li, Q., He, B., Song, D.: Model-contrastive federated learning. In: IEEE Conference on Computer Vision and Pattern Recognition, CVPR 2021, virtual, 19–25 June 2021, pp. 10713–10722. Computer Vision Foundation / IEEE (2021)
12. Li, X., Huang, K., Yang, W., Wang, S., Zhang, Z.: On the convergence of FedAvg on non-IID data. In: 8th International Conference on Learning Representations, ICLR 2020, Addis Ababa, Ethiopia, 26–30 April 2020 (2020)

13. Lim, S., Kim, I., Kim, T., Kim, C., Kim, S.: Fast autoaugment. In: Advances in Neural Information Processing Systems, vol. 32: Annual Conference on Neural Information Processing Systems 2019, NeurIPS 2019, Vancouver, BC, Canada, 8–14 December 2019, pp. 6662–6672 (2019)
14. Lin, T., Kong, L., Stich, S.U., Jaggi, M.: Ensemble distillation for robust model fusion in federated learning. In: Advances in Neural Information Processing Systems, vol. 33: Annual Conference on Neural Information Processing Systems 2020, NeurIPS 2020, 6–12 December 2020, virtual (2020)
15. López, V., Fernández, A., Moreno-Torres, J.G., Herrera, F.: Analysis of preprocessing vs. cost-sensitive learning for imbalanced classification. open problems on intrinsic data characteristics. Expert Syst. Appl. **39**(7), 6585–6608 (2012)
16. McMahan, B., Moore, E., Ramage, D., Hampson, S., y Arcas, B.A.: Communication-efficient learning of deep networks from decentralized data. In: Proceedings of the 20th International Conference on Artificial Intelligence and Statistics, AISTATS 2017, 20–22 April 2017, Fort Lauderdale, FL, USA. Proceedings of Machine Learning Research, vol. 54, pp. 1273–1282. PMLR (2017)
17. Mirza, M., Osindero, S.: Conditional generative adversarial nets. CoRR abs/1411.1784 (2014)
18. Odena, A., Olah, C., Shlens, J.: Conditional image synthesis with auxiliary classifier GANs. In: Proceedings of the 34th International Conference on Machine Learning, ICML 2017. Proceedings of Machine Learning Research, Sydney, NSW, Australia, 6–11 August 2017, vol. 70, pp. 2642–2651. PMLR (2017)
19. Seiffert, C., Khoshgoftaar, T.M., Hulse, J.V., Napolitano, A.: Rusboost: a hybrid approach to alleviating class imbalance. IEEE Trans. Syst. Man Cybern. Part A **40**(1), 185–197 (2010)
20. Smith, V., Chiang, C., Sanjabi, M., Talwalkar, A.S.: Federated multi-task learning. In: Advances in Neural Information Processing Systems, vol. 30: Annual Conference on Neural Information Processing Systems 2017, Long Beach, CA, USA, 4–9 December 2017, pp. 4424–4434 (2017)
21. Sun, Y., Kamel, M.S., Wong, A.K.C., Wang, Y.: Cost-sensitive boosting for classification of imbalanced data. Pattern Recognit. **40**(12), 3358–3378 (2007)
22. Wang, H., Kaplan, Z., Niu, D., Li, B.: Optimizing federated learning on non-IID data with reinforcement learning. In: 39th IEEE Conference on Computer Communications, INFOCOM 2020, Toronto, ON, Canada, 6–9 July 2020, pp. 1698–1707. IEEE (2020)
23. Wang, L., Xu, S., Wang, X., Zhu, Q.: Addressing class imbalance in federated learning. In: Thirty-Fifth AAAI Conference on Artificial Intelligence, AAAI 2021, Thirty-Third Conference on Innovative Applications of Artificial Intelligence, IAAI 2021, The Eleventh Symposium on Educational Advances in Artificial Intelligence, EAAI 2021, Virtual Event, 2–9 February 2021, pp. 10165–10173. AAAI Press (2021)
24. Xiao, H., Rasul, K., Vollgraf, R.: Fashion-MNIST: a novel image dataset for benchmarking machine learning algorithms. CoRR abs/1708.07747 (2017)
25. Zhao, Y., Li, M., Lai, L., Suda, N., Civin, D., Chandra, V.: Federated learning with non-IID data. CoRR abs/1806.00582 (2018)
26. Zhou, Z., Liu, X.: Training cost-sensitive neural networks with methods addressing the class imbalance problem. IEEE Trans. Knowl. Data Eng. **18**(1), 63–77 (2006)

Deep-Steiner: Learning to Solve the Euclidean Steiner Tree Problem

Siqi Wang$^{(\boxtimes)}$ (ID), Yifan Wang (ID), and Guangmo Tong (ID)

University of Delaware, Newark, DE 19716, USA
{wsqbit,yifanw,amotong}@udel.edu

Abstract. The Euclidean Steiner tree problem seeks the min-cost network to connect a collection of target locations, and it underlies many applications of wireless networks. In this paper, we present a study on solving the Euclidean Steiner tree problem using reinforcement learning enhanced by graph representation learning. Different from the commonly studied connectivity problems like travelling salesman problem or vehicle routing problem where the search space is finite, the Euclidean Steiner tree problem requires to search over the entire Euclidean space, thereby making the existing methods not applicable. In this paper, we design discretization methods by leveraging the unique characteristics of the Steiner tree, and propose new training schemes for handling the dynamic Steiner points emerging during the incremental construction. Our design is examined through a sanity check using experiments on a collection of datasets, with encouraging results demonstrating the utility of our method as an alternative to classic combinatorial methods.

Keywords: Reinforcement learning · Combinatorial optimization · The steiner tree problem

1 Introduction

Network connection is an important issue in wireless networks [8,15,35], and a key problem in such studies is to build a connected network with the minimum cost, for example, the location-selection problem [31], the relay node placement problem [10], and the network connectivity restoring problem [39]. Such problems can often be nicely reduced to the classic Euclidean Steiner tree (EST) problem, where we seek to connect a collection of points in the Euclidean space using Steiner minimal trees. The EST problem is well-known to be NP-hard, even in the two-dimensional Euclidean space [16], and various algorithms have been developed for effective and efficient solutions [3,13,22,25,40,41,47]. Recently, a trending direction is to design reinforcement learning diagrams for solving combinatorial optimization problems in a data-driven manner. This is driven by as least two compelling reasons: philosophically, we are wondering if effective heuristics can be automatically inferred by artificial intelligence [34]; practically, heuristics produced by reinforcement learning are tuned by the empirical distribution of the inputs, and can therefore offer better performance for a specific

© ICST Institute for Computer Sciences, Social Informatics and Telecommunications Engineering 2023
Published by Springer Nature Switzerland AG 2023. All Rights Reserved
Z. J. Haas et al. (Eds.): WiCON 2022, LNICST 464, pp. 228–242, 2023.
https://doi.org/10.1007/978-3-031-27041-3_16

application scenario [5] [34]. In this paper, we revisit the EST problem and design reinforcement learning methods.

Challenges. Learning-based methods have recently shown promising results in solving combinatorial optimization problems [5,26,28]. In principle, searching the best solution to combinatorial optimization problems can be modeled as a Markov decision process (MDP) in which the optimal policy is acquired using reinforcement learning [11]. Enhanced by deep learning techniques, the policies can be further parameterized through neural networks for learning better representation [28] [36]. The existing works have studied problems like the travelling salesman problem (TSP) and the vehicle routing problem where the searching space is finite, and therefore, they focus primarily on policy parameterization and training [28] [36]. The key challenge in solving the EST problem is that the searching space is unstructured: the Steiner points could be any subset of the Euclidean space. Therefore, as opposed to the TSP problem where the searching space is composed of all permutations of the nodes, the solutions to the EST problem cannot be readily enumerated. A straightforward method is to discretize the Euclidean space using grid networks by which the Steiner points are assumed to be on the joints. However, such a simple method is intuitively not optimal because it is unable to take account of any combinatorial properties of the Steiner trees. In this paper, we make an attempt to address the above challenges by presenting a reinforcement learning framework called Deep-Steiner for solving the EST problem. Our work in this paper can be summarized as follows:

- **Space discretization.** Leveraging the unique properties of Steiner trees, we design methods for creating a compact candidate set for the Steiner points. The resulted candidate set is dynamically constructed during the incremental searching, thereby being superior to methods adopting fixed searching spaces (e.g., grid network). In addition, the complexity of our candidate set can be easily tuned through hyper-parameters, admitting a controllable efficacy-efficiency trade-off.
- **Policy parameterization and training schemes.** We present methods for parameterizing the searching policy using attention techniques to dynamically update the point and graph embeddings. Our methods iteratively update the point and graph embeddings and then select a Steiner point until meeting the stopping criterion, which is different from previous methods that only compute the embeddings once. In addition, we design new reinforcement schemes for parameter training, where three stopping criteria are proposed for different training purposes.
- **Implementation and experiments.** Extensive experiments have been conducted to examine the proposed methods on different datasets and different training schemes. We have acquired encouraging results showing that the proposed method is non-trivially better than the baselines, which might be the first piece of evidence that demonstrates the potential of data-driven approaches for addressing combinatorial optimization problems with complex searching spaces. Our source code is made publicly available[1].

---

[1] https://github.com/EricW1996/EAI-Deepsteiner.

2   Related Work

Steiner Tree in Wireless Networks. In the field of wireless network, many research problems are closely related to the Steiner tree problem. For example, the relay node placement problem can be reduced to the EST problem with bounded edge length [10,30]. Furthermore, solving the EST problem is also a key to many other problems, including the problem of restoring the network connectivity [39], the minimum connected dominating set problem [33], the problem of broadcast routing [29], and the minimum length multicast tree problem [18].

Traditional Methods. Traditional approaches for solving the EST problem can be classified into three branches: exact algorithms, approximation algorithms, and heuristic methods. Warme *et al.* propose the GeoSteiner algorithm [45], which is the most successful exact algorithm for the EST problem. Their algorithm is based on the generation and concentration of the full Steiner tree. For heuristic algorithms, Thompson *et al.* provide an edge insertion algorithm using local search methods [41], and an improved version is designed later by Dreyer *et al.* [13]. Smith *et al.* propose a heuristic algorithm running in $O(n \log n)$ based on the generation and concentration of the full Steiner tree [40]. Bereta et al. propose a memetic algorithm to find optimal Steiner points [7]. These heuristic algorithms can generate an approximate solution in a polynomial time, suggesting that good handcrafted rules are helpful to solve the EST problems.

Learning to Solve Combinatorial Optimization Problem. Using machine learning to learn heuristic algorithms opens new horizons for solving combinatorial optimization problems. Vinyals *et al.* [43] propose a supervised learning method and design the pointer network model to learn a heuristic for computing the Delaunay triangulation and solving TSP. Later, Bello *et al.* [5] propose a reinforcement learning method to solve TSP; following this idea, Kool *et al.* [28] propose a deep reinforcement learning method based on the Transformer architecture. Motivated by the success on solving TSP, various combinatorial problems have been revisited by the machine learning community, e.g., the 3D bin packing problem [21], the minimum vertex cover problem [26], and the maximum cut problem [4,26]. More related works can be found in recent surveys [6,32].

Steiner Tree Over Graph vs Euclidean Steiner Tree. Being closely related to the EST problem, the Steiner tree over graph problem seeks to build the min-cost network using Steiner points from a given point set, implying the searching space is finite. Therefore, most of the existing techniques can be easily applied to the Steiner tree over graph problem. For example, Du *et al.* [14] propose a reinforcement learning method and Ahmed *et al.* [1] study the same problem through supervised learning methods. Another related one is the rectilinear Steiner minimum tree problem, where the network is required to be composed of horizontal and vertical lines, and therefore, the grid network is a natural choice for creating the searching space [9]. Unfortunately, such a simple method does not work well for the EST problem, as evidenced later in experiments.

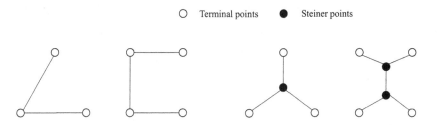

Fig. 1. The left two figures illustrate the minimal spanning trees. The right two figures illustrate the Steiner trees.

3   Problem Setting

Formally, the EST problem is defined as follows.

Definition 1 (The Euclidean Steiner tree (EST) problem). *Given a point set S (called terminal set) in a two-dimensional Euclidean space $\mathbb{R}^2$, construct a tree with the minimum Euclidean distance to connect S, where points not in S (called Steiner points) are allowed to use to construct the tree.*

An illustration of the comparison between minimal spanning trees and the Steiner tree is given in Fig. 1.

Concerning a distribution $\mathcal{D}$ over the input instance S, we wish to learn a function T that can compute a Steiner tree $T(S)$ over S with the minimum length. As a statistical learning problem, we seek to minimize the true error:

$$L(T) = \mathbb{E}_{S \sim \mathcal{D}}\Big[\operatorname{len}\big(T(S)\big)\Big]$$

where $\operatorname{len}(T(S))$ denotes the tree length under the Euclidean distance.

4   Deep-Steiner

In this section, we present a reinforcement learning method called Deep-Steiner to learn the desired function T.

4.1   Overall Structure

Notably, supposing that the optimal Steiner points have been identified, the optimal solution must be a minimum spanning tree over the Steiner points plus the terminal nodes. Therefore, the key part is to determine the Steiner points. The overall framework of Deep-Steiner is conceptually simple, as shown in Algorithm 1. Given the input instance S, Deep-Steiner decides the Steiner points in an iterative manner. In each iteration i, based on the current selected points $I_{i-1} \subseteq \mathbb{R}^2$ including both the terminal points and Steiner points, a new Steiner point is selected from a certain candidate set $C_i \subseteq \mathbb{R}^2$ by a policy $\pi : C_i \to \mathbb{R}^2$, with $I_0 = S$ being the initial input. In particular, the policy selects the best node

---

Algorithm 1. Deep-Steiner

Input: S and p_θ
Output: A Steiner tree associated with S
1: $I_0 = S, i = 1$
2: **while** $\text{len}(\text{MST}(I_i)) \leq \text{len}(\text{MST}(I_{i-1}))$ and $i \leq |S| - 2$ **do**
3:    Generate candidate set C_i based on I_{i-1}
4:    $v^* = \arg\max_{v \in C_i} p_\theta(v|I_{i-1})$, $I_i = I_{i-1} \cup \{v^*\}$, $i = i+1$
5: **end while**
6: **return** $\text{MST}(I_{i-1})$

---

from the candidate set C_i according to a distribution $p_\theta(v|I_{i-1})$ over $v \in C_i$ (conditioned on I_{i-1}), where p_θ is parameterized by deep neural networks. In completing the framework, we first present methods for generating the candidate set (Sect. 4.2) and then present the design of p_θ (Sect. 4.3). Finally, we discuss training methods for computing the parameters θ involved in p_θ (Sect. 4.4).

4.2 Candidate Set C_i

We now present methods for constructing the candidate set C_i based on the current selected points I_{i-1}. To eschew searching the continuous space $\mathbb{R}^2$, one straightforward idea is to use the grid network, which has been widely adopted in existing methods [2, 9, 38]. Nevertheless, the grid pattern is not informed by the structure of the Steiner trees and therefore can lead to suboptimal performance, as shown in the experiments later. For a better candidate space, we are inspired by the following property of the Steiner trees.

Lemma 1. *[17] The Steiner points in the Steiner minimal tree must have a degree of three, and the three edges incident to such a point must form three $120°\,C$ angles.*

The above property suggests that the optimal Steiner points must be on the $120\,°C$-arc between two points in $\mathbb{R}^2$, which has greatly reduced the searching space. We denote such arcs as Steiner arcs.

Definition 2 (Steiner arc). *Given two points $a \in \mathbb{R}^2$ and $b \in \mathbb{R}^2$, the set $\text{Arc}_{a,b} = \{x : x \in \mathbb{R}^2, \angle axb = 120\}$ is the Steiner Arc induced by a and b.*

With the above concept, the initial space we acquire consists of all the Steiner arcs between the points in I_{i-1}. As such a space is still continuous, we divide the arc into k^* equal-size parts, for some $k^* \in \mathbb{Z}$, and select the endpoints to acquire an enumerable space. Formally, the resulted candidates associated with one arc $\text{Arc}_{a,b}$ are given as follows.

$$\text{Arc}_{a,b}^{k^*} =$$
$$\left\{ x_1, ..., x_{k^*} : x_i \in \text{Arc}_{a,b}, |x_{i-1} - x_i| = |x_i - x_{i+1}|, x_0 = a, x_{k^*+1} = b, i \in [k^*] \right\}$$

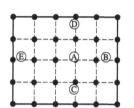
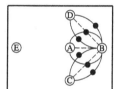
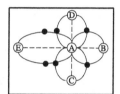

Fig. 2. The left figure illustrates the candidate points based on the grid network. The middle figure shows the candidate points generated based on the Steiner arcs between node B and its nearest neighbors; the right figure presents the candidate points generated by the MST-based methods.

Enumerating over all possible pairs in I_{i-1}, the total candidate points are in the order of $O(k^* \cdot |I_{i-1}|^2)$, which is still infeasible when being involved in training deep architectures (Sect. 4.3). Therefore, we adopt the following two methods to further reduce the searching space:

- **KNN-based candidate space.** Notice that the Steiner minimal tree has the optimality condition that each subgraph tree is also a minimum spanning tree over the involved points. Intuitively, for two points in I_{i-1} that are not local neighbors, their Steiner arc cannot include any Steiner points in the optimal solution to the input instance S. Therefore, for each point v in I_{i-1}, only the Steiner arcs between v and its nearest neighbors are selected. Let $N_v^{k'} \subseteq I_{i-1}$ be the set of the $k' \in \mathbb{Z}$ nearest neighbors of v in I_{i-1}. We have the following candidate space:

$$C_i = \bigcup_{v \in I_{i-1}} \bigcup_{u \in N_v^{k'}} \text{Arc}_{v,u}^{k^*} \tag{1}$$

- **MST-based candidate space.** Following the same intuition of the KNN-based method, we now seek to eliminate unqualified Steiner arcs by using the minimum spanning tree $\text{MST}(I_i)$ over I_i. That is, for each pair of the nodes in I_{i-1}, we only select the Steiner arc $\text{Arc}_{u,v}$ when edge (u, v) appears in $\text{MST}(I_i)$. Formally, we have the following space:

$$C_i = \bigcup_{(u,v) \in \text{MST}(I_{i-1})} \text{Arc}_{v,u}^{k^*} \tag{2}$$

One can easily see that the candidate space resulted from the above methods is linear in $|I_{i-1}|$ and determined by some hyperparameters k^* and k' that control the complexity-efficient trade-off. Such a trade-off will be experimentally studied later. An illustration of the candidate points generated by different methods is given in Fig. 2.

4.3 Policy π and Distribution p_θ

Given the candidate set C_i in each iteration of Algorithm 1, our policy computes one Steiner point based on a parameterized distribution $p_\theta(v|I_{i-1})$, with the hope that a higher value of $p_\theta(v|I_{i-1})$ translates the better quality of the final Steiner tree. To this end, the parameters θ will be trained using reinforcement learning (Sect. 4.4). In what follows, we present our design of $p_\theta(v|I_{i-1})$. The overall design of p_θ has two modules: the encode computes the hidden embedding of each point in C_i as well as the entire graph; the decoder translates the embeddings into a distribution over C_i.

Encoder. Given the candidate C_i and the currently selected points I_{i-1}, where each point is represented by its coordinates, we first compute the hidden representations following the framework proposed in [28] to capture useful latent relationships between the points in terms of building a Steiner minimal tree.

Let $X = C_i \cup I_{i-1} = \{x_1, ..., x_n\}$ be the entire point set. For each $x_j \in X$, the embedding is computed through the attention mechanism [42] composed of a sequence of $L \in \mathbb{Z}$ neural layers, where its d-dimensional hidden representation at layer $l \in [L]$ is denoted by $\mathbf{A}_{j,l} \in \mathbb{R}^{d\times 1}$. Initially, we have $\mathbf{A}_{j,0} = \mathbf{W}^{(0)} \cdot x_j + \mathbf{b}^{(0)}$ with $\mathbf{W}^{(0)} \in \mathbb{R}^{d\times 2}$, and $\mathbf{b}^{(0)} \in \mathbb{R}^{d\times 1}$ being learnable parameters. To obtain $\mathbf{A}_{j,l+1}$ from $\mathbf{A}_{j,l}$, we first use multi-head attention [42] to aggregate the information from the neighbors of x_j:

$$\text{MHA}_{j,l+1}(\mathbf{A}_{1,l}, \mathbf{A}_{2,l}, ..., \mathbf{A}_{n,l}) = \sum_{m=1}^{M} \mathbf{W}^{(1)}_{m,l} \cdot \mathbf{A}'_{j,m}$$

which is composed of $M \in \mathbb{Z}$ self-attentions $\mathbf{A}'_{j,m}$ [42] computed by

$$\mathbf{A}'_{j,m} = \sum_{k=1}^{n} \frac{\exp(\mathbf{q}^{\mathsf{T}}_{j,m}\mathbf{k}_{k,m}/\sqrt{d_s}) \cdot \mathbf{v}_{k,m}}{\sum_{k'=1}^{n} \exp(\mathbf{q}^{\mathsf{T}}_{j,m}\mathbf{k}_{k',m}/\sqrt{d_s})}$$

where $d_s = d/M$ is the normalizer, $\mathbf{q}_{j,m} \in \mathbb{R}^{d_s \times 1}$, $\mathbf{k}_{j,m} \in \mathbb{R}^{d_s \times 1}$, and $\mathbf{v}_{j,m} \in \mathbb{R}^{d_s \times 1}$ are hidden vectors obtained through linear transformation from $\mathbf{A}_{j,l}$:

$$\mathbf{q}_{j,m} = \mathbf{W}^{(2)}_{m,l+1} \cdot \mathbf{A}_{j,l}, \quad \mathbf{k}_{j,m} = \mathbf{W}^{(3)}_{m,l+1} \cdot \mathbf{A}_{j,l}, \quad \mathbf{v}_{j,m} = \mathbf{W}^{(4)}_{m,l+1} \cdot \mathbf{A}_{j,l}$$

with $\mathbf{W}^{(1)}_{m,l+1} \in \mathbb{R}^{d\times d_s}$, $\mathbf{W}^{(2)}_{m,l+1} \in \mathbb{R}^{d_s \times d}$, $\mathbf{W}^{(3)}_{m,l+1} \in \mathbb{R}^{d_s \times d}$, and $\mathbf{W}^{(4)}_{m,l+1} \in \mathbb{R}^{d_s \times d}$ being learnable parameters. With the transmission of MHA, the representation $\mathbf{A}_{i,l+1}$ of point x_j at the next layer $l + 1$ is finally obtained through batch normalization and one feed-forward layer:

$$\hat{\mathbf{A}}_{j,l} = \text{BN}_{l+1}\left(\mathbf{A}_{j,l} + \text{MHA}_{j,l+1}(\mathbf{A}_{1,l}, \mathbf{A}_{2,l}, ..., \mathbf{A}_{n,l})\right)$$

$$\mathbf{A}_{j,l+1} = \text{BN}_{l+1}\left(\hat{\mathbf{A}}_{j,l} + \text{FF}_{l+1}(\hat{\mathbf{A}}_{j,l})\right)$$

where BN is the standard batch normalization process [23] and FF is the standard feed-forward network with ReLu activations [19] of dimension 512. Finally, the graph embedding $\mathbf{A}_G \in \mathbb{R}^d$ is calculated as the average sum of the final embeddings over I_{i-1} rather than over X, which is different from [28]:

$$\mathbf{A}_G = \frac{1}{|I_{i-1}|} \sum_{j:x_j \in I_{i-1}} \mathbf{A}_{j,L}$$

Decoder. With the final point embeddings $\mathbf{A}_{j,L}$ and the graph embedding $\mathbf{A}_G$, the encoder derives a parameterized distribution over C_i by combining the embeddings through exponential families:

$$p_\theta(x_j \in C_i | I_{i-1}) = \frac{\exp(\mathbf{q}^\mathsf{T} \cdot \mathbf{k}_j / \sqrt{d_s})}{\sum_{k:x_k \in X_i \cap C_i} \exp(\mathbf{q}^\mathsf{T} \cdot \mathbf{k}_k / \sqrt{d_s})}$$

where the hidden representation $\mathbf{q} \in \mathbb{R}^{d_s \times 1}$ and $\mathbf{k}_j \in \mathbb{R}^{d_s \times 1}$ are obtained via linear transformation based on the embeddings:

$$\mathbf{q} = \mathbf{W}^{(5)} \cdot \mathbf{A}_G \quad \text{and} \quad \mathbf{k}_j = \mathbf{W}^{(6)} \cdot \mathbf{A}_{j,L}$$

where $\mathbf{W}^{(5)} \in \mathbb{R}^{d_s \times d}$ and $\mathbf{W}^{(6)} \in \mathbb{R}^{d_s \times d}$ are learnable.

Parameter Space. In summary, the proposed model has three hyperparameters: $M \in \mathbb{Z}$ controlling the complexity of multi-head attention, $L \in \mathbb{Z}$ determining the number of layers in the encoder, and $d \in \mathbb{Z}$ specifying the hidden dimensions. On top of that, the distribution p_θ is parameterized by a collection of learnable matrices, including $\mathbf{W}^{(0)}$, $\mathbf{b}^{(0)}$, $\mathbf{W}_{m,l}^{(i)}$ ($i \in [1,4]$, $m \in [M]$ and $l \in [L]$), $\mathbf{W}^{(5)}$, and $\mathbf{W}^{(6)}$.

4.4 Training

We now present methods for computing the parameter using REINFORCE with baseline [28,46]. The framework is given in Algorithm 2. Each epoch consists of a sequence of batch training. In each batch training (line 4–20), given a batch size $B \in \mathbb{Z}$, we sample a collection of instances, and for each instance, we predict the Steiner trees based respectively on the current parameter θ and the best parameter θ_{bs}. With the predicted Steiner trees, we obtain a new parameter θ_{new} by maximizing

$$\sum_{i=1}^{B} (\text{len}(T_\theta(S_i)) - \text{len}(T_{\theta_{bs}}(S_i))) \cdot \nabla_\theta \log p_\theta(T_\theta(S_i) | S_i) \tag{3}$$

using the Adam algorithm [27], where $p_\theta(T_\theta(S_i)|S_i) = \prod_j p_\theta(I_j|I_{j-1})$ is likelihood of the prediction and I_j is the sequence of points used to construct $T_\theta(S_i)$. The above optimization implies that the model should produce a Steiner tree with small length and large likelihood. At the end of each epoch, the parameter will be updated only if it passes the paired t-test with $\alpha = 0.05$ on $10,000$ validation instances to examine whether or not the performance improvement is statistically significant [20]. Now the only part left is the process to generate predictions during the training process (line 6–17 in Algorithm 2), where we keep selecting Steiner points but use different stopping criteria for different training purposes. We consider three stopping criteria:

- **First-increment.** Similar to the inference process (Algorithm 1), we stop adding Steiner points if the resulted minimum spanning tree becomes larger instead of smaller. The rationale behind such a strategy is that parameter updating would become useless if the current tree is nowhere close to the optimal one.

Algorithm 2. REINFORCE with Rollout Baseline

Input: batch size B, significance α

Output: parameter θ_{bs}

1: initial parameter θ, $\theta_{bs} \leftarrow \theta$
2: **for** each epoch **do**
3:    **for** each batch training **do**
4:       Sample a batch of instance $\{S_1, ..., S_B\}$
5:       **for** $j \in [B]$ **do**
6:          $I_0 = S_j$, $i = 1$
7:          **while** stopping criterion is not met **do**
8:             Generate candidate set C_i based on I_{i-1}
9:             $v' \sim p_\theta(v|I_{i-1})$, $I_i = I_{i-1} \cup \{v'\}$, $i = i + 1$
10:          **end while**
11:          $T_\theta(S_i) = \mathrm{MST}(I_{i-1})$
12:          $I_0 = S_j$, $i = 1$
13:          **while** stopping criterion is not met **do**
14:             Generate candidate set C_i based on I_{i-1}
15:             $v^* = \arg\max_{v \in C_i} p_{\theta_{bs}}(v|I_{i-1})$, $I_i = I_{i-1} \cup \{v^*\}$, $i = i + 1$
16:          **end while**
17:          $T_{\theta_{bs}}(S_i) = \mathrm{MST}(I_{i-1})$
18:       **end for**
19:       $\nabla\mathcal{L} \leftarrow \sum_{i=1}^{B}(\mathrm{len}(T_\theta(S_i)) - \mathrm{len}(T_{\theta_{bs}}(S_i))) \cdot \nabla_\theta \log p_\theta(T_\theta(S_i)|S_i)$
20:       $\theta \leftarrow \mathrm{Adam}(\theta, \nabla\mathcal{L})$
21:    **end for**
22:    **if** t-test$(\theta, \theta_{bs}, \alpha)$ passes **then**
23:       $\theta_{bs} \leftarrow \theta$
24:    **end if**
25: **end for**

- **First-selection.** Under this stopping criterion, we stop adding Steiner points after selecting one Steiner point, which means that we focus on training the policy to select the nodes that are locally optimal. Since our inference process runs in a greedy manner, local optimality is necessary to achieve nontrivial performance compared to random methods.
- **All-selection.** Under such a method, we always select $|S| - 2$ Steiner points, which is motivated by the well-known fact that the Steiner minimal tree over $|S|$ points can have at most $|S| - 2$ Steiner points [17].

5   Experiment

In this section, we present our empirical studies.

5.1   Experiment Setting

Model Setting. We examine our method with different candidate generation methods (Sect. 4.2) and different stopping criteria (Sect. 4.4). Following the standard practice [37], we initialize the parameters using a pre-trained TSP-20 model

[28]. Balancing between quality and computational cost, the best hyperparameters are set as follows. $k^* = 9$ for arc partition; $k' = 3$ for KNN-based candidate space; $d = 128, L = 5, M = 8$ for the attention model; the batch size B is 32.

Datasets. For synthetic dataset $(n, \mathcal{D})$, each instance is generated by randomly selecting n points following a certain distribution $\mathcal{D}$ over $\mathbb{R}^2$. Our experiments involve three synthetic datasets:

$$D_1 = (10, U(0, 1)^2), D_2 = (20, U(0, 1)^2), D_3 = (10, N(0.5, 0.2)^2),$$

where U is the uniform distribution and N is the Gaussian distribution. Such samples have been widely adopted in existing works [24, 28]. In addition, we adopt the DEG-10 dataset containing a thousand instances with ten terminal points [48], which is a benchmark used in the 11th DIMACS Implementation Challenge [12].

Baseline Methods. The optimal solution is calculated by Geo-Steiner [44]. The second baseline outputs the minimum spanning tree of the input instance, which is a simple and effective approximation to the Steiner minimal tree. In addition, we include a highly effective heuristic method proposed by Bereta *et al.* [7], which is an iterative framework and can often produce near-optimal solutions provided with a sufficient number of iterations. Finally, two random methods are adopted as baselines. Rand-1 samples $r \in \mathbb{Z}$ random Steiner points from the distribution $\mathcal{D}$, where r is sampled from $[0, |S| - 2]$. Rand-2 is the same as Algorithm 1 except that the Steiner points are randomly selected from the candidate set; such a method is used to prove that our policy is indeed nontrivial.

Training and Testing. Our experiments were executed on Google Colab with NVIDIA Tesla V100. The training size is $10, 240$. For each method, we examine its performance by comparing the predicted Steiner trees to the optimal solution over $10, 000$ testing instances, i.e., $\frac{\text{len}(T_\theta(S)) - \text{len}(T_{\text{opt}}(S))}{\text{len}(T_{\text{opt}}(S))}$.

5.2   Result and Analysis

Overall Observations. Tables 1 and 2 show the performance in terms of effectiveness and efficiency. The results confirm that our method is non-trivially better than Rand-1 and minimum spanning trees, and furthermore, it is comparable to the best heuristic and can generate solutions close to the optimal ones. Compared to Berata's method, the main advantage of our method lies in time efficiency (as shown in Table 2), which suggests that methods based on reinforcement learning are promising in dealing with NP-hard combinatorial optimization problems with complex searching spaces.

On Candidate Generation Methods. According to Table 1, the proposed methods are clearly better than grid based methods in generating good candidate points. In addition, MST-based methods are better than the KNN-based on small graphs but not on large graphs. The main reason is that the candidate set generated by KNN-based methods is larger than that of the MST-based methods,

Table 1. Main results. Each cell shows the performance of one method on one dataset, together with the standard deviation. The missing data means that the training time of one epoch is more than 2.5 h, which is considered to be impractical.

Methods	D_1	D_2	D_3
Geo-Steiner	0	0	0
Bereta's method (10 iterations)	1.67 ± 0.02%	2.43 ± 0.01%	1.67 ± 0.02%
Bereta's method (20 iterations)	1.08 ± 0.01%	1.92 ± 0.01%	1.13 ± 0.02%
Bereta's method (50 iterations)	0.59 ± 0.01%	1.18 ± 0.01%	0.61 ± 0.01%
Minimum spanning tree	3.15 ± 0.03%	3.19 ± 0.01%	3.06 ± 0.02%
Rand-1	25.05 ± 3.31%	24.08 ± 2.06%	48.44 ± 19.1%
KNN+First-selection	2.41 ± 0.02%	2.13 ± 0.01%	2.62 ± 0.02%
KNN+First-increment	2.94 ± 0.02%		2.82 ± 0.02%
KNN+All-selection	3.02 ± 0.02%		2.92 ± 0.02%
KNN+Rand-2	3.64 ± 0.03%	3.24 ± 0.01%	3.45 ± 0.03%
MST+First-selection	1.39 ± 0.01%	2.46 ± 0.01%	1.77 ± 0.01%
MST+First-increment	2.30 ± 0.02%	3.01 ± 0.01%	2.07 ± 0.01%
MST+All-selection	2.95 ± 0.02%		2.92 ± 0.02%
MST+Rand-2	4.20 ± 0.04%	3.62 ± 0.02%	3.89 ± 0.04%
Grid+First-selection	2.98 ± 0.02%	3.16 ± 0.01%	2.88 ± 0.02%
Grid+First-increment	3.08 ± 0.02%	3.16 ± 0.01%	2.93 ± 0.02%
Grid+All-selection	3.07 ± 0.02%		2.91 ± 0.02%
Grid+Rand-2	3.31 ± 0.03%	3.21 ± 0.01%	3.23 ± 0.03%

Table 2. Running time. Each cell shows the average time cost to generate one prediction.

Methods	D_1	D_2	D_3
Geo-Steiner	211.2 ms	303.2 ms	205.2 ms
Bereta's method (10 iterations)	118.8 ms	331.7 ms	125.2 ms
Bereta's method (20 iterations)	310.0 ms	898.5 ms	315.4 ms
Bereta's method (50 iterations)	1021.5 ms	2217.1 ms	945.6 ms
Minimum spanning tree	1.6 ms	5.8 ms	1.7 ms
Rand-1	2.8 ms	10.7 ms	2.9 ms
KNN+First-selection	200.6 ms	285.1 ms	148.3 ms
KNN+Rand-2	9.4 ms	41.9 ms	8.7 ms
MST+First-selection	142.1 ms	254.9 ms	130.7 ms
MST+Rand-2	14.3 ms	22.3 ms	12.9 ms
Grid+First-selection	39.3 ms	72.1 ms	35.8 ms
Grid+Rand-2	7.0 ms	20.4 ms	7.0 ms

which means that, compared to the MST-based methods, KNN-based methods need more training epochs to get converged (especially on larger graphs) but can have a better performance once it is converged, for example, on small graphs. Indeed, we observed that both methods have almost converged on small graphs, while the loss of the KNN-based methods was still decreasing after 100 training epochs on large graphs.

Table 3. Generalization performance. Each cell shows the performance of one method generalized to one dataset, together with the standard deviation)

Methods	D_1	D_2	D_3	DEG
Model trained on D_1	$1.39 \pm 0.01\%$	$2.72 \pm 0.01\%$	$1.63 \pm 0.01\%$	$1.47 \pm 0.01\%$
Model trained on D_2	$2.11 \pm 0.02\%$	$2.46 \pm 0.01\%$	$2.43 \pm 0.05\%$	$2.14 \pm 0.02\%$
Model trained on D_3	$1.75 \pm 0.01\%$	$2.81 \pm 0.01\%$	$1.77 \pm 0.01\%$	$1.81 \pm 0.02\%$
Minimum spanning tree	$3.15 \pm 0.03\%$	$3.19 \pm 0.01\%$	$3.06 \pm 0.02\%$	$3.29 \pm 0.02\%$

On Stopping Criteria. According to Table 1, our proposed stopping criteria perform non-trivially better than the Rand-2, which confirms that our models indeed learn to improve the policy during training. An interesting observation is that First-selection has the best performance among the possible stopping criteria. One plausible reason is that in generating predictions in the training phase, compared to First-selection, First-increment and All-selection tend to construct larger trees on which the loss function is defined, which means that the corresponding models seek to learn a policy that can draw a Steiner tree, as opposed to the case of the First-selection where the model simply wants to learn how to select the best local Steiner point. For All-selection, it is less optimal also because it often forces the model to select some unnecessary candidates, as most of the Steiner minimal trees do not have $|S| - 2$ Steiner points.

Ability to Generalize Between Distributions. In order to investigate the generalization performance between distributions, we train the MST+First-selection on one dataset and evaluate its performance on different datasets. The result of this part is given in Table 3. The main observation is that even with distributions shifts, our method can still generate Steiner trees that are non-trivially better than the minimum spanning trees, which suggests that the embeddings we acquire do not heavily rely on the points distributions.

6   Conclusion

In this paper, we propose Deep-Steiner, a deep reinforcement learning method, to solve the EST problem. In particular, we design space discretization methods based on the unique properties of minimal Steiner trees, policy parameterization methods using attention techniques, and new training schemes with different stopping criteria. As evidenced by experiments, our method can generate decent solutions without incurring high computation and memory costs compared to traditional algorithms. One future work is to explore new representation methods in order to improve the performance on small graphs. In addition, it remains unknown how to overcome the memory issues in handling large instances, which is another interesting future work.

References

1. Ahmed, R., Turja, M.A., Sahneh, F.D., Ghosh, M., Hamm, K., Kobourov, S.: Computing Steiner trees using graph neural networks. arXiv preprint arXiv:2108.08368 (2021)
2. Ammar, A., Bennaceur, H., Châari, I., Koubâa, A., Alajlan, M.: Relaxed Dijkstra and A* with linear complexity for robot path planning problems in large-scale grid environments. Soft. Comput. **20**(10), 4149–4171 (2016). https://doi.org/10.1007/s00500-015-1750-1
3. Arora, S.: Polynomial time approximation schemes for Euclidean traveling salesman and other geometric problems. J. ACM (JACM) **45**(5), 753–782 (1998)
4. Barrett, T., Lvovsky, A., Clements, W., Foerster, J.: Exploratory combinatorial optimization with reinforcement learning. In: AAAI 2020–34th AAAI Conference on Artificial Intelligence, pp. 3243–3250 (2020)
5. Bello, I., Pham, H., Le, Q.V., Norouzi, M., Bengio, S.: Neural combinatorial optimization with reinforcement learning. ArXiv: abs/1611.09940 (2017)
6. Bengio, Y., Lodi, A., Prouvost, A.: Machine learning for combinatorial optimization: a methodological tour d'horizon. Eur. J. Oper. Res. **290**(2), 405–421 (2021)
7. Bereta, M.: Baldwin effect and Lamarckian evolution in a memetic algorithm for Euclidean Steiner tree problem. Memetic Comput. **11**(1), 35–52 (2019). https://doi.org/10.1007/s12293-018-0256-7
8. Caro, D.A.: Wireless Networks for Industrial Automation. ISA, Haryana (2005)
9. Chen, P.Y., et al.: A reinforcement learning agent for obstacle-avoiding rectilinear Steiner tree construction. In: Proceedings of the 2022 International Symposium on Physical Design, pp. 107–115 (2022)
10. Cheng, X., Du, D.Z., Wang, L., Xu, B.: Relay sensor placement in wireless sensor networks. Wirel. Netw. **14**(3), 347–355 (2008)
11. Deudon, M., Cournut, P., Lacoste, A., Adulyasak, Y., Rousseau, L.-M.: Learning heuristics for the TSP by policy gradient. In: van Hoeve, W.-J. (ed.) CPAIOR 2018. LNCS, vol. 10848, pp. 170–181. Springer, Cham (2018). https://doi.org/10.1007/978-3-319-93031-2_12
12. DIMACS, t.D.S.F.o.I.S., Analysis, D.D., by the Institute for Computational, in Mathematics (ICERM), E.R.: 11th dimacs implementation challenge (2014). https://dimacs11.zib.de/downloads.html
13. Dreyer, D.R., Overton, M.L.: Two heuristics for the Euclidean Steiner tree problem. J. Glob. Optim. **13**(1), 95–106 (1998)
14. Du, H., Yan, Z., Xiang, Q., Zhan, Q.: Vulcan: Solving the Steiner tree problem with graph neural networks and deep reinforcement learning. arXiv preprint arXiv:2111.10810 (2021)
15. Fujiwara, T., Iida, N., Watanabe, T.: A hybrid wireless network enhanced with multihopping for emergency communications. In: 2004 IEEE International Conference on Communications (IEEE Cat. No. 04CH37577), vol. 7, pp. 4177–4181. IEEE (2004)
16. Garey, M.R., Graham, R.L., Johnson, D.S.: The complexity of computing Steiner minimal trees. SIAM J. Appl. Math. **32**(4), 835–859 (1977)
17. Gilbert, E.N., Pollak, H.O.: Steiner minimal trees. SIAM J. Appl. Math. **16**(1), 1–29 (1968)
18. Gong, H., Zhao, L., Wang, K., Wu, W., Wang, X.: A distributed algorithm to construct multicast trees in WSNs: an approximate Steiner tree approach. In: Proceedings of the 16th ACM International Symposium on Mobile Ad Hoc Networking and Computing, pp. 347–356 (2015)

19. Goodfellow, I., Bengio, Y., Courville, A.: Deep Learning. MIT Press, Cambridge (2016). https://www.deeplearningbook.org
20. Hsu, H., Lachenbruch, P.A.: Paired t test. Wiley StatsRef: statistics reference online (2014)
21. Hu, H., Zhang, X., Yan, X., Wang, L., Xu, Y.: Solving a new 3d bin packing problem with deep reinforcement learning method. arXiv preprint arXiv:1708.05930 (2017)
22. Hwang, F.K., Richards, D.S.: Steiner tree problems. Networks 22(1), 55–89 (1992)
23. Ioffe, S., Szegedy, C.: Batch normalization: Accelerating deep network training by reducing internal covariate shift. In: International Conference on Machine Learning, pp. 448–456. PMLR (2015)
24. Joshi, C.K., Laurent, T., Bresson, X.: An efficient graph convolutional network technique for the travelling salesman problem. arXiv preprint arXiv:1906.01227 (2019)
25. Juhl, D., Warme, D.M., Winter, P., Zachariasen, M.: The Geosteiner software package for computing Steiner trees in the plane: an updated computational study. Math. Program. Comput. 10(4), 487–532 (2018)
26. Khalil, E., Dai, H., Zhang, Y., Dilkina, B., Song, L.: Learning combinatorial optimization algorithms over graphs. In: Advances in Neural Information Processing Systems, vol. 30 (2017)
27. Kingma, D.P., Ba, J.: Adam: a method for stochastic optimization. In: ICLR (Poster) (2015)
28. Kool, W., van Hoof, H., Welling, M.: Attention, learn to solve routing problems! In: International Conference on Learning Representations (2018)
29. Li, D., Jia, X., Liu, H.: Energy efficient broadcast routing in static ad hoc wireless networks. IEEE Trans. Mob. Comput. 3(2), 144–151 (2004)
30. Lin, G.H., Xue, G.: Steiner tree problem with minimum number of Steiner points and bounded edge-length. Inf. Process. Lett. 69(2), 53–57 (1999)
31. Lu, X.X., Yang, S.W., Zheng, N.: Location-selection of wireless network based on restricted Steiner tree algorithm. Proc. Environ. Sci. 10, 368–373 (2011)
32. Mazyavkina, N., Sviridov, S., Ivanov, S., Burnaev, E.: Reinforcement learning for combinatorial optimization: a survey. Comput. Oper. Res. 134, 105400 (2021)
33. Min, M., Du, H., Jia, X., Huang, C.X., Huang, S.C.H., Wu, W.: Improving construction for connected dominating set with Steiner tree in wireless sensor networks. J. Glob. Optim. 35(1), 111–119 (2006)
34. Nazari, M., Oroojlooy, A., Takáč, M., Snyder, L.V.: Reinforcement learning for solving the vehicle routing problem. In: Proceedings of the 32nd International Conference on Neural Information Processing Systems, pp. 9861–9871 (2018)
35. Obayiuwana, E., Falowo, O.E.: Network selection in heterogeneous wireless networks using multi-criteria decision-making algorithms: a review. Wirel. Netw. 23(8), 2617–2649 (2017)
36. Peng, B., Wang, J., Zhang, Z.: A deep reinforcement learning algorithm using dynamic attention model for vehicle routing problems. In: Li, K., Li, W., Wang, H., Liu, Y. (eds.) ISICA 2019. CCIS, vol. 1205, pp. 636–650. Springer, Singapore (2020). https://doi.org/10.1007/978-981-15-5577-0_51
37. Qiu, X.P., Sun, T.X., Xu, Y.G., Shao, Y.F., Dai, N., Huang, X.J.: Pre-trained models for natural language processing: a survey. Sci. China Technol. Sci. 63(10), 1872–1897 (2020). https://doi.org/10.1007/s11431-020-1647-3
38. Saeed, R.A., Recupero, D.R.: Path planning of a mobile robot in grid space using boundary node method. In: ICINCO (2), pp. 159–166 (2019)

39. Senel, F., Younis, M.: Relay node placement in structurally damaged wireless sensor networks via triangular Steiner tree approximation. Comput. Commun. **34**(16), 1932–1941 (2011)
40. Smith, J.M., Lee, D., Liebman, J.S.: An o (n log n) heuristic for Steiner minimal tree problems on the Euclidean metric. Networks **11**(1), 23–39 (1981)
41. Thompson, E.A.: The method of minimum evolution. Ann. Hum. Genet. **36** (1973)
42. Vaswani, A., et al.: Attention is all you need. In: Advances in Neural Information Processing Systems, pp. 5998–6008 (2017)
43. Vinyals, O., Fortunato, M., Jaitly, N.: Pointer networks. Adv. Neural Inf. Process. Sys. **28**, 2692–2700 (2015)
44. Warme, D., Winter, P., Zachariasen, M.: Geosteiner (2003)
45. Warme, D.M.: Spanning Trees in Hypergraphs with Applications to Steiner Trees. University of Virginia, Charlottesville (1998)
46. Williams, R.J.: Simple statistical gradient-following algorithms for connectionist reinforcement learning. Mach. Learn. **8**(3), 229–256 (1992)
47. Winter, P., Zachariasen, M.: Euclidean Steiner minimum trees: an improved exact algorithm. Netw.: Int. J. **30**(3), 149–166 (1997)
48. Wong, Y.C., Chu, C.: A scalable and accurate rectilinear Steiner minimal tree algorithm. In: 2008 IEEE International Symposium on VLSI Design, Automation and Test (VLSI-DAT), pp. 29–34. IEEE (2008)

Author Index

© ICST Institute for Computer Sciences, Social Informatics and Telecommunications Engineering 2023
Published by Springer Nature Switzerland AG 2023. All Rights Reserved
Z. J. Haas et al. (Eds.): WiCON 2022, LNICST 464, pp. 243–244, 2023.
https://doi.org/10.1007/978-3-031-27041-3

Printed in the United States
by Baker & Taylor Publisher Services